GARDEN
PLANTS

ILLUSTRATED ENCYCLOPEDIA

GARDEN PLANTS

SUSAN BERRY AND STEVE BRADLEY

LORENZ BOOKS

ABOVE: The brilliant red poppies stand
out in a wild flower meadow in summer.

This edition published in 2000 by
Lorenz Books
Anness Publishing Inc.,
27 West 20th Street,
New York, NY 10011;
(800) 354-9657

© 1996, 2000 Anness Publishing Ltd

ISBN 0-7548-0558-1

Publisher: Joanna Lorenz
Project Editor: Antony Atha
Plant Consultant: Tony Lord
Editors: Jacky Jackson, Penny Clarke
Designer: Patrick McLeavey & Partners
Jacket Design: Balley Design Associates
Commissioned Photography: Sue Atkinson

Previously published as *Best Plants for Your Garden*

Printed and bound in Hong Kong

10 9 8 7 6 5 4 3 2 1

Contents

Introduction

A cottage-style border showing a blend of perennials and small shrubs including alliums, poppies, astrantia, elaeagnus, cistus and hostas.

For all gardeners, making the right selection of plants is the single most important ingredient for success in gardening. To do this, you need to be informed on several different levels: you need to·be able to identify the overall look you are hoping to achieve and the kind of garden you want to create, and you also need to understand the conditions·that determine which plants will grow successfully. One of the most important lessons for any novice gardener to grasp is that you cannot grow exactly what you want wherever you please.

Although you always want to try to manage nature, or at least influence it as much as you dare, the most successful gardeners are those who look at how plants grow in their natural habitat, and apply this to their own garden, working with nature wherever possible. The greater understanding you have of where plants grow best, and the more you understand their needs, the easier it becomes to grow them. The section on page 8 explains these requirements in more detail.

PLANNING YOUR GARDEN

When planning a garden you must have some understanding of what your soil is like – whether it is acid or alkaline, heavy clay or light sand – and whether the climate is hot or cool, wet or dry. Immense strides have been made in plant breeding, and recent innovations have allowed gardeners far greater freedom of choice than they had previously now that in many instances plants are bred to be both beautiful and tough. Even so, nature still plays by far the most important role, and a plant that naturally thrives in a damp or wet habitat will not flourish in hot dry sun as well. Its entire organism has evolved over thousands of years to cope with the particular conditions in which it originated, and usually it is only in similar conditions that it will continue to thrive.

Fortunately, some plants do withstand quite a wide range of climatic variations and are particularly well adapted, thriving surprisingly well in conditions very far removed from those of their natural habitat. The sensible gardener tries to pay attention to these needs, and to select his or her plants from within the range of those that are broadly suitable.

Whether planning an entire garden or just designing a border, you will probably want to include a range of different types to give height and variety to your plan. Try to remember that foliage is as important as flowers in the overall structure and shape of the garden, and make sure you pick a framework of plants with good shape or attractive foliage, on which the more ephemeral elements of the design such as perennials and annuals can be hung.

Flowers, while eye-catching, are not always the major element in the success of any garden design. It is also the way in which the garden is laid out and constructed: the organization of its hard surfaces including terraces and paths; any hedges and screens; the creation of a vertical element, in the form of climbing plants, shrubs and trees. These also give shelter and create pockets of dry shade which a further range of plants will enjoy. A selection of climbers, wall shrubs and hedges is listed in chapter 7. Nature often tends to provide these variations unaided, but if they do not exist in your garden, you will have to make your own varied but viable micro-climate, thereby increasing the range you can grow, and also your own enjoyment.

Not many gardens have a naturally damp area which could support moisture-loving plants but a boggy patch or even a pond is easy to make and certainly gives you the opportunity to include these attractive plants.

Another important element when planning a garden is winter interest. Try to ensure you have a good number of evergreen shrubs or trees which will provide a structure for the garden during the winter months. Without them, the garden can look impossibly bleak and dull, when the foliage of most herbaceous perennials has disappeared, leaving you with bare stems and branches. In a new garden, ground cover can be an important element in the plan to help prevent the bare soil becoming engulfed in weeds. You can opt either for plants that naturally spread to cover the soil, or for those shrubs and perennials that have a spreading habit, thereby effectively suppressing weeds by their shady canopy. Chapter 8 suggests a range of plants that are suitable for ground cover.

CULTIVATION

Whatever plants you choose, you need to ensure that you look after them correctly. This means not only do you plant them where they are most likely to thrive, but you also attend to any special requirements, in terms of watering, feeding and pruning.

Most plants look far better when planted in largish groups rather than dotted about singly, and propagation is one of the easiest and cheapest ways to increase your stock of plants. When purchasing your plants initially, it is a good idea to pick plants that can be propagated easily and that are fairly fast to establish, so that building up your stock of plants and also furnishing the bare spaces in your garden are achieved relatively quickly.

Although many plants are more or less pest- and disease-free, others are singularly prone to various complaints and to attacks by a particular kind of insect. Hostas, for example, are notoriously easy prey to slugs, while tender young shoots, leaves and buds of many plants will quickly become infested with aphids in summer. You can do a lot to control these problems if you are forewarned when you select your plants. Hostas, for example, can be surrounded with a layer of grit, which deters slugs and snails, or, if you are not averse to chemical methods, you can use slug pellets. Particular problems for individual plants are indicated in each entry.

Like most humans, plants respond best to regular, systematic sensible care, and very rarely to the feast or famine principle of gardening. Try not to neglect your plants for a long period of time and then make up for it in one mammoth session of attention, whether it is feeding, watering, pruning or whatever. It is far better to keep a watchful eye on your plants, noting any problems as they arise, and nipping them in the bud, if you will forgive the expression, before they become more serious. Even the vexed problem of pruning is better if tackled after flowering on a week-by-week basis, rather than in one massive hit in late autumn or early spring.

HOW TO USE THIS BOOK

This book is divided into ten sections which focus on some of the common conditions and basic needs of modern gardeners, with the idea that once you have identitifed these, you can then find some suitable plants for your purpose.

The plants we have selected in this book have been chosen on the basis of good overall performance: they are all reasonably easy to grow and have more than one good feature. Within the specific categories of need or condition identified, you will find a cross-section of the following types: trees, shrubs, herbaceous perennials, and climbers – the plants which usually make up the core planting of any garden, and bulbs, tuberous plants and roses which everyone will want to grow have their own sections. Annuals, which can be grown from seed in one season, and therefore are not a permanent feature in the garden, get only relatively minor coverage here.

At the end of each section there is a cross reference list which itemises other plants that might be grown. Most plants will tolerate differing soil types and the chart on page 9 shows you plants can be chosen if you need to consider more than one feature.

WHAT PLANTS NEED

Knowledge of what a plant requires in terms of light, water, temperature, soil type and nutrients is essential for good gardening. In addition, you also need to identify which of these requirements your garden can naturally provide, and how you can change the micro-environment within your garden if the conditions are not suitable for the plants you aspire (and in many instances perspire) to grow. For instance, in a dark situation, thinning existing plants will allow in more light, and in a damp garden, improving the soil drainage will encourage plants which prefer drier conditions. Alternatively, you may prefer to use your garden's natural dampness and enjoy the range of moisture-loving plants listed in chapter 4.

The plants you may wish to grow originate from many different areas of the world, where very different growing conditions exist. In their natural environment, some will grow in dense shade on the forest floor while others are exposed to intense bright sunlight for long periods of time. This wide diversity of natural habitat explains why the many different ornamental plants we grow require different conditions. The ability to adapt to unfamiliar conditions is a major reason for the popularity of many common plants. Of course, some plants are much more adaptable than others; classic examples are the forsythia, which seems to be flowering everywhere in the spring, and *Buddleja davidii*, which has been so successful at colonizing areas that many people now regard it as a weed.

Salvias, lilies, sambucus and daisies emphasized by the white of Geranium clarkei *'Kashmir White' make a quiet corner in a mixed border.*

Plants pushing out onto gravel paths create a charming informality. Here Lavandula stoechas *and* Lychnis coronaria *catch the evening sun.*

LIGHT

Light is essential to all plants, as it provides the energy needed by the plant to manufacture food during daylight hours. Other activities within the plant are also influenced by light; for instance, the response to the hours of daylight within the 24–hour cycle will determine the time of year that flowers are produced. This response to the day-length is called photoperiodism, and explains why plants flower at specific times of the year, regardless of the prevailing weather conditions. As day-length appears to be a plant's main method of knowing which season is which, it is a factor which gardeners would love to be able to tamper with, but this can only realistically be done at great expense in a fully controlled environment, as in the production of pot plants such as poinsettias for Christmas.

The amount of light is also the main stimulus for autumn leaf fall in deciduous trees and shrubs, the trigger which starts this response being the shortening days of autumn. The various color changes within the leaf are brought about by the chemical changes which occur when plant nutrients are drawn out of the leaf back into the stem. (See chapter 9 for autumn and winter foliage plants.) As a gardener you are able to influence (to some extent) the light intensity your plants receive by providing shade to reduce light levels. Alternatively, to raise light levels in a darkened corner, you could use mirrors and create light-reflective surfaces such as white gravel and paving . However, there is a selection of plants in chapter 5 that enjoy a shady situation, while plants that love sunny conditions are listed in chapter 6.

Generally speaking, most plants consist of roots, stems, leaves, flowers and usually fruits, many of which contain seeds. None of

these parts functions in isolation. There is a close relationship between the individual parts of the plant and the plant's overall growth rate. Some plants are also scented and these are a particular favorite with gardeners. A selection of these is listed in chapter 10.

THE SOIL

Although it is not easy to describe what soil actually is, we know that plants grow better when planted in the right type of soil. A basic understanding can help to create a good root environment for the plants you wish to grow. Soil is required by the gardener to have certain properties: the ability to hold moisture and air so that the plant's roots are not deprived of oxygen; the correct balance of nutrients; and the appropriate level of lime or acidity.

What makes growing plants more of a challenge is that many garden soils play host to a number of unwanted 'additives' such as weed seeds, stones (and occasionally builder's debris), pests and diseases. Heavy, clay soils are also difficult to work with and choosing plants that thrive in this situation is essential. Chapter 3 suggests a range of plants for clay soils.

Acidity and alkalinity are measured on a scale of pH which ranges from 0 to 14, with 0 being the most acid and 14 being the most alkaline. The influence of pH affects the solubility of minerals and hence their availability to plants. Acid conditions tend to encourage phosphorus deficiency and sometimes contain excess manganese and aluminum, while alkaline conditions can lead to a lack of manganese, boron, and phosphorus. Soil pH can also influence the number and type of beneficial soil-borne organisms, as well as the incidence of pests and diseases. For example, worms dislike a low pH, but leatherjackets and wireworms are more commonly found in acid conditions. What is the optimum pH? Again, the pH range for good plant growth varies depending upon the preference of the individual plants. Some plants are more sensitive than others and have quite specific requirements: lime-loving plants that prefer alkaline soil are known as calcicoles, and lime-haters that like an acid soil are called calcifuges. These plants are listed in chapter 1 for acid soils and chapter 2 for limy soils.

Many gardeners wish to grow the widest range of plants possible and the temptation is to try to manipulate the pH of the soil. Although this may be possible, to lower the soil pH is difficult, costly, and usually only a short-term measure, whereas raising soil pH is relatively easy and, if done correctly, can have beneficial effects on a long-term basis. If you really cannot resist the temptation to grow lime-hating plants and your soil has a pH reading of 6.0 or over, then by far the best option is to grow them in containers. That way you can exercise complete control over the pH of the soil mix.

The question of what plants you can grow in your garden is now, therefore, a matter of turning to the appropriate section for your particular requirements.

Best Plants for a Variety of Conditions

The following selection of plants has been chosen from those featured in this book and represent the trees, shrubs, climbers and herbaceous perennials which have a range of useful features; they are, therefore, good all-arounders.

	Acid soil	Alkaline soil	Clay soil	Moisture-loving	Shade	Dry/Sunny	Climbers/Hedges	Ground cover	Winter interest	Scent	Growth rate	Season of interest	Classification	Evergreen
Acanthus spinosus	◆	◆								◆	F	2	HP	
Acer palmatum	◆				◆					◆	S	3	T	
Actinidia kolomikta	◆						◆				M	2–3	C	
Agapanthus	◆					◆		◆			M	2–3	HP	
Amelanchier					◆					◆	S	1–3	S	
Arbutus	◆							◆	◆		M	134	T	
Aucuba	◆	◆			◆						M	2–3	S	•
Berberis					◆	◆	◆				M	2–3	S	●
Bergenia	◆								◆		S	1	HP	•
Buxus sempervirens					◆	◆		◆	◆		S	1–4	S	•
Calluna	◆					◆		◆	◆		S	2–4	S	•
Camellia	◆				◆			◆			S	12	S	•
Campsis		◆					◆	◆		◆	F	2–3	C	
Cercidiphyllum	◆				◆				◆	◆	M	3	T	
Cercis		◆	◆				◆	◆		◆	M	123	S	
Crataegus		◆	◆	◆			◆	◆		◆	F	2–3	T	
Eccremocarpus	◆						◆	◆			F	2–3	C	•
Epimedium	◆				◆	◆			◆	◆	M	2–3	HP	•
Escallonia	◆	◆	◆				◆	◆			F	2–3	S	•
Festuca	◆				◆				◆		M	1–4	HP	•
Ficus carica		◆				◆	◆	◆			S	2–3	S	
Filipendula				◆	◆					◆	M	2–3	HP	
Garrya					◆			◆	◆		M	1	S	•
Gaultheria	◆							◆		◆	S	234	S	•
Gleditsia		◆	◆		◆					◆	M	2–3	T	
Hamamelis	◆								◆	◆	M	1&3	S	
Hosta			◆	◆	◆				◆		◆	F	2–3	HP

	Acid soil	Alkaline soil	Clay soil	Moisture-loving	Shade	Dry/Sunny	Climbers/Hedges	Ground cover	Winter interest	Scent	Growth rate	Season of interest	Classification	Evergreen
Ilex					◆			◆			S	2–4	T	•
Imperata			◆		◆	◆			◆	◆	M	3–4	HP	
Iris pseudacorus			◆	◆	◆						M	1–2	HP	
Kalmia latifolia	◆				◆						M	1–2	S	•
Laburnum		◆	◆		◆					◆	M	2–3	T	
Lathyrus		◆	◆				◆			◆	F	2–3	CHP	
Lavandula		◆				◆		◆	◆	◆	M	2	S	•
Lilium	◆							◆			F	1–2	HP	
Mahonia		◆			◆	◆	◆	◆	◆	◆	M	3–4	S	•
Osmunda			◆	◆	◆					◆	M	3	HP	
Parrotia		◆							◆		S	1&3	T	
Parthenocissus					◆	◆		◆			F	2–3	C	
Pieris	◆					◆					M	1–2	S	•
Prunus		◆							◆		M	1&3	T	
Pyracantha		◆	◆		◆	◆	◆			◆	M	2–3	S	•
Rhus hirta		◆			◆	◆	◆			◆	M	3	S	
Rosa rugosa		◆	◆			◆	◆			◆	F	2&3	S	
Rosmarinus		◆						◆			M	2	S	•
Salvia officinalis		◆	◆			◆				◆	M	2–3	S	
Senecio 'Sunshine'		◆	◆		◆	◆	◆			◆	M	2–3	S	•
Stachys		◆	◆			◆					M	2	HP	
Stewartia	◆					◆	◆			◆	M	2	S	
Taxus		◆				◆					M	3–4	T	•
Viburnum		◆	◆		◆		◆	◆	◆	◆	M	341	S	●
Vitis		◆	◆				◆	◆		◆	F	3–4	C	
Wisteria		◆	◆				◆	◆		◆	F	2–3	C	
Zenobia	◆						◆			◆	S	2–3	S	

KEY

Growth rate
S – Slow
M – Medium
F – Fast

Season of interest
1 – Spring
2 – Summer
3 – Autumn
4 – Winter

Classification
T – Tree
S – Shrub
HP – Herbaceous Perennial
C – Climber
CHP – Climbing Hardy Perennial

Evergreen
• – Some varieties are evergreen

Plants
for Acid Soils

For gardens, borders and containers with an acid soil, here is a selection of the many excellent garden plants that prefer this condition, of which camellias and rhododendrons are perhaps the best known. Acid soil occurs frequently in areas of high rainfall but can also be found under conifers where their needles drop.

ABOVE: Kalmia latifolia, *a magnificent rhododendron-like shrub which can only be grown successfully in acid soil.*

OPPOSITE: *A mixed heather border. Heathers are ideal for planting in acid soil and require little upkeep once established.*

ABOVE: *A rich mixture of magnolias and rhododendrons — two of the best candidates for acid soil — makes an enticing late spring display. Some magnolias, however, will grow satisfactorily in alkaline conditions.*

Plants that prefer to grow in an acid soil are often wrongly referred to as ericaceous plants, because many acid-loving plants belong to the family, *ericaceae*, including heathers (*erica*), arbutus, kalmia, pieris and, of course, rhododendrons. It is worth remembering that many other attractive plants such as camellia, eucryphia, hamamelis and some magnolias are also acid-loving but are not of the family *ericaceae*. The correct term for plants which prefer acid soil is calcifuges.

Some excellent garden plants grow only in acid soil, so if your garden has this condition, you can look forward to growing some real treasures. Acid-loving plants are often associated with the tendency to be spring flowering as are camellias and hamamelis, but many of these plants, for example fothergilla and stewartia, are renowned for their autumn foliage color, and if you can grow a range of heathers it is possible to have plants in flower practically all year around.

You can check on the pH of your soil to determine its acidity by using a home soil testing kit. It is a matter of a few minutes to discover whether or not your soil is suitable. As a rough guide, if your soil measures more than 6.5 on the pH scale it is unsuitable for growing acid-lovers. Of course, even if this is the case, you can always grow the plants you want in containers where you have greater control over the growing medium.

In nature, the most acid soils are usually found on heather moorland, or in coniferous forests. Remember, soil type is not always directly linked to soil pH. Acid soils can be free-draining and sandy, or heavy and sticky, or even organic with a high peat content. Clay soils may be acid or alkaline, depending on their make-up. Peat-based soils are almost always acid. Some soils, even if originally alkaline, can gradually become more acid as a result of the lime being washed out of the upper layers, close to the soil surface. This is owing to the fact that rainwater is slightly acidic, and the lime in the soil dissolves and is washed (leached) down through the soil. Soils in high rainfall areas are more likely to be acid than alkaline and many of the gardens famous for their rhododendrons are found in the west of the country.

Plants which grow naturally in acid soils, marked pH in the text, will usually struggle when grown in anything else. This is because of the different availability of plant nutrients at lower pH levels as plants vary in their ability to absorb these nutrients. Most acid-loving plants are unable to take up enough iron from the soil if the pH is too high. Initially, this shows as a yellowing (chlorosis) between the leaf veins, and in many cases is followed by the death of the plant unless additional iron is supplied.

LEFT: *Heathers are ideal subjects for acid soils, and when mixed together in a large bed, provide a wonderful tapestry of color and shape. The best impact is gained when, as here, several different cultivars are combined in one area of the garden.*

Abies koreana

Korean fir
HEIGHT: 10ft (3m) • Hardy
FLOWERING SEASON: None

Commonly known as the Korean fir, this conifer is a small, slow-growing tree, with a broad-based, conical shape, the base of the tree being as wide as its overall height. Each leaf or 'needle' is an attractive dark green above with a silvery white underside. It produces striking, violet-purple cones 2-3in (5-7.5cm) long, even on young plants. Propagation is by seed, sown into pots and placed outdoors in February. Prone to attack by the adelgid, which distorts young growths.

Acer rubrum

Red maple
HEIGHT: 50ft (15m) • Hardy
FLOWERING SEASON: Spring

The red maple forms a large round-headed deciduous tree with dark green leaves which turn bright red in the autumn. There are tiny red flowers which appear on the branches in the spring but these are insignificant. Like all maples the best autumn color is found when the tree is grown on acid soil but it is easy to cultivate and flourishes in any ordinary well-tilled soil.

Andromeda polifolia 'Compacta'

HEIGHT: 6-9in (15-23cm) • Hardy • pH
FLOWERING SEASON: Late summer/early autumn

This charming dwarf evergreen shrub has slender stems covered in narrow, bluish-green leaves each with a white underside. The soft pink flowers are produced in clusters on the tips of the shoots. It belongs to the heather family and grows wild in peat bogs in northern Europe. It does not flourish when there is lime in the soil. Propagate by semi-ripe cuttings taken in late summer. The plant may suffer from vine weevil grubs, which eat the roots and cause wilting and collapse if they attack in large numbers.

Arbutus × andrachnoides

HEIGHT: 50ft (15m) • Hardy
FLOWERING SEASON: Late autumn/early spring

A hybrid between *A. andrachos* and *A. unedo*, the Killarney strawberry tree, this attractive, slow-growing, broad-leafed evergreen forms an open spreading tree with striking orange-red bark which peels and flakes from the trunk and older branches to reveal the new bark beneath. The white, urn-shaped flowers, produced in large upright spikes in late autumn/early spring appear as the orange-red fruits of the previous year ripen. In a severe winter some of the leaves and shoots may be damaged. Propagation is by semi-ripe cuttings taken in late summer.

Arctostaphylos uva-ursi

Bearberry
HEIGHT: 4in (10cm) • Hardy • pH
FLOWERING SEASON: Summer

This is a low evergreen shrub with a spreading habit and small, oval, bright green leaves, that is ideal as a ground-cover plant. The small heather-like flowers are white flushed pink, followed by a display of small scarlet berries in autumn and winter. It likes acid soil and shelter from cold winds. A particularly interesting form is *A. u.* 'Point Reyes', which has pale pink flowers against a backdrop of gray-green leaves. Propagation is by semi-ripe cuttings with a heel taken in August and inserted into a cold frame.

Aristolochia durior

Birthwort/Dutchman's pipe
HEIGHT: 27ft (9m) • Not fully hardy
FLOWERING SEASON: Summer

A vigorous climber, its unusual tubular flowers are yellowish-green with a brownish-purple interior, they are 1.5-2in (3-5cm) long with the bottom half bent upwards to resemble a smoker's pipe, hence the common name Dutchman's pipe. The large, dull green leaves are heart-shaped and up to 12in (30cm) in length, borne on thin, woody twining stems. It provides a good wall covering when given support. Propagation is by softwood tip cuttings taken in July. Prune by thinning shoots in March.

Begonia × carrierei

Begonia
HEIGHT: 9in (23cm) • Half-hardy
FLOWERING SEASON: Summer/autumn

These plants, with their colorful leaves and attractive flowers, are popular for containers or summer bedding schemes. They are available with either green or bronze leaves, and produce masses of red, pink or white flowers from June until the first frosts. There are several mixed color selections, including 'New Generation', which has shades of salmon, rose, pink, scarlet and white. Propagation is by seed sown in spring, or by softwood tip cuttings taken in summer.

Berberidopsis corallina

Coral plant
HEIGHT: 14ft (4.5m) • Moderately hardy
FLOWERING SEASON: Late summer

A beautiful evergreen climber with woody, twining stems, the heart-shaped, dark green leaves have a thick leathery texture, and a single row of spine-like teeth along the margin. The common name, coral plant, refers to the small, round, deep red flowers on thin red stalks that hang in bunches. This plant grows best in a shaded slightly sheltered situation with a moist soil. Propagation is by seed sown indoors in spring or semi-ripe stem cuttings taken in late summer.

Calluna vulgaris 'J H Hamilton'

Ling/Scottish heather
HEIGHT: 2ft (60cm) • Hardy • pH
FLOWERING SEASON: Midsummer/late autumn

A low-growing evergreen, bushy shrub with small, hairy leaves carried on thin, woody stems. The leaves may vary in color from mid green or gray to yellow, orange or a bright reddish-brown, and many varieties, such as *C. v.* 'Sunrise', display their most attractive colors through the winter. The small bell-like flowers range from white to dark mauve, and are carried in spikes on the tips of shoots and branches. Propagate by cuttings taken in autumn after flowering.

Camellia japonica 'R L Wheeler'

Camellia
HEIGHT: 12ft (4m) • Moderately hardy • pH
FLOWERING SEASON: Spring

C. japonica, the common camellia, can grow as large as 30ft (10m) although it may take some years to attain this height. *C.j.* 'R L Wheeler' is one of the most popular cultivars with a robust upright growth habit and large dark-green leaves. The flowers are rose-pink, semi-double with striking circles of gold stamens. Camellias can be grown successfully in tubs where there is limited space in a small garden and they may require some shelter in very cold weather. Prune in the spring after flowering if they outgrow their space.

Camellia × williamsii 'Donation'

Camellia
HEIGHT: 10ft (3m) • Moderately hardy • pH
FLOWERING SEASON: Late winter/late spring

These shrubs or small trees are attractive, easy to grow, and valued highly for their spectacular flowers and glossy foliage. The flowers come in a wide range of shades of white, pink or red, and occasionally a combination of two or more colors in early spring. The flowers may be single, semi-double or double depending upon the cultivar. Camellias grow well in a sheltered situation. Propagation is by semi-ripe cuttings taken in early autumn.

Cassiope 'Muirhead'

HEIGHT: 12in (30cm) • Hardy • pH
FLOWERING SEASON: Spring

These dwarf evergreen shrubs have a low compact or spreading habit, and each shoot is covered in densely overlapping, scale-like dark green leaves. The small bell-like flowers, which vary from white to white-tinged red, hang singly or in pairs on the stems and branches. They need a damp sheltered site with some shade in order to establish and grow well and they do not like lime in the soil. The cultivar 'Edinburgh' is possibly the easiest to grow. Propagation is layering or semi-ripe cuttings taken in late summer or early autumn.

Cercidiphyllum japonicum

Katsura tree
HEIGHT: 25ft (8m) • Hardy
FLOWERING SEASON: Spring

This graceful tree is grown for the color and
beauty of its unusual round or heart-shaped
leaves which are red as they unfold and
change to mid green within a few days. The
main display comes in autumn when the
leaves turn pale yellow before becoming a
soft pink. In addition, the plants give off an
aroma of 'candy floss' as these color changes
occur. The young shoots may be damaged by
late frosts. Propagation is by seed sown in a
cold frame during the autumn and winter.

Clethra arborea

Lily-of-the-valley tree of Madeira
HEIGHT: 25ft (8m) • Half-hardy
FLOWERING SEASON: Mid-late summer

This handsome tree has a dense bushy habit,
and its oval, evergreen leaves are a rich green
with a toothed margin. The long clusters of
white, bell-shaped flowers are very fragrant
and look very similar to the blooms of lily-
of-the-valley. To produce its best display,
clethra should be grown in a moist peaty soil
in semi-shade. It also produces good autumn
color. Propagation is by softwood cuttings
taken in summer or by freshly collected seed
sown in autumn.

Cornus canadensis

Creeping dogwood
HEIGHT: 6in (15cm) • Hardy • pH
FLOWERING SEASON: Summer

Strictly speaking, this low spreading plant is
not a shrub, as the shoots die down each
winter and are replaced by fresh shoots the
following spring. The mid green leaves are
carried in clusters at the tips of the thin
green stems. An ideal ground-cover plant, it
forms a carpet of small starry white flowers
followed by tight clusters of vivid red fruits
in the autumn. Propagation is by division of
established plants in winter. Late spring frosts
may damage the leaves.

Cornus kousa var. *chinensis*

Dogwood
HEIGHT: 10ft (3m) • Hardy
FLOWERING SEASON: Summer

This is a graceful shrubby plant, the dull
green, oval leaves have a pronounced wavy
margin and are carried along the branches in
opposite pairs. The multitude of flower-like
bracts which are carried on spreading
branches make a lovely display in early
summer and are followed by strawberry-like
fruits ripening in autumn and winter. The
attractive cultivar *C. k.* 'Satomi' has deep pink
bracts and leaves that turn reddish-purple in
early autumn. Propagation for species is from
fresh seed, sown in the autumn.

Cornus nuttallii

Mountain dogwood/Pacific dogwood
HEIGHT: 25ft (8m) • Hardy
FLOWERING SEASON: Late spring/early summer

This large, free-flowering plant has attractive
creamy-white bracts surrounding small
yellow-green flowers. The bracts become
flushed pink as they age. The roughly oval
leaves are a dull green throughout the
summer, changing to rich bronze and
crimson hues in the autumn. The cultivar
C. n. 'Gold Spot' has mottled yellow leaves.
It prefers a sheltered position in rich well-
drained soil. Propagation is from fresh seed,
sown in a cold frame in the autumn, but
germination may take eighteen months.

Corydalis cheilanthifolia

Fumitory
HEIGHT: 10in (25cm) • Hardy
FLOWERING SEASON: Late spring/early summer

This evergreen perennial forms a decorative
plant with its pretty fern-like olive-green
foliage which is initially produced in a low-
growing rosette. The dense spikes of light
yellow flowers are held erect above the leaves.
It can be an attractive feature in the border
for most of the year, and once established
will self-seed on an annual basis. It prefers
light well-drained soil and will tolerate some
shade. Propagation is by seed sown in
autumn, or by division of the thick fleshy
roots in winter when the plant is dormant.

Corylopsis pauciflora

HEIGHT: 6ft (1.8m) • Hardy • pH
FLOWERING SEASON: Spring

This beautiful flowering shrub produces drooping strands of highly fragrant primrose-yellow flowers which appear in spring before the leaves. The broadly oval leaves have bristled margins when they first appear and are a pinkish-bronze, changing to bright green as they mature. They like a sunny sheltered position and the delicate flowers may be damaged by late spring frosts. Propagation is by softwood cuttings in the summer or by seed sown in a cold frame in the autumn to root slowly during the winter.

Cryptomeria japonica

Japanese cedar
HEIGHT: 60ft (18m) • Hardy
FLOWERING SEASON: Spring

A large, fast-growing tree with a broad conical habit and soft, orange-red bark which shreds into fine strips as the tree ages. The thin, needle-like leaves are mid green deepening to dark green and densely packed in spirals along the branches. The cultivar *C. j.* 'Elegans', has decorative foliage which changes from green to reddish-bronze in the autumn and winter. To propagate, put semi-ripe, heeled cuttings in early autumn in a cold frame to root slowly over winter.

Cypripedium reginae

Showy lady's slipper orchid
HEIGHT: 2ft (60cm) • Hardy
FLOWERING SEASON: Spring/summer

This deciduous, hardy perennial is commonly referred to as the showy lady's slipper orchid. It has pale green, deeply grooved, long strap-like leaves, which look rather like hosta leaves. The flowers are predominantly white with a pink and white pouch forming the 'toe' of the slipper. They are carried on green stems or spikes, with as many as four flowers to a spike. Although attractive when flowering, these plants take time to establish. Propagation is by division in the spring.

Daboecia cantabrica

St Dabeoc's heath
HEIGHT: 2ft (60cm) • Hardy
FLOWERING SEASON: Summer/autumn

This is one of the most charming dwarf shrubs, with tough, thin stems. The small, lance-shaped leaves are dark green above and silvery-gray beneath. The small, urn-shaped, rose-purple flowers are produced in long strand-like bunches. The cultivar *D. c.* 'Snowdrift' has white flowers. Young soft growths may be damaged by late spring frosts. The plant responds well to hard pruning. Propagate by taking semi-hardwood cuttings in late summer, or layering year-old shoots in the spring.

Darlingtonia californica

Pitcher plant
HEIGHT: 3ft (1m) • Hardy
FLOWERING SEASON: Spring/summer

This pitcher plant has fleshy rhizomes below ground and a dense rosette of yellowish-green, white-spotted leaves, modified at the tip to form a hooded tube or mouth, in which insects are trapped. The solitary flowers, a yellowish-green flushed with dark red-purple, are carried above the pitchers on long, leafless stalks. They are followed by a small fruit which contains many seeds. This plant prefers moist sheltered conditions such as a bog garden. Propagate by seed or division in the spring.

Desfontainia spinosa

HEIGHT: 5ft (1.5m) • Moderately hardy • pH
FLOWERING SEASON: Summer/autumn

A magnificent slow-growing evergreen shrub, of dense growth and fairly erect habit, with small, holly-like leaves which are a shiny dark green. The flowers, which are carried singly at the base of each leaf, are slender scarlet tubes with a yellow mouth and a waxy texture. This plant needs some shade and likes moist, acid soil. It grows particularly well in mild western areas of the country. The cultivar *D. s.* 'Harold Comber', produces larger flowers that are a deeper red. Propagation is by semi-ripe cuttings taken in the summer and placed in a heated frame.

Embothrium coccineum

Chilean fire bush
HEIGHT: 18ft (6m) • Moderately hardy •pH
FLOWERING SEASON: Early summer

This semi-evergreen tree has a narrow upright habit and stiff erect branches. The glossy, deep green leaves are slightly elliptical and have a leathery appearance. Clusters of brilliant orange-red spiky flowers are produced in great profusion along the branches. A hardier selection, the *E. c.* Lanceolatum Group, has slightly larger flowers but it is more deciduous. Propagate by sowing seeds in spring or by taking root cuttings in winter and putting them in a cold frame.

Enkianthus campanulatus

HEIGHT: 8ft (2.4m) • Hardy •pH
FLOWERING SEASON: Early summer

This is a deciduous shrub with dense, erect branches and smooth red twigs. The finely toothed leaves are a dull green, broadly elliptical and produced in clusters on the tips of the branches. In the autumn they turn yellow and then a brilliant red before falling. The small, urn-shaped flowers are sulfur yellow veined with red and are produced in small hanging clusters. They often last for up to three weeks. They like sun or semi-shade and moist soil. Propagation is by semi-ripe cuttings taken in late summer or early autumn.

Epimedium grandiflorum

Barrenwort
HEIGHT: 12in (30cm) • Hardy
FLOWERING SEASON: Spring/summer

These attractive, low-growing perennials make excellent ground cover, especially in moist, well-drained soil in partial shade. The heart-shaped leaves are bright green, tinted pinky-red when young, changing to a darker green as they mature. In the autumn these leaves display vivid tints of yellow, orange, red and bronze. The small, cup-shaped flowers are carried in clusters above the leaves; colors vary depending upon the cultivar. Propagation is by division in early spring.

Erica carnea 'Springwood White'

Heather/Alpine heath
HEIGHT: 12-18in (30-45cm) • Hardy
FLOWERING SEASON: All year round

Heathers are popular evergreen plants because year-round flowering is possible if a range of the different cultivars is planted. Most heathers prefer full sun and acid soil but *E. carnea* and its cultivars will tolerate some lime and shade. 'Springwood White' is the most vigorous white cultivar and bears large flowers from late winter into spring. Heathers look their best grown in a mass and should be pruned immediately after flowering by removing the old flowers with shears.

Erica × darleyensis 'Darley Dale'

Heather
HEIGHT: 12-18in (30-45cm) • Hardy
FLOWERING SEASON: All year round

Many heathers have most attractive foliage as well as their flowers: *E. cinerea* 'Golden Drop' has golden foliage with copper-red new growth and *E. carnea* 'Aurea' has golden-yellow leaves and pink flowers. *E. × d.* 'Darley Dale' has pale mauve-pink flowers which last from late autumn into spring, *E. × d* 'Kramer's Red' has deep ruby flowers and *E. × d.* 'Silberschmelze' is silver-white. Propagate by hardwood cuttings taken in September.

Eucryphia × nymansensis 'Nymansay'

Eucryphia
HEIGHT: 20ft (6m) • Moderately hardy
FLOWERING SEASON: Late summer/early autumn

The mid to dark green evergreen leaves have a leathery texture and a crinkled margin; they are carried singly or in groups on a short leaf stalk. The most notable is *E. × nymansensis*, a hybrid between *E. cordifolia·× E. glutinosa*; the cultivar 'Nymansay' forms a small tree of erect habit, which matures quickly, producing pure white flowers. *E. lucida* 'Pink Cloud' has pale pink flowers with a thin white margin to each petal. Propagation is by taking semi-ripe cuttings with a heel in September.

Fothergilla major

HEIGHT: 6ft (1.8m) • Hardy • pH
FLOWERING SEASON: Spring

This is a slow-growing shrub with a thin straggly appearance. The broadly oval leaves are a glossy dark-green on the upper surface, with a bluish-white bloom beneath. In the autumn they turn yellow and vivid orange-red before the winter frosts. The flowers, which are very fragrant and look like small, white bottle-brushes, appear before the leaves. They prefer sandy, lime-free soil and a sheltered position. Propagation is by layering young shoots in autumn. Prone to damage and branch death by the coral spot fungus.

Gaultheria mucronata

HEIGHT: 3ft (1m) • Hardy • pH
FLOWERING SEASON: Late spring/early summer

Formerly known as pernettyas, gaultherias are a genus of evergreen shrubs. G. mucronata has small, glossy, dark green leaves which are oval and end in a sharp point. The flowers are generally white, followed by clusters of small round fruit, which vary from white and pink to purple and red. Cultivars include: G. m. 'Bell's Seedling' which has bright cherry-red fruits and G. m. 'Lilacina', with pale lilac fruit. Both male and female plants are needed for berries. Propagation is by semi-ripe cuttings taken in September.

Gaultheria shallon

Shallon
HEIGHT: 4ft (1.2m) • Hardy • pH
FLOWERING SEASON: Late spring/early summer

This vigorous evergreen plant produces broad, oval leaves which are thick, leathery and borne on slender, upright, reddish-green stems. The small, pinkish-white flowers which are produced at the base of the leaves and form large drooping clusters, are followed by dark purple fruits in the autumn. This plant is very invasive and requires plenty of room, but it is ideal for growing in shade, and makes excellent ground cover. Propagate by dividing established plants in winter.

Gentiana sino-ornata

Gentian
HEIGHT: 6in (15cm) • Hardy • pH
FLOWERING SEASON: Autumn

This evergreen perennial is possibly the best autumn-flowering gentian. In the spring a number of thin green trailing stems appear which sprawl across the ground, each of which, lengthening during the summer, produces in the autumn a brilliant blue flower, handsomely striped on the outside. G. sino-ornata needs moist, acid soil. Propagation is by 'thongs', where the roots, complete with a small segment of stem, are pulled from the parent plant and potted on or replanted in early spring.

Halesia monticola

Snowdrop tree/Silver bell tree
HEIGHT: 25ft (8m) • Hardy
FLOWERING SEASON: Spring

A hardy, deciduous tree which has a spreading habit, this attractive plant is grown primarily for its distinctive clusters of white, bell-shaped flowers, which appear in spring before the leaves. The flowers are usually followed by small, green, winged and roughly pear-shaped fruit in the autumn. The broadly oval leaves are a light to mid green. The tree prefers moist acid to neutral soil and propagation is by softwood cuttings taken in summer or by seed sown in a cold frame in autumn.

Hamamelis × intermedia

Witch hazel
HEIGHT: 10ft (3m) • Hardy
FLOWERING SEASON: Winter/spring

This very distinctive and beautiful deciduous shrub produces its fragrant flowers in winter. They have small strap-like petals chiefly in shades of yellow, although some cultivars have darker flowers: H. × intermedia 'Ruby Glow' has copper-red flowers and H. × i. 'Diane' deep red ones. They prefer sun or semi-shade and well-drained acid to neutral soil. The large, mid green leaves are broadly oval and give a magnificent autumn display. Propagation is by softwood cuttings in late summer or grafting in midwinter.

Holboellia coriacea

HEIGHT: 18ft (6m) • Moderately hardy
FLOWERING SEASON: Late spring

An evergreen climber that supports itself by means of twining woody stems carrying glossy green leaves composed of three sub-divided stalked leaflets. The flowers of both sexes are borne on the same plant; the male flowers are purple and the female ones are greenish-white with purple tints. As a result, in the autumn, blackish-purple, sausage-shaped fruits containing black seeds usually develop. It grows in any well-drained soil in sun or semi-shade. Propagate by semi-ripe stem cuttings taken in late summer.

Hydrangea macrophylla 'Générale Vicomtesse de Vibray'

HEIGHT: 5ft (1.5m) • Moderately hardy
FLOWERING SEASON: Summer/autumn

Mop-head (hortensias) and lace-cap hydrangeas have broad, flat blooms, which in lace-caps are surrounded by one or more rows of pink, white or blue sepals. They grow in most soils but the color varies from pink to blue according to the amount of acid in the soil. As their name implies they like moisture. Remove the dead flower heads in spring after the frosts and cut up one third of the shoots on mature plants to ground level. Propagate by stem cuttings taken in August.

Indigofera heterantha

Indigo
HEIGHT: 5ft (1.5m) • Moderately hardy
FLOWERING SEASON: Early summer/autumn

A charming member of the pea family, this plant produces spikes of purplish-pink flowers on arching branches throughout the summer. It prefers well-drained loamy soil and a sunny position. The plant can be grown against a wall as a climber or in open ground where it should be cut back in the spring. If cut down by frosts it will regenerate. Propagate by cuttings of young shoots taken in July and inserted in a cold frame or by seed in May.

Kalmia latifolia

Calico bush
HEIGHT: 10ft (3m) • Hardy • pH
FLOWERING SEASON: Summer

A magnificent rhododendron-like evergreen shrub with a dense bushy habit, the alternate leaves, which are a glossy dark green and have a tough leathery appearance, are borne on thin, whippy, green stems. The unusual crimped buds open to produce large clusters of bright pink, cup-shaped flowers in summer. The cultivars *K. l.* var. *alba* and *K. l.* 'Silver Dollar' have white flowers flushed pink. It prefers full sun and moist acid soil. Propagation is by semi-ripe stem cuttings taken in late summer.

Kirengeshoma palmata

HEIGHT: 3ft (1m) • Hardy • pH
FLOWERING SEASON: Late summer/autumn

An upright hardy herbaceous perennial which has lush, bright green, palm-like leaves. The creamy-yellow, shuttlecock-shaped flowers are produced in clusters above the large, roundish leaves on tall, erect purplish-maroon stems and appear in late summer. This plant does best in conditions where there is some light shade with protection from the wind, while a damp but well-drained, preferably lime-free, soil is essential. It should be planted in the spring and propagation is by division of the rootstock in early spring.

Koelreuteria paniculata

Golden-rain tree/Pride of India
HEIGHT: 30ft (9m) • Moderately hardy
FLOWERING SEASON: Late summer

A handsome deciduous tree with large mid green leaves divided into numerous leaflets which turn yellow in autumn. It has large terminal clusters of yellow flowers in late summer followed by inflated triangular pinkish-brown seed pods and requires a position in full sun and well-drained, fertile soil. It is best propagated by seeds sown when ripe in the autumn in sandy soil in a cold frame. The tree is named after Joseph G Koelreuter, a professor of natural history at Karlsruhe in the eighteenth century.

Leucothoe fontanesiana

HEIGHT: 5ft (1.5m) • Hardy • pH
FLOWERING SEASON: Spring

An elegant evergreen shrub which is ideal as ground cover. The graceful, arching shoots carry leathery, strap-like leaves, which are a glossy dark green in the spring and summer, becoming tinted a beet-red or bronze in autumn and winter. The small white flowers are urn-shaped and hang in small clusters along the entire length of the stem. *L. f.* 'Rainbow' has leaves splashed with cream, yellow and pink. Likes moist acid soil and shade or partial shade. Propagation is by semi-ripe cuttings taken in late summer.

Liquidambar styraciflua 'Worplesdon'

Sweet gum
HEIGHT: 25ft (8m) • Hardy
FLOWERING SEASON: Spring

A large tree with maple-like, glossy, dark green leaves which turn orange and yellow in autumn. Initially forming a slender pyramid with the lower branches having upturned ends, it develops a broadly conical shape with age. The trunk becomes deeply grooved and fissured, changing from dark brown to dark gray. Small green flowers may be produced in spring. Propagation is by grafting under protection in spring.

Lupinus luteus

Yellow lupin
HEIGHT: 2½ft (75cm) • Hardy
FLOWERING SEASON: Summer

This striking annual has mid green stems thickly covered with soft hairs, the pale to mid green oval leaves are narrower towards the base and sparsely covered in a coating of fine soft hair. The bright yellow flowers, which are arranged in a circle or whorl at the end of the stem, are followed by small, black, hairy pods, each containing about five slightly flattened black seeds. Propagation is by seed sown in situ in the spring; pre-soak the seed in water for about twenty-four hours.

Magnolia × soulangeana 'Lennei'

Magnolia/Lily tree
HEIGHT: 20ft (6m) • Hardy
FLOWERING SEASON: Early spring

Contrary to perceived opinion there are a number of magnolias which will tolerate chalky soil, *M. delavayi, M. kobus* and *M. wilsonii* are three of them. That said the majority thrive best in neutral to acid soil and like to be sheltered from east winds which may otherwise damage the flowers when they emerge in the spring. The × *soulangeana* hybrids like 'Lennei' are among the hardiest and have a color range of pink through rose-purple to white.

Magnolia stellata

Star magnolia
HEIGHT: 10ft (3m) • Hardy
FLOWERING SEASON: Spring

The star magnolia is a shapely bush which carries many fragrant, star-like, white flowers in great profusion in spring before coming into leaf. The leaves are narrow and deep green. Magnolias come from North America, the Himalayas and Japan and are named after Pierre Magnol. Among the finest are *M. campbellii, M. acuminata* (the cucumber tree), *M denudata* (the lily tree) and *M. grandiflora* (page 148). They can be propagated by semi-ripe cuttings taken in summer or by seed sown in autumn.

Meconopsis betonicifolia

Blue poppy
HEIGHT: 4ft (1.2m) • Hardy
FLOWERING SEASON: Summer

The mid green leaves are oblong in shape and covered with soft bristles. The vivid, sky-blue flowers, with their central core of golden-yellow stamens, are carried on tall, slender stems, in hairy, pod-like buds. This plant requires a deep, rich, preferably acid compost and a cool, sheltered, shady site. Propagate this perennial from seed, sown into a cold frame in the autumn, and kept sheltered over winter. Do not allow these plants to flower in the first year after germination and divide them every four years.

Menziesia ciliicalyx 'Spring Morning'

HEIGHT: 3-5ft (1-1.5m) • Hardy • pH
FLOWERING SEASON: Early summer

This very attractive flowering shrub is a native of Japan and is a real treasure when grown in association with rhododendrons. The leaves are pale to mid green in color and have a bristled margin. *M. c.* 'Spring Morning' has pale creamy urn-shaped flowers while *M. c.* var. *purpurea* has purple ones. They appear during May and June. It likes semi-shade and moist acid soil. Propagation is by semi-ripe cuttings taken with a heel during mid to late summer.

Ourisia macrophylla

HEIGHT: 10in (25cm) • Hardy
FLOWERING SEASON: Midsummer

A low-growing plant with creeping rhizomatous rootstocks below ground, and mid green rounded leaves with a notched margin that form dense mats. This plant produces erect, slender stems, which carry white (sometimes streaked with pink) tubular flowers up to 1in (2.5cm) long, very like those of a miniature penstemon, on a spike above the leaves. This plant must have partial shade and a well-drained soil. Propagation is by division in spring or by seed sown in late spring.

Oxydendrum arboreum

Sorrel tree
HEIGHT: 27ft (9m) • Hardy • pH
FLOWERING SEASON: Summer

This deciduous spreading tree is grown mainly for its spectacular yellow and crimson autumn leaf colors. In spring and summer they are elliptical in shape and a glossy dark green. The white flowers are produced in long, dangling clusters on the tips of the shoots in summer. In winter the bark is an attractive rusty-red, which turns to gray as it ages. It likes sun and moist acid soil. Propagation is by softwood cuttings taken in summer or by fresh seed sown in autumn.

Picea pungens 'Koster'

Colorado spruce
HEIGHT: 50ft (15m) • Hardy
FLOWERING SEASON: Spring

The type forms a medium-sized tree with a conical profile. New growth is orange-brown, while the sharply pointed mature 'needles' are grayish-green. The dangling light-brown cones are bluish-green when young. The most popular cultivar, *P. p.* 'Koster', forms a small tree with silvery-blue leaves. Most species can be propagated by seed sown outdoors in the spring, the named selections are grafted under cover in early spring. Prone to attack by the adelgid, which sucks sap and distorts young growths.

Pieris japonica 'Firecrest'

HEIGHT: 10ft (3m) • Hardy • pH
FLOWERING SEASON: Spring

These compact evergreen shrubs have narrow leaves and white or pink bell-shaped flowers that look much like lily-of-the-valley. Most are grown for their spring display of bright foliage, ranging from lime-green to crimson or bronze. They like a shady site and moist acid soil. The cultivar *Pieris* 'Forest Flame' has young leaves which start red, change through pink and cream before turning green. *P. j.* 'Variegata' is a slow-growing cultivar with white and green variegated leaves, flushed pink when young. Propagation is by semi-ripe cuttings in August.

Pseudolarix amabilis

Golden larch
HEIGHT: 45ft (15m) • Hardy • pH
FLOWERING SEASON: Inconspicuous

This is a beautiful, deciduous and open-crowned tree that is very slow-growing, partly because the growing tips of young trees are often killed by late spring frosts, yet will eventually make a good height. The long, larch-like leaves are light green and turn a clear golden-yellow, orange and then reddish-brown in autumn. It bears erect cones with spreading scales which carry the seeds. This plant is particularly sensitive to lime in the soil. Propagation is by seed sown under protection in spring.

Plants for Acid Soils

Pseudotsuga menziesii

Douglas fir
HEIGHT: 75ft (25m) • Hardy
FLOWERING SEASON: Inconspicuous

This large vigorous tree develops a deeply grooved, corky bark as it ages, and a flat, broadly spreading crown also develops as the tree reaches maturity. The broad 'needle' leaves are aromatic and arranged in two horizontal lines along the branchlets, they are a rich dark green above with two silvery lines on the underside. The blue-leaved variety, *P. m.* var. *glauca,* will tolerate drier soils. Propagate by seed sown under protection in spring.

Rhododendron 'Kirin'

Azalea
HEIGHT: 5ft (1.5m) • Hardy • pH
FLOWERING SEASON: Spring

Botanically speaking all azaleas are classified as rhododendrons but most gardeners commonly reserve the name of azalea for those species which lose their leaves in winter. Just to complicate things a number of azaleas are evergreen and 'Kirin' is one of those. All rhododendrons and azaleas prefer moist, neutral to acid soil, with some dappled shade. Propagate by half-ripe cuttings taken with a thin heel from the current year's growth in July or by layering.

Rhododendron davidsonianum

Rhododendron
HEIGHT: 5–10ft (1.5–3m) • Hardy • pH
FLOWERING SEASON: Late spring

Rhododendrons in full bloom are one of the most glorious sights of spring and the best known gardens, Kew, the Savill Garden, Exbury and Bodnant are well worth visiting to appreciate the massed blooms.
R. davidsonianum is a relatively slow growing species with clusters of pale pink to pale mauve funnel-shaped flowers. As all rhododendrons are shallow rooting it is a good idea to mulch with half-decayed leaves in May to keep the soil moist in summer.

Rhodohypoxis baurii

HEIGHT: 4in (10cm) • Not fully hardy
FLOWERING SEASON: Spring/summer

This low-growing herbaceous perennial has a tufty habit and a crown of erect, spear-shaped hairy leaves. The small, flattish, six-petalled flowers, which vary from white to pale pink or red, are carried on slender, erect stems, each flower has six petals which meet at the center so the flower has no eye. The ideal conditions for this plant are full sun and a moist, sandy, peaty soil. Propagation can be achieved by seed sown in spring for the species, but named cultivars, such as *R. b.* 'Douglas', must be propagated by division in early spring.

Staphylea colchica

Bladder nut
HEIGHT: 11ft (3.5m) • Hardy
FLOWERING SEASON: Late spring

A large deciduous shrub which comes from the Causasus which bears handsome clusters of white flowers in May. These are followed by inflated seed pods up to 2in (5cm) long. It has bright green leaves each having three to five oval leaflets, and requires sun or semi-shade and moist fertile soil. *S. holocarpa* 'Rosea' has pink flowers. The species can be propagated by seed sown in autumn and selected forms by softwood cuttings taken with a slight heel of old wood in July. Trim young plants to encourage a bushy habit.

Stewartia sinensis

HEIGHT: 20ft (6m) • Hardy
FLOWERING SEASON: Summer

This small deciduous tree has attractive brown stems and unusually peeling ornamental bark; it belongs to the camellia family. The broad, spear-shaped, mid green leaves have a leathery texture and provide a vivid display of red and yellow in the autumn. The pure white, cup-shaped flowers have prominent yellow anthers in the center. These plants grow best in a sunny spot with their roots shaded, and are very intolerant of root disturbance. Propagation is by softwood cuttings taken in the summer, or by seed sown in a cold frame in autumn.

Styrax officinalis

Storax
HEIGHT: 12ft (4m) • Hardy • pH
FLOWERING SEASON: Early summer

This attractive deciduous shrub has a loose, open habit and spear-shaped leaves that are dark green on the upper surface and silver-white beneath. The short drooping clusters of large, white, fragrant, bell-shaped flowers are carried on the tips of the shoots in early summer. This plant prefers a sheltered position in full sun or partial shade, and a moist well-drained soil. Propagation is by softwood cuttings taken in summer, or by seed sown in a cold frame in autumn.

Taxodium distichum

Bald cypress/Swamp cypress
HEIGHT: 75ft (25m) • Hardy
FLOWERING SEASON: Winter

A strikingly beautiful, slow-growing deciduous tree which has fibrous, reddish-brown, peeling bark. The branches are a bright orange-brown with gray-green young shoots. The bright yellow-green leaves are small and narrow, turning a russet brown in autumn. This tree is ideal for growing close to water, so that the beautiful autumn colors are reflected on the surface. Propagation is by seed sown in spring or by hardwood cuttings taken in autumn.

Trillium grandiflorum

Trinity flower/Wood lily/Wake robin
HEIGHT: 18in (45cm) • Hardy
FLOWERING SEASON: Spring/summer

This clump-forming perennial develops into a dome-shaped plant with large, oval, deeply veined, dark green leaves. The pure white, funnel-shaped flowers, which gradually become flushed pink as the flower ages, are produced singly on short arching stems from spring until summer. There are also species with pink flowers and double white flowers. It likes shade and moist soil. Propagation is by division of the rhizomes after the leaves have died down.

Tropaeolum speciosum

Flame creeper
HEIGHT: 15ft (4.5m) • Hardy
FLOWERING SEASON: Summer/autumn

This deciduous herbaceous perennial climber has long-stalked, brilliant scarlet, trumpet-shaped flowers which are made up of five rounded wavy petals opening out flat, produced singly on curling stems. The stems, with their notched and circular mid green leaves, form an attractive plant even before the flowers start to appear. These plants are slow to establish but are worth the wait and like to have their roots in the shade. Prune in spring by cutting out the dead stems. Propagate by division in March.

Tsuga heterophylla

Western hemlock
HEIGHT: 70-100ft (20-30m) • Hardy
FLOWERING SEASON: None

A large, fast-growing tree with drooping branches and shoot tips. The young shoots are white and hairy bearing leaves which are dark green above and silver on the underside. The dark brown bark is scaly and deeply grooved. These trees perform best in sheltered areas with a heavy rainfall and in a partially shaded position. Propagation is by seed sown under protection in the spring, or for named cultivars, by semi-ripe cuttings taken in autumn. Other species are smaller. They dislike urban pollution.

Uvularia grandiflora

Bellwort/Merry-bells
HEIGHT: 18in (45cm) • Hardy • pH
FLOWERING SEASON: Spring

This clump-forming herbaceous perennial has narrow, pointed leaves which appear in the spring and only partially unfold to reveal clusters of graceful, bell-shaped, yellow flowers. These are carried on olive-green, succulent-looking stems, and after flowering the leaves unroll completely. A slower-growing species, *U. perfoliata*, has yellow flowers with twisted petals. Semi-shade is essential for this plant and it prefers moist peaty soil. Propagation is by division in early spring before flowering.

Vaccinium corymbosum

Blueberry/Whortleberry/Cowberry/Bilberry
HEIGHT: 5ft (1.5m) • Hardy • pH
FLOWERING SEASON: Spring

This small deciduous shrub forms a dense suckering thicket of upright multi-branched shoots, covered in bright green, spear-shaped leaves, which turn to bronze and scarlet in the autumn. The flowers are urn-shaped and vary in color from white to white-blushed-pink. They are followed in the autumn by sweet, edible, black berries which are covered by blue bloom. *V. c.* 'Pioneer' is grown for its vivid red autumn foliage. Propagation is by semi-ripe cuttings taken in late summer.

Viburnum plicatum 'Mariesii'

HEIGHT: 6ft (1.8m) • Hardy
FLOWERING SEASON: Spring/summer

This is a spectacular, large, wide-spreading shrub with a tendency to produce its branches in stacked layers, which gives a tiered effect. The oval leaves, which are deeply crinkled and a bright green through the summer, change to yellow and reddish-purple in autumn. The white flowers are carried in large flat heads, making the shrub look as if a layer of snow has just fallen on it. Propagation is by semi-ripe cuttings taken in late summer or by layering young shoots in early autumn.

Zenobia pulverulenta

Zenobia
HEIGHT: 6ft (1.8m) • Hardy • pH
FLOWERING SEASON: Summer

This is a beautiful small deciduous or semi-evergreen shrub with an open habit and thin, twiggy stems that are covered in a bluish-white bloom. The strap-like leaves are a glossy blue-green with a bluish-white underside when young. Large white flowers, very similar to those of the lily-of-the-valley, that hang in clusters from the leaf joints are produced in summer. The blooms give off a faint scent of aniseed. Propagation is by semi-ripe cuttings taken in late summer.

More Plants for Acid Soils

It is important to distinguish between those plants which are lime-haters and have to have acid soil to thrive and other plants which are quite tolerant of some acidity in the soil. The lime-haters are marked pH in the plant details and if you garden on clay or chalk it really is a waste of time trying to grow them.

Otherwise if your soil is not too acid and your climate isn't too wet then there is very little restriction on what you can grow. Your roses may not be quite as bountiful, and your stone fruit may not yeild quite as much as someone who lives a hundred miles away and is lucky enough to garden on the best loam but they will be fine for the average gardener. You may be best to avoid the Mediterranean plants like cistus and lavender. Acid soil can always be sweetened by adding lime and the productivity improved by digging in compost or manure.

The following plants included in other chapters in this book are just some of those that can also be grown in acid soils. Space prevents the inclusion of roses and bulbs which are also perfectly viable.

TREES

Acers (in variety)
Alnus incana
Amelanchier canadensis
Carpinus betulus
Chamaecyparis lawsoniana (and most conifers)
Crataegus (in variety)
Fagus (in variety)
Hamamelis mollis
Larix decidua
Liriodendron tulipifera
Magnolia grandiflora
Sorbus (in variety)

SHRUBS

Aucuba japonica
Berberis (in variety)
Ceanothus (in variety)
Choisya ternata
Cornus (in variety)
Cotinus coggygria
Euonymus fortunei cvs
Forsythia suspensa
Lavatera 'Barnsley'
Ligustrum ovalifolium
Mahonia (in variety)
Osmanthus (in variety)
Rhododendron – including *azaleas* (in variety)
Sambucus (in variety)
Sarcococca (in variety)
Syringa (in variety)
Vaccinium glaucoalbum
Viburnum (in variety)

PERENNIALS, GROUND COVER PLANTS & CLIMBERS

Aconitum 'Bressingham Spire'
Alchemilla mollis
Aquilegia alpina
Aronia arbutifolia
Artemesia absinthium
Aruncus dioicus
Astrantia major
Bergenia cordifolia
Buddleja (in variety)
Campanula (in variety)
Centhranthus ruber
Ceratostigma willmottianum
Echinops bannaticus
Filipendula palmata
Galium odoratum
Geranium (in variety)
Gunnera manicata
Iris germanica
Jasminum officinale
Lamium maculatum
Lapageria rosea
Ligularia (in variety)
Myosotis sylvestris
Phlomis fruticosa
Polygonatum × *hybridum*
Primula (in variety)
Santolina chamaecyparissus
Tradescantia (in variety)
Veronica prostrata
Vinca minor 'Argenteovariegata'
Viola (in variety)

PLANTS *for* ALKALINE SOILS

Alkaline soil occurs naturally in limestone areas, but is also created by the inclusion of builder's rubble in the soil, often around the bases of walls, where clematis thrives. Although gardeners with this soil are fortunate in that lime-loving plants are more numerous than acid-loving plants, dry, alkaline soil does need added leaf mold and compost to increase the nutrient content and water-retaining capacity.

ABOVE: Saponaria ocymoides, *with the charming common name of 'Tumbling Ted', is an ideal mat-forming perennial for a dry bank.*

OPPOSITE: *An informal border of yarrow, violas, geraniums and iris makes an attractive display. Most of the summer-flowering perennials do well on alkaline soil giving the gardener a wide range to choose from.*

ABOVE: Linum narbonense *(flax) is a charming, small, clump-forming perennial with flowers ranging from light to deep blue in summer. It likes light soil.*

It is understandable that those gardeners who can grow rhododendrons, and the many other lovely plants needing similar soil, think they are so lucky, but if you look at the vast range of lime-loving plants available, you will soon realize that, as a group they can provide interest and beauty at least on a par with the acid-loving plants.

Plants that prefer to grow in an alkaline soil, that is, with a pH of 7.0 or higher, are called Calcicole plants. Use a soil-testing kit to check your soil's pH. If you look at the number of popular native plants which grow well on alkaline soils, you will see that there is a wide range of attractive trees and shrubs, including clematis, lonicera (honeysuckle), sorbus and viburnums, that like these conditions. The list of plants also includes many herbaceous perennials, and many members of the pea family often excel on these soils, including cytisus and genista (broom), gleditsia, lathyrus (the sweet pea), and robinia.

In some areas, gardens made up of a shallow layer of soil over solid caliche or limestone have several characteristic features which make them difficult to garden. The presence of the base rock so near the surface of the soil makes it difficult to position plants at any depth without resorting to the use of a pickaxe or other heavy duty implement. Even this does not alter the fact that you are planting into rock and not soil, so that plant roots will have great difficulty penetrating it. This can lead to poor anchorage, particularly of trees, although some trees like beech (*Fagus sylvatica*), which does grow on shallow, alkaline soil, have developed a naturally broad, shallow root system in order to cope with the lack of soil.

During dry periods, these thin layers of soil can hold only limited reserves of water, and the upper levels of the rock become extremely dry. However, once established, many plants will produce an extensive root system which penetrates the soft rock, so that when rain does fall, they can absorb the maximum amount before it drains through the soil. Adding bulky organic matter to improve the soil is usually best done soon after a period of rain.

Many gardens have certain areas with more alkaline soil than other parts, in particular where builder's rubble has accumulated, often near house walls or patios. This is particularly true of many town gardens in areas around garden walls where old lime mortar may turn the soil from acid to alkaline. In a case like this, move plants if they do not do well in the position chosen for them originally. These are ideal situations for lime-loving plants, especially clematis, but it is essential when growing clematis that you shelter their roots from hot sun. Many gardeners are frightened of moving plants particularly in summer. Even if it is not recommended if you take plenty of soil with the plant, dig a deep hole, and puddle the plant in thoroughly, it is usually perfectly satisfactory.

ABOVE: *An informal woodland walk in spring in a garden with alkaline soil. Hellebores seen on the left do best in partial shade.*

LEFT: *The glorious rugosa rose, R. 'Roseraie de L'Haÿ' will flourish in alkaline soil. It is sometimes grown successfully as a low hedge.*

Acanthus spinosus

Bear's breeches
HEIGHT: 3ft (1m) • Hardy
FLOWERING SEASON: Summer

This herbaceous perennial is often described
as an 'architectural' plant. It has large arching
leaves, which are a glossy dark-green and
strap-like, with sharp spines on the points of
the toothed margins. The tall spikes of white
and purple tubular flowers, which alternate
between layers of green spiny bracts, are
borne throughout summer. The dead
flowerheads look attractive during winter
when frost-covered. Propagate by root cuttings in early spring, or division in winter.

Acer negundo 'Flamingo'

Ash-leaved maple/Box elder
HEIGHT: 50ft (15m) • Hardy
FLOWERING SEASON: Spring

A vigorous tree with ash-like leaves that are
bright green in summer, turning to golden-
yellow in autumn. In the spring, bright
greenish-yellow flowers are produced in flat
clusters on the branches before the leaves.
A. n. var. *violaceum* has purple leaves and
shoots, and the cultivar *A. n.* 'Variegatum'
has mid green leaves marbled with creamy-
white flecks and pink shoot tips in the spring.
Propagation is by seed sown in the spring or
budding in the summer (for cultivars).

Achillea filipendulina 'Gold Plate'

Yarrow
HEIGHT: 3ft (1m) • Hardy
FLOWERING SEASON: Late summer/early autumn

This herbaceous perennial has a compact
upright habit, with broad, finely divided,
slightly hairy, dull green leaves. The lemon-
yellow flowers are held erect above the
foliage in bold flat clusters 5-6in (12-15cm)
across. The cultivar *A. f.* 'Gold Plate' has
deep golden-yellow flowers. Propagate by
lifting the clumps in early spring, dividing
them into smaller portions of 4-5 shoots and
replanting them in the growing site.

Actinidia kolomikta

HEIGHT: 12ft (4m) • Hardy
FLOWERING SEASON: Late summer

This deciduous climbing shrub with twining
stems has heart-shaped, dark green leaves
marked with pink and white at the tip.
Actinidias generally prefer shade but
A. kolomikta will grow well on a sheltered
fence or wall in full sun and preferably a
neutral, well-drained soil. It has small white,
slightly fragrant flowers in June. The young
leaves are prone to damage by late spring
frosts. Propagation is by semi-ripe cuttings in
July and August. In February prune by thinning out overcrowded growths, and shorten
excessively vigorous shoots.

Aesculus pavia

Red buckeye/Horse chestnut
HEIGHT: 10ft (3m) • Hardy
FLOWERING SEASON: Early summer

This is a round-headed shrub, with large,
mid green, palm-like leaves made up of five
leaflets. The snapdragon-like flowers are
bright red with a yellow throat, and carried
on erect spikes up to 6in (15cm) long. There
are two good cultivars: *A. p.* 'Atrosanguinea',
which has deeper red flowers, and *A. p.*
'Humilis', which has a low, spreading habit.
A. hippocastanum is the common horse chestnut or conker tree. Propagation is by seed
sown in spring, budding in summer or grafting indoors in spring (for named cultivars).

Amelanchier canadensis

Snowy mespilus
HEIGHT: 20ft (6m) • Hardy
FLOWERING SEASON: Late spring

This is a deciduous, suckering shrub or small
tree with a dense, upright habit and dark
whippy shoots. The oval, mid to dark green
leaves with toothed margins are woolly
when young, and turn vivid shades of yellow,
orange and red in autumn. Brilliant white,
star-shaped flowers, are carried in bold erect
spikes in spring before the leaves have developed, followed by small, purple, currant-like
fruits in late summer. Propagation is by seed
sown in early autumn. Fireblight may cause
shrivelling of young shoots and flowers.

Anchusa azurea

Blue alkanet
HEIGHT: 3ft (1m) • Hardy
FLOWERING SEASON: Mid/late summer

A hardy herbaceous perennial with mid green, strap-like leaves covered in fine bristly hairs. The small, dish-shaped flowers are produced in long blunt spikes carried high above the foliage. Among the most popular cultivars are: 'Loddon Royalist', with rich gentian-blue flowers or the sky-blue variety 'Opal'. This plant thrives in full sun or partial shade, but must have a well-drained site. Propagation is by root cuttings 2in (5cm) long in February.

Aquilegia alpina

Columbine/Alpine columbine
HEIGHT: 18in (45cm) • Hardy
FLOWERING SEASON: Spring/early summer

Aquilegias are hardy perennial plants which bear long-spurred beautifully-coloured flowers from late spring throughout the summer. *A. alpina* has clear violet-blue flowers while *A. vulgaris*, 'Granny's bonnets', has flowers ranging from white through pink to purple. They prefer sun or partial shade and thrive in most garden soils provided that they do not dry out. Propagate by seed sown in spring or autumn but named forms seldom come true from seed and they cross freely.

Astrantia major

Masterwort
HEIGHT: 2ft (60cm) • Hardy
FLOWERING SEASON: Summer

One of the most under-rated garden perennials astrantias are easy to grow and tolerant of most soils and conditions provided the soil does not become waterlogged. They prefer slight shade. The flowers are pinkish-white and are borne in profusion throughout the summer above mid green leaves. Cut the plants down to soil level in late autumn and divide every three or four years. Propagate by dividing the plants into rooted pieces in March or October.

Aucuba japonica

HEIGHT: 6–12ft (2–4m) • Hardy
FLOWERING SEASON: Late spring

This evergreen shrub is easy to grow and will tolerate both dense shade and atmospheric pollution. The leaves, which are narrow, oval and have several teeth or notches at the tip, are glossy, leathery and a rich dark green. Of the various coloured leaf cultivars, *A. j.* 'Crotonifolia', with green and yellow mottled leaves, and *A. j.* 'Picturata' with a vivid golden splash in the center of each leaf, are the most popular. To obtain fruits both male and female plants have to be grown. Propagation is by semi-ripe cuttings in September and October.

Berberis darwinii

Darwin's barberry
HEIGHT: 10ft (3m) • Hardy
FLOWERING SEASON: Late spring

This berberis is one of the hardiest of shrubs originating from Chile. It has an upright habit. Its dark, shining evergreen leaves have three spiny points, which make it look like a miniature holly in winter. In spring the leaves are almost lost beneath a shower of brilliant orange-yellow blossom, which is followed by small, blue-black fruits which have a gray bloom to them. It prefers full sun and moist well-drained soil. Propagate by taking heel cuttings in late summer or by semi-ripe cuttings taken in the autumn.

Brunnera macrophylla

Siberian bugloss
HEIGHT: 18in (45cm) • Hardy
FLOWERING SEASON: Late spring

This is a low-growing woodland plant which prefers at least partial shade. In the late spring it bears delicate sprays of small, star-shaped, bright blue flowers with an orange-yellow eye in the center. The flowers are followed by roughly textured heart-shaped, slightly hairy, matt green leaves. The cultivar *B. m.* 'Dawson's White' has ivory-white margins to the dark green leaves. It needs shade to keep its color. Propagation is by division in the spring or, for species, seed sown in the autumn.

Campanula lactiflora

Bellflower
HEIGHT: 4ft (1.2m) • Hardy
FLOWERING SEASON: Summer

This herbaceous perennial has light green, oval leaves carried on strong, upright green stems. Bell-shaped flowers of light lavender-blue are produced on branching stems in summer. There are a number of named cultivars: *C. l.* 'Prichard's Variety' has deep lavender-blue flowers and *C. l.* 'Loddon Anna' soft pink ones. Propagation is by division in the early spring. The stems of these plants are so strong that they very rarely require staking. They like some shade.

Campsis × tagliabuana 'Mme Galen'

HEIGHT: 30ft (9m) • Moderately hardy
FLOWERING SEASON: Late summer/early autumn

This vigorous free-flowering hybrid is ideal for sunny walls and fences, and pergolas or other similar structures. It has up to twelve trumpet-like, salmon-red flowers, carried in clusters on the shoot tips from late summer until the first frosts. The light to mid green foliage consists of oval leaflets with toothed margins. Good yellow autumn color. The stem is light gray-green when young, ageing to creamy-brown. Propagation is by root cuttings taken in early spring.

Caryopteris × clandonensis 'Heavenly Blue'

HEIGHT: 3ft (1m) • Moderately hardy
FLOWERING SEASON: Late summer/autumn

A perennial sub-shrub caryopteris produce masses of small blue flowers at the end of the summer above silvery, gray-green, lance-shaped leaves. They prefer full sun and light well-drained soil with the addition of some peat to the soil and appreciate the shelter of a wall if grown in colder parts of the country. Cut the plant back hard in the spring. *C. incana* has deeper more purple flowers. Propagate by taking cuttings from non-flowering shoots at the ends of July.

Ceanothus impressus

Californian lilac
HEIGHT: 6ft (1.8m) • Moderately hardy
FLOWERING SEASON: Mid spring/early summer

This colorful, bushy evergreen shrub has small, dark green leaves which are slightly paler and downy on the underside. It produces many dense clusters of tiny, deep blue flowers. An excellent plant for its vibrant blue color, for the best effect it should be grown as a wall shrub. This is one of the hardiest of the evergreen ceanothus that can be grown in cooler climates, it likes a sheltered sunny position and well-drained soil. Propagation is by semi-ripe cuttings taken in summer or autumn.

Centranthus ruber

Red valerian
HEIGHT: 2½ft (75cm) • Hardy
FLOWERING SEASON: Mid/late summer

This perennial has thick, oval, gray-green leaves, carried on erect, fleshy, stems with the flowers developing at the tip. Branching heads of fierce red or deep pink, star-shaped flowers are borne in slightly domed clusters. There is a white-flowered form, *C. r. albus*, which also has pale green leaves. This plant will grow in virtually any soil: almost pure lime, brick dust or even builder's rubble. Propagation is by seed sown in autumn or spring, or by division in spring. Valerian is very invasive and must be controlled.

Cercis siliquastrum

Judas tree/Redbud tree
HEIGHT: 20ft (6m) • Hardy
FLOWERING SEASON: Late spring/early summer

This is a large, slow-growing shrub or small tree, which has deeply veined, broad, heart-shaped leaves, often purple-green when young with a blue sheen later, and turning yellow in autumn. The pretty, small, purple-pink, pea-shaped flowers are produced in vast quantities on both old and new wood from late spring to early summer. Small dark-brown, pod-like fruits are produced in autumn. It has been cultivated in British gardens since 1596. Propagation is by seed which is sown in spring.

Cistus × cyprius

Rock rose/Gum cistus
Height: 5ft (1.5m) • Moderately hardy
Flowering Season: Early summer

Beautiful half-hardy evergreen shrubby plants, rock roses like full sun, a warm sheltered position and light well-drained soil. Each flower lasts for one day but the plants carry flowers in succession throughout June and July. *C.* × *cyprius* has white flowers with a prominent red spot at the base of each petal, *C. albidus* has pale pink flowers and *C. creticus* has bright pink flowers. Propagate by semi-ripe cuttings in summer or hardwood cuttings in winter.

Clematis texensis

Height: 7ft (2m) • Hardy
Flowering Season: Late summer/early autumn

This is one of the less vigorous clematis and is ideal for growing into trees, bushy shrubs or hedges. The blue-green leaves have up to eight oval leaflets with the leaf stalk being the part of the plant which twines to support the plant. In the late summer single, scarlet-red, tulip-shaped flowers are produced. The hybrid *C.* 'The Princess of Wales' has attractive deep pink blooms. Like all clematis it prefers rich well-drained soil with its roots in the shade. Propagation is by semi-ripe cuttings taken in midsummer.

Corydalis lutea

Fumitory
Height: 8in (20cm) • Hardy
Flowering Season: Spring/autumn

This low-growing, clump-forming herbaceous perennial has gray-green, evergreen leaves, which are finely dissected and fern-like. The leaves of this plant often hang limply, giving the impression that the plant is wilting. From late spring spikes of yellow tubular flowers which open out to form a split funnel shape are carried above the leaves on thin green stems. Propagation is by seed sown in autumn or by division in early spring when the plants are dormant.

Crataegus laevigata 'Paul's Scarlet'

Hawthorn
Height: 15ft (4.5m) • Hardy
Flowering Season: Spring

This small tree, often called 'may', has gray-green, twiggy stems with small, very sharp spines, and an open spreading habit. The deeply lobed oval leaves are mid green in the summer, turning yellow in autumn. The clusters of white flowers which have a musky scent are followed by clusters of small red fruits in autumn and winter. The cultivar *C. l.* 'Paul's Scarlet' has double red flowers. Propagation is by budding in summer or grafting in spring.

Cupressus arizonica var. glabra 'Blue Ice'

Arizona cypress
Height: 60ft (18m) • Hardy
Flowering Season: Early autumn

This is a large coniferous tree of broadly conical habit. It has smooth, purple bark which flakes off to reveal yellow patches of new bark beneath. The blue-gray leaves are short, stubby and closely packed together, completely hiding the twigs. There are a number of slow-growing forms with attractive foliage. The cultivar *C. a.* var. *g.* 'Compacta' is a true dwarf conifer. Propagation is by semi-ripe cuttings, taken with a heel in September and October.

Delphinium 'Lord Butler'

Delphinium/Perennial larkspur
Height: 5ft (1.5m) • Hardy/half hardy
Flowering Season: Summer

Hardy perennials which bloom in mid-summer with tall spikes of flowers which are, by tradition, blue, but are available in a color range from white, through mauve to indigo. They do best in deep well-drained soil enriched with compost or manure and full sun. They require staking which must be done early and it is a good idea to thin out the shoots. Cut down the flower spikes after flowering and divide every four years in spring. Raise from seed or take basal cuttings in spring.

Deutzia scabra 'Plena'

HEIGHT: 8ft (2.5m) • Hardy
FLOWERING SEASON: Early/midsummer

This is a bushy deciduous shrub with an erect habit and attractive peeling nut-brown bark on the older stems. The narrow, oval leaves are mid to dark green in color. Dense spikes of scented, cup-shaped white flowers are produced in summer. Of the cultivars *D. s.* 'Candidissima' has white, double flowers, and *D. s.* 'Plena' has white blooms flushed rose-pink. Prefers full sun and fertile well-drained soil. Propagation is by semi-ripe cuttings taken in late summer, or by hardwood cuttings taken in winter.

Dianthus 'Doris'

Carnation/Pink
HEIGHT: 16in (40cm) • Hardy
FLOWERING SEASON: Summer/autumn

These plants have tufted, cushion-forming mounds of silver-gray foliage, with the leaves arranged in pairs on the silver-gray stems. They are ideal for the front of a border as they produce flushes of delicately scented, brightly coloured blooms, in colours ranging from white, through pink to dark red, in summer and again in autumn. They like sun and well-drained soil. Propagation is by division every three years, or by layering or cuttings in late summer.

Doronicum plantagineum

Leopard's bane
HEIGHT: 3ft (1m) • Hardy
FLOWERING SEASON: Spring/summer

This is a sturdy little plant with bright green, heart-shaped leaves. Above the leaves rise the stems, each carrying up to four large, bright yellow, daisy-like flowers. Three popular hybrids are: *D.* × *excelsum* 'Harpur Crewe' which has larger golden-yellow flowers, *D.* × *e.* 'Miss Mason', which is shorter and more compact, and the double-flowered *D.* × *e.* 'Spring Beauty'. They grow in sun or shade and any well-drained soil. Propagation is by division in the autumn or early spring.

Dryas octopetala

Mountain avens
HEIGHT: 3in (7.5cm) • Hardy
FLOWERING SEASON: Late spring/early summer

This tough, evergreen perennial, has a prostrate, spreading habit, and it develops into a dense mat of dark green, leathery leaves, the underneath of which is gray. The leaves are deeply lobed, giving them an oak-like appearance. The small, cup-shaped flowers are creamy-white and carried on stems just above the leaves from April. They are followed by attractive silvery-gray seed-heads: a good plant for ground cover in a rock garden. Propagation is by seed sown fresh or semi-ripe cuttings in midsummer.

Eccremocarpus scaber

Chilean glory flower
HEIGHT: 8–10ft (2.5-3m) • Moderately hardy
FLOWERING SEASON: Summer/autumn

This plant makes a vigorous climber when established, quickly covering whatever support it can find with its green slender stems. It supports itself with tendrils which are modifications of the dull green leaves. The small, orange, tubular flowers appear in large bunches from June onwards. *E. s. roseus* is a pink form, and *E. s. aurantiacus* a yellow one. Often grown as an annual it likes full sun and any well-drained soil but parts of the plant will die back each winter. Propagation is by seed sown in March.

Eremurus himalaicus

Foxtail lily/King's spear
HEIGHT: 8ft (2.5m) • Hardy
FLOWERING SEASON: Early summer

This is a truly majestic perennial. The bright green, narrow, strap-like leaves are produced in spring, but die down in summer as the flower spike develops. Tall spikes of white, cup-shaped flowers are produced from May onwards; *E. robusta* has soft pink flowers and *E.* × *isabellinus* Shelford Hybrids produce pink, orange or white flowers. Propagation is by seed sown in autumn, or by division in spring. These plants prefer sun and well-drained soil and come into growth early in spring, so may suffer some frost damage.

Erysimum cheiri

Wallflower
HEIGHT: 2ft (60cm) • Hardy
FLOWERING SEASON: Spring

Evergreen shrubby perennial, with woody stems forming a low mound. The strap-like leaves are dark green and slightly paler on the underside. The flat, four-petalled flowers are carried above the leaves in dense spikes. Of several named cultivars the most popular is *E. c.* 'Harpur Crewe', with double, mustard-yellow, fragrant flowers; this lasts about five years. Propagation is by softwood cuttings taken in summer. Clubroot causes stunted top growth and death.

Exochorda × macrantha 'The Bride'

Pearl bush/Bride bush
HEIGHT: 5ft (1.5m) • Hardy
FLOWERING SEASON: Late spring/early summer

A deciduous, arching, free-flowering shrub that flourishes in sun. It likes loamy soil and should have a top dressing of farmyard compost every other year. It eventually forms a thick mound covered with large, attractively-shaped, white flowers in late spring. Pruning is not really necessary but the plant benefits from thinning the old shoots after flowering. Exochordas are spectacular enough to merit an isolated place in the garden. Propagation is by cuttings of young shoots taken in late summer.

Forsythia suspensa

Golden bell
HEIGHT: 8ft (2.5m) • Hardy
FLOWERING SEASON: Spring

These ubiquitous shrubs, with their open, spreading habit and long, gently arching, gray-brown branches are a familiar sight in spring. The light to mid green leaves which are roughly oval in shape, turn butter-yellow in autumn. Delicate, pale to golden yellow flowers are produced abundantly in spring on the previous year's growth before the leaves emerge. They should be pruned after flowering. Propagation is by hardwood cuttings taken in the winter.

Geranium 'Johnson's Blue'

Cranesbill
HEIGHT: 2½ft (75cm) • Hardy (most)
FLOWERING SEASON: Late spring

The leaves of many of these versatile herbaceous perennials are their main attraction. Deeply notched to form a palm-like shape, they are carried on tough, thin leaf stalks and in many varieties turn orange-scarlet in autumn. The flowers appear as large clusters of small, saucer-shaped blooms. There are a large number of geraniums and among the easiest to grow are: *G.* 'Johnson's Blue' and *G. endressii*. They prefer a sunny position in well-drained garden soil. Propagation is by division in early spring.

Geranium pratense

Meadow cranesbill
HEIGHT: 2ft (60cm) • Hardy
FLOWERING SEASON: Midsummer

This low-growing perennial is another popular member of the large genus of hardy cranesbills. It has mid green, deeply lobed leaves with a scalloped margin, held above the ground on thin green leaf stalks. The saucer-shaped flowers have five petals, and are violet-blue with clearly marked red veins on each petal. The cultivar 'Mrs Kendall Clark' is very free flowering, with clear blue flowers. Propagation is by division in early spring. In autumn the leaves of these plants turn orange before dying down for winter.

Gypsophila 'Rosenschleier' syn. 'Rosy Veil'

Baby's breath/Chalk plant
HEIGHT: 3ft (1m) • Hardy
FLOWERING SEASON: Summer

These cottage garden favorites have thin, strap-like, gray-green leaves very like those of the carnation, carried on thick, gray-green stems. Masses of very small flowers are produced in large clusters. Dwarf and pink-flowered cultivars are available as well as a double cultivar, *G. paniculata* 'Bristol Fairy'. *G. repens* 'Rosea' is very low-growing, 4-6in (10-15cm), and spreads to form a dense mat, with small, rose-pink flowers produced in abundance. Propagation is by root cuttings.

Hydrangea aspera
Villosa Group

Hydrangea
HEIGHT: 10ft (3m) • Hardy
FLOWERING SEASON: Late summer/autumn

The Villosa Group hydrangeas are rather gaunt shrubs with narrow bluish green leaves above and gray down underneath. In late summer they carry large flower heads with a mass of small purple-pink flowers in the center surrounded by larger pinkish-white flowers on the outside. The whole effect is most striking and attractive. They prefer partial shade and moist soil. Propagation is by softwood cuttings taken in summer.

Iris germanica

Common German flag
HEIGHT: 2½ft (75cm) • Hardy
FLOWERING SEASON: Spring/summer

This tough evergreen plant has dark green, strap-like leaves up to 2ft (60cm) in length. The primrose-scented flowers have silky purple petals with a yellow center. They are carried on short stems in late spring. Among many good hybrids are: *I.* 'Black Swan', with deep, blue-black flowers with a dark blue beard, and the free-flowering *I.* 'Wabash', which has white standards and violet-blue falls. Bearded irises of which this is one will grow in most ordinary soils enriched by compost. Propagation is by division of established plants immediately after flowering.

Juniperus virginiana
'Sulphur Spray'

Pencil cedar
HEIGHT: 21ft (7m) • Hardy
FLOWERING SEASON: Spring

These versatile hardy conifers come in a vast array of cultivars. The low-growing, 'prostrate' cultivars make very good ground cover for low maintenance gardens. In contrast, *J. scopulorum* 'Skyrocket', with its silvery blue-green foliage, is probably the most narrow and upright conifer in cultivation. The wood of *J. virginiana* was used to make lead pencils. Propagation is by semi-ripe cuttings with a heel taken in September.

Kerria japonica 'Pleniflora'

Jew's mallow
HEIGHT: 10ft (3m) • Hardy
FLOWERING SEASON: Spring

A hardy leaf losing shrub with bright green leaves and arching shoots with yellow, spiky, pompom-type flowers carried on the branches in spring. They are often grown against a wall where they may have to be tied back. Kerria is one of the easiest shrubs to grow and tolerates all soil conditions but does best in sun where the soil has been deeply dug and enriched by compost or manure. Mature plants form clumps and propagation is by dividing the clumps in late autumn.

Kolkwitzia amabilis

Beauty bush
HEIGHT: 10ft (3m) • Hardy
FLOWERING SEASON: Late spring/early summer

This medium-sized shrub is commonly known as the beauty bush, a name it thoroughly deserves. The small, bell-shaped flowers, which are a soft-pink with a trace of yellow in the open throat, hang in small clusters on the thin twiggy branches. The light olive-green leaves are tinged red when young. The thin, twiggy shoots are erect when young but develop a drooping habit as they become older. Prefers full sun and fertile well-drained soil. Propagated from semi-ripe cuttings taken in midsummer.

Lavatera 'Barnsley'

Tree mallow
HEIGHT: 6ft (1.8m) • Moderately hardy
FLOWERING SEASON: Summer/autumn

A popular vigorous garden plant which may keep its leaves in mild winters, in the summer it carries a multitude of pinkish-white flowers with a deeper pink circle at the center. The leaves are a grayish green. *L.* 'Rosea' is bright pink. Lavateras must have well-drained soil and do not do well in heavy clay or soil that is very acidic. They like a sunny position. Cut the whole plant down to within 1ft (30cm) of the ground in the spring. Propagate by semi-ripe cuttings in summer or hardwood cuttings in winter.

Lonicera × *brownii* 'Dropmore Scarlet'

Scarlet trumpet honeysuckle
HEIGHT: 10ft (3m) • Hardy
FLOWERING SEASON: Mid/late summer

These attractive twining climbers have fragrant flowers which are tubular, opening out to a broad mouth, carried individually or in clusters. The colours range from white through pale yellow to gold, pink and scarlet. The pale to mid green leaves vary in shape from broadly oval to almost circular. *L. periclymenum* cultivars are very popular. Propagation is by semi-ripe cuttings taken in autumn.

Lupinus Russell Hybrids

Lupin
HEIGHT: 4ft (1.2m) • Hardy
FLOWERING SEASON: Summer

One of the delights of the herbaceous border in high summer, lupins are easy to grow and flourish in most soils. They prefer a sunny position. They come in a variety of colours which range from yellow to purple, blue and red. They are best raised from seed sown in the spring and planted out in position in the autumn, or they can be propagated by basal cuttings taken in the spring. The plants are not long-lived and will require replacing every 3 or 4 years. Prone to attack by aphids.

Morus nigra

Black mulberry
HEIGHT: 24ft (7.5m) • Hardy
FLOWERING SEASON: Early spring

This remarkable tree has large, gray-green pointed leaves, with a coarsely toothed margin and a coarse texture. The leaves give a striking display of autumn color. The catkin-like flowers are quite inconspicuous and often go unnoticed, but are followed in autumn by reddish-purple, blackberry-like fruit, almost black when ripe, which is juicy and very tasty. Propagation is by hardwood cuttings taken in early winter and rooted out in the open ground.

Nigella damascena

Love-in-a-mist/Devil-in-a-bush
HEIGHT: 2ft (60cm) • Hardy
Flowering Season: Summer

A hardy annual grown for its attractive blue flowers, the flowers are set among very finely divided leaf stems which add considerably to their charms. *N. d.* 'Miss Jekyll' has darker blue flowers and *N. d.* 'Persian Jewels' has white, pink or blue flowers. The flowers are followed by decorative seed pods much used in flower arranging but if these are not required it is best to dead head the plant as this prolongs the flowering period. Likes sun and fertile well-drained soil. Sow seed in spring for flowers that summer.

Osmanthus delavayi

HEIGHT: 8ft (2.5m) • Hardy
FLOWERING SEASON: Spring

An evergreen shrub, *O. delavayi* is from China and was originally introduced in 1890. It has oval, toothed leaves which are a dark, glossy green. It produces clusters of small tubular white flowers which are highly fragrant. It will grow in sun or partial shade and prefers well-drained soil, but ideally needs a site sheltered from cold winds. The species, *O. heterophyllus*, makes a good hedging plant. If growing *O. heterophyllus* as a hedge, trim it regularly. To propagate take half-ripe cuttings in summer or layer branches in autumn.

Ostrya carpinifolia

Hop hornbeam
HEIGHT: 50ft (15m) • Hardy
FLOWERING SEASON: Mid spring

This attractive tree has grayish-purple bark on the main trunk and reddish-brown shoots which carry the glossy, dark green, oval leaves, which turn butter-yellow in the autumn. The flowers are long yellow catkins which hang from the bare branches in large quantities in spring. Green, hop-like fruits appear in autumn which later turn brown, they have a small nut-type seed under each 'hop' scale. For small gardens, the smaller *O. virginiana* is more useful. Propagation is by seed sown in late autumn or early spring.

Philadelphus coronarius 'Variegatus'

Mock orange
HEIGHT: 6ft (1.8m) • Hardy
FLOWERING SEASON: Summer

This deciduous, bushy shrub has a dense, upright habit and mid green, oval leaves. The small, creamy-white flowers are noted for their heady fragrance. A number of cultivars have coloured leaves: *P. c.* 'Aureus' has golden-yellow leaves, which turn lemon-green as they age, and *P. c.* 'Variegatus' green leaves edged with white. Propagation is by softwood cuttings taken in summer or hardwood cuttings taken in autumn and winter.

Paeonia delavayi

Tree peony
HEIGHT: 6ft (1.8m) • Hardy
FLOWERING SEASON: Summer

The tree peony is a deciduous shrub with erect branches and an open suckering habit, the pale-brown bark flakes from the stems as they age. Large, oval leaves are finely divided into pointed sections with reddish-green stalks. The small, cup-shaped, single red flowers have golden stamens in the center, and are followed by green, black-seeded fruits in autumn. Propagation is by seed sown in autumn or semi-ripe cuttings taken in summer.

Phillyrea latifolia

HEIGHT: 10ft (3m) • Hardy
FLOWERING SEASON: Late spring/early summer

An evergreen shrub which has small but very fragrant flowers. The small, elliptical strap-like leaves are a shiny dark green and leathery. The small, scented white flowers are carried in clusters at the end of the young, branching stems. They are sometimes followed by blackcurrant-like fruits in autumn. Many of the branches tend to arch over so that a loose mound-like shrub is formed. It likes a sunny position and well-drained soil. Propagation is by semi-ripe cuttings taken in early summer.

Phlomis fruticosa

Jerusalem sage
HEIGHT: 3ft (1m) • Hardy
FLOWERING SEASON: Summer

An attractive, summer-flowering shrub, which forms a dense evergreen mound of straggly twiggy branches. The unusually shaped yellow flowers are produced in large ball-shaped trusses on the shoot tips. Broadly oval gray-green, coarsely textured leaves have a felty surface which turns slightly yellow in autumn. The young erect stems are also covered in felt, which disappears by the end of the first year of growth. Prune in late spring after the last frosts. Propagation is by softwood cuttings taken in late summer.

Populus alba 'Raket'

White poplar
HEIGHT: 80ft (25m) • Hardy
FLOWERING SEASON: Early spring

A deciduous tree with a broad, spreading habit, dark gray-green fissured bark, and young shoots which are covered with a thick white felt. The main attraction is the foliage: dark green leaves which have a silver down on the underside turn golden yellow in autumn. The cultivar *P. a.* 'Richardii' is much slower-growing and has small golden leaves which are white beneath. Poplar trees like coastal districts. Propagation is by hardwood cuttings taken in autumn. Silver leaf fungus kills large branches.

Potentilla fruticosa 'Hopley's Orange'

HEIGHT: 4ft (1.2m) • Hardy
FLOWERING SEASON: Spring/summer

This is a compact, bushy shrub with masses of spindly branches, with orange-brown bark which turns gray-brown and flakes with age. Deeply lobed, mid green leaves are in dense clusters over the younger branches. Flowers are small, buttercup-yellow and borne in clusters of no more than three blooms. Numerous named cultivars include the low-growing, *P. f.* 'Red Ace', with vermilion flowers and *P. f.* 'Abbotswood', with dark green foliage and white flowers. Propagation is by semi-ripe cuttings taken in autumn.

Prunus sargentii

Sargent cherry
HEIGHT: 25ft (8m) • Hardy
FLOWERING SEASON: Early/mid spring

This tree produces vast quantities of clear, single, shell-pink flowers in large clusters, which are complemented by the emerging glossy, bronze-red foliage of the new season's growth. Even more striking is the dramatic change of foliage color in early autumn when the leaves turn yellow, orange and crimson shades before falling. Most ornamental cherries are propagated by budding or grafting in commercial nurseries, and offered for sale as young trees.

Robinia hispida

Rose acacia
HEIGHT: 6ft (1.8m) • Hardy
FLOWERING SEASON: Late spring/early summer

This attractive deciduous shrub has a loose, open habit and slightly arching branches, which are brittle and break very easily. The dark green leaves, which consist of up to thirteen small, oval leaflets arranged along a green central leaf stalk, turn butter-yellow in autumn. The large, sweet pea-like flowers are deep rose-pink, and are borne in long dangling clusters. It is ideal for training up against a wall or fence. The shrub tolerates most soils except for waterlogged sites and prefers full sun. Propagation is by seed sown in spring.

Romneya coulteri

Californian tree poppy
HEIGHT: 6ft (1.8m) • Moderately hardy
FLOWERING SEASON: Late summer

A striking and beautiful summer flowering perennial which needs the shelter of a south or south-west wall. It has large fragrant white flowers with prominent centres of golden-yellow stamens which appear in late summer. The leaves are deeply divided and gray-green in color. It needs well-drained soil enriched by compost or leaf mould. Cut back the stems in the spring. Propagation is by root cuttings taken in the spring or by seed sown in the autumn.

Rosmarinus officinalis

Rosemary
HEIGHT: 6ft (1.8m) • Moderately hardy
FLOWERING SEASON: Spring/autumn

This popular aromatic shrub has an erect open habit, with narrow, aromatic, evergreen leaves that are mid to dark green in color with pale green undersides. The tubular flowers, which range in color from white to blues, pinks and mauves, are produced in small clusters at the leaf joints. These plants do not respond favorably to hard pruning, just trim back any straggling shoots. They grow best in well-drained soil and full sun. Propagation is by semi-ripe cuttings taken in August and September.

Sambucus racemosa

Red-berried elder
HEIGHT: 9ft (3m) • Hardy
FLOWERING SEASON: Late spring

This is a large deciduous shrub with a broad, spreading habit. It is grown for its lush foliage and colorful fruits. The leaves are mid green and divided into five oval leaflets joined at the base to form a 'hand'. They turn pale yellow in autumn. In spring, large flat heads of white flowers are produced, to be fol-lowed by huge clusters of bright red berries in autumn. The cultivar *S. r.* 'Plumosa Aurea' has golden, finely-cut leaves. Elders grow almost anywhere. Propagation is by hardwood cuttings taken in winter.

Scabiosa 'Butterfly Blue'

Scabious
HEIGHT: 2ft (60cm) • Hardy
FLOWERING SEASON: Summer/autumn

A clump-forming herbaceous perennial with leaves that are divided into narrow segments. The large flowers, which range from white through blue to mauves and pinks, are borne on long, slender, leafless stems. *S. caucasica* 'Clive Greaves' is a rich mauve; 'Miss Willmott' is the best white cultivar. Two recent introductions are the more compact species 'Butterfly Blue' and 'Pink Mist'. It likes a sunny position and well-drained soil. Propagation is by softwood cuttings taken in spring and summer, or division in spring.

Spiraea betulifolia

Meadowsweet
HEIGHT: 3ft (1m) • Hardy
FLOWERING SEASON: Spring

Spiraeas are hardy deciduous shrubs grown
for their leaf color and the masses of small
flowers that appear in spring and summer.
S. 'Arguta' known as the 'Bridal wreath', has
arched branches covered with white flowers
in May as has *S. betulifolia*. *S. japonica*
'Goldflame' is a more upright arching shrub
with orange-red young leaves in the spring
and heads of deep rose-pink flowers. Spiraeas
can be grown in most soils and semi-shade.
Propagate by semi-ripe cuttings in summer.

Stachyurus chinensis

HEIGHT: 12ft (4m) • Hardy
FLOWERING SEASON: Winter

These winter-flowering shrubs do well on
most soils and deserve to be more common
than they are. When young, the plant has an
upright habit, later forming a network of
branching, purple-green shoots. The dark
green, purple-tinged leaves are deeply
veined, large, oval and end in a point. The
small, pale yellow flowers, which are in long
catkin-like structures, are borne freely along
the bare branches in winter and spring.
Propagation is by layering of low branches
or semi-ripe cuttings taken in summer.

Symphoricarpos × doorenbosii 'Mother of Pearl'

Snowberry
HEIGHT: 5ft (1.5m) • Hardy
FLOWERING SEASON: Summer

The common snowberry, *S. albus* has small
pink flowers in summer followed by white
round berries which can be seen on bushes
all winter as they are often ignored by the
birds. *S. × d.* 'Mother of Pearl' has pink
berries and *S. orbiculatus*, the coral berry, has
white flowers and red berries. They can be
grown in all soils and in shade as well as sun.
They can make a useful informal hedge.
Propagate by semi-ripe cuttings in summer.

Syringa × henryi

Lilac
HEIGHT: 5-15ft (1.5-4.5m) • Moderately hardy
FLOWERING SEASON: Summer

Attractive, deciduous shrubs, lilacs have mid
green leaves, arranged along the twiggy
branches in opposite pairs. The small flowers
are carried in spikes at the tips of shoots, they
are very fragrant, tubular and range in color
from deep pink through mauve to white.
There are a number of species and cultivars
available and care should be taken to select
one that does not grow too large. They
flourish in light or heavy fertile soil and
prefer a sunny site. Propagation is by semi-
ripe cuttings taken in mid to late summer.

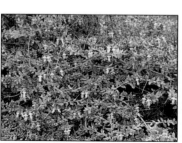

Teucrium fruticans

Shrubby germander
Height: 6ft (1.8m) • Moderately hardy
Flowering Season: Summer

An evergreen shrub sometimes called the
tree germander which has rather untidy
pointing branches. These carry blue-gray
silvery aromatic leaves which are white
underneath. In the summer blue flowers
appear along the length of each branch. It
likes full sun and fertile well-drained soil and
is a useful addition to any mixed border. It
does not require pruning except to remove
straggly branches and any dead wood in the
spring. Propagate by semi-ripe cuttings
taken in the summer.

Thuja occidentalis 'Sunkist'

Eastern white cedar
HEIGHT: 60ft (18m) • Hardy
FLOWERING SEASON: Early spring

This is a vigorous, long-lived tree with a neat
conical shape. The bark, which is light to
reddish-brown, peels and flakes off as the tree
ages. The flat leaves are made up of many
small, scale-like sections, and have a strong
'pineapple' aroma which is released when
the leaves are crushed. The cones are small
and brown. *T. plicata* 'Zebrina' has yellow
bands on the leaves which are so close
together that the plant appears to be golden.
Propagation is by semi-ripe cuttings taken
in spring or autumn.

Verbascum chaixii

Mullein
HEIGHT: 3ft (1m) • Hardy
FLOWERING SEASON: Summer

This evergreen perennial has large, nettle-like leaves which are gray-green in color and covered with a fine, gray felt. The slender spires of yellow flowers with purple centres are produced in July and August and the white-flowered cultivar *V. c.* 'Album', is even more striking. Propagation is by seed in spring or late summer or by root cuttings in winter. Blackfly are often a problem but mullein moth caterpillars are possibly the most devastating pest.

Viburnum tinus

Laurustinus
HEIGHT: 5ft (1.5m) • Hardy
FLOWERING SEASON: Winter

This evergreen shrub has an upright habit when young but becomes a rather open, round-topped, spreading plant as it ages. The broadly oval, dark green leaves have paler undersides and are arranged in pairs along the dark, greenish-brown stems which end in flat clusters of small, white, slightly fragrant tubular flowers. Possibly the best plant is *V. t.* 'Eve Price', which has flowers that are deep rose-pink in bud, opening to white flushed with pink. It tolerates most soils and some shade. Propagation is by semi-ripe cuttings taken in early summer.

Weigela florida 'Foliis Purpureis'

Bush honeysuckle
HEIGHT: 3ft (1m) Hardy
FLOWERING SEASON: Spring/early summer

A deciduous, low-growing, bushy shrub which has funnel-shaped flowers, bright pink on the outside and a paler pink shading to white within. The leaves are a dullish dark green. Weigelas will grow in almost any soil and while they prefer sun they will tolerate some shade. Prune established plants after flowering by cutting out up to one third of the branches to ground level. Propagate by semi-ripe cuttings in summer.

More Plants for Alkaline Soil

Many plants can be grown on alkaline soil. The list is very large and we can only give a small selection of the most suitable plants but it should be noted that most bulbs (see pages 138–145) do well on lime.

Gardening on alkaline soil is governed by the depth of soil over the underlying lime or limestone strata, alkaline soil is inclined to be dry and hungry. It can be improved by adding copious quantities of farmyard manure, leaf mold, garden compost and turf and the fertility can be improved by adding dried blood and balanced artificial fertilizers.

TREES

Abies koreana
Acer (in variety)
Betula (in variety)
Carpinus betulus
Catalpa bignonioides
Cercidiphyllum japonicum
Chimonanthus praecox
Corylus (in variety)
Crataegus (in variety)
Davidia involucrata
Fagus (in variety)
Ficus carica
Fraxinus angustifolia

Koelreuteria paniculata
Larix decidua
Liquidambar styraciflua 'Worplesdon'
Malus (in variety)
Pyrus (in variety)
Sorbus (in variety)

SHRUBS

Aronia arbutifolia
Artemesia absinthium
Berberis (in variety)
Buddleja (in variety)
Chaenomeles japonica
Choisya ternata
Cornus (in variety)
Cotinus coggygria
Escallonia (in variety)
Euonymus fortunei cvs.
Jasminum officinale
Lavandula (in variety)
Ligustrum ovalifolium
Mahonia (in variety)
Myrtus communis
Osmanthus (in variety)
Philadelphus (in variety)
Ribes laurifolium
R. 'Königin von Dänemark'
R. 'Madame Legras de Saint Germain'
(Old-fashioned and Alba roses are particularly suitable for poor soil and conditions)
Rosmarinus officinalis
Salvia officinalis
Sarcococca hookeriana
Senecio (*Brachyglottis*) 'Sunshine'

Stepanandra tanakae
Syringa (in variety)
Viburnum (in variety)

PERENNIALS & GROUND COVER PLANTS

Alchemilla mollis
Amenone × hybrida
Aruncus dioicus
Aster novi-belgii
Astilbe (in variety)
Bergenia (in variety)
Campanula carpatica
Catananche caerulea
Ceratostigma willmottianum
Crambe cordifolia
Dianthus (in variety)
Dicentra (in variety)
Digitalis (in variety)
Echinops bannaticus
Geranium (in variety)
Helianthemum (in variety)
Iris (in variety)
Lamium maculatum
Leucanthemum × superbum
Nepeta × faassenii
Penstemon (in variety)
Perovskia atriplicifolia
Phlox paniculata
Polygonatum × hybridum
Primula auricula 'Adrian'
Pulmonaria saccharata
Santolina chamaecyparissus
Veronica prostrata
Vinca (in variety)

PLANTS
for CLAY SOILS

Although part of the garden landscape in many areas, clay soil can be difficult to deal with, becoming waterlogged in winter and baked hard in summer. Plants suffer alternately from too much water or from drought. Here is a selection of plants that are attractive and tough enough to cope with these far from ideal conditions.

ABOVE: Houttuynia cordata *'Chameleon', a robust ground-covering perennial with lovely leaf color that likes moisture and appreciates some sun. It grows well beside water.*

OPPOSITE: *Foxgloves make an impressive bank at the back of a border with yellow hemerocallis, geranium and lady's mantle at the front.*

ABOVE: *Big clump-forming hostas, such as* Hosta crispula *with its wavy-edged, cream-splashed leaves, are successful on clay, as are the drifts of* Persicaria bistorta, *with its spires of pink flowers in summer.*

Clay is one of those substances that is wonderful in small quantities, but a real nuisance if you have too much of it. It is an essential part of a good soil, because it holds onto the nutrients that plants need for healthy growth, and retains moisture, so that plants growing in it suffer less from drought in all but the driest of summers. Unfortunately, despite these advantages, really heavy, wet, sticky clay soil is often totally unworkable, and it is also cold in spring, which can quickly rot delicate plants.

These difficulties come about as a direct result of the composition of the soil. The particles that make up a clay soil are the smallest found in mineral soils, with the result that the water retained in the tiny spaces between the particles binds them together into an unresponsive mass. Physically working this soil is largely a matter of timing; try to do it when it is too wet and it will smear and form a 'pan' at the depth you go down to, forming an impenetrable layer for plant roots and draining water alike. Leave it until it is too dry, on the other hand, and you are working with what feels like lumps of rock. Once you have experienced both situations, it will become apparent that you must establish the ideal state in which to tackle your soil.

Clay soils have a tendency to either become sticky and greasy when they are wet, or to bake hard and crack open when they dry out. This cracking process leaves deep crevices which speed up the drying-out process by exposing a greater surface area from which the moisture can evaporate. Any rain which falls then simply runs off without soaking in. At this stage, you would expect the plants to wilt and die, but even though the soil seems to be rock hard, enough water is still being held by the soil particles to sustain the plants for a while.

While water retention is a distinct advantage in summer, it is usually just the opposite in winter. So much water may be retained in the soil, and for such long periods, that plant roots have to be able to tolerate very damp conditions, often with little air to help compensate. Many members of the rose family thrive in these conditions; and aronia, chaenomeles (quince), cotoneaster, crataegus (hawthorn), malus (crab apple) and pyracantha do particularly well.

If the soil can be improved to make it more workable by the addition of organic matter to loosen it up, it will retain plant nutrients for longer periods than other soils, so that plants are able to use more of them before they are leached away by rain. Fertilizer applications are then more effective and the nutrients released by organic matter as it rots are used more effectively.

Finally, clay soils can be acid, neutral or alkaline, which will also affect your choice of plants, so a soil test is helpful if the vegetation in the immediate surroundings fail to give any clues. Although clay soils are more stable in their acidity and alkalinity, they are much more difficult to change. More often than not the limiting factor as to what you can grow on a clay soil will in fact be the soil pH reading rather than the clay content of your soil.

There are many bulbs, herbaceous perennials and marginal plants such as aruncus, lysimachia, mimulus, and tradescantia which prefer the cool, moist conditions that clay soils offer. As with any situation where one condition overrides the others, once you have chosen the plants which thrive under those circumstances, you can have as good a display as anywhere else. Grow plants with a vigorous constitution as those are the ones likely to do best.

BELOW: Persicaria bistorta, *at the front of the border, with iris,* geranium phaeum *and* philadelphus *behind are all plants that will flourish in heavy soil. Roses are particularly suitable plants to grow if you garden on clay.*

Abelia × *grandiflora*

HEIGHT: 5ft (1.5m) • Hardy
FLOWERING SEASON: Late summer/late autumn

This hybrid shrub has glossy green, oval leaves carried on thin branches, giving the plant a loose, spreading appearance. The tubular flowers, borne in open clusters on the shoot tips, are slightly fragrant and a soft pink, which fades to white with age. Regular pruning is not required. It likes well-drained soil and a sheltered sunny position, some protection may be necessary in severe winters. This plant is easy to propagate from 4in (10cm) tip cuttings placed in a cold frame in August.

Acer platanoides

Norway maple
HEIGHT: 100ft (30m) • Hardy
FLOWERING SEASON: Spring

This is a vigorous tree with typical, palmate maple leaves. Bright green in summer, they turn a bright golden-yellow in the autumn. In the spring bright golden flowers are produced in broad flat clusters on the branches before the leaves. Two good cultivars are the purple-leaved *A. p.* 'Crimson King' and *A. p.* 'Drummondii', which has mid green leaves with a creamy-white margin. Propagation is by seed sown in the spring or, for named cultivars, budding in the summer.

Alcea rosea Chater's Double Group

Hollyhock
HEIGHT: 8ft (2.5m) • Hardy
FLOWERING SEASON: Summer

Hollyhocks are hardy biennial plants although in some cases they are short lived perennials. They are a familiar sight throughout cottage gardens in the country and their large upright flower spikes make a focal point in any border. They should be raised from seed sown in a prepared bed in May and planted out in position in October. Hollyhocks like well-drained soil and a sunny position. Rust may be a problem.

Alnus incana

Gray alder
HEIGHT: 60ft (18m) • Hardy
FLOWERING SEASON: Early spring

This is a deciduous tree with reddish-brown shoots and a wide conical habit. The broadly oval leaves are dark green on the upper surface, gray beneath and deeply veined, with slightly puckered margins. In late winter and early spring, dangling yellow catkins are produced close to the shoot tips. Alders grow in most conditions and this tree is ideal for poor soils and cold exposed sites. There is a golden-leafed cultivar *A. i.* 'Aurea'. Propagation is by seed sown in spring, or, for named cultivars, grafting.

Amaranthus caudatus

Love-lies-bleeding/Joseph's coat
HEIGHT: 3-4ft (1-1.2m) • Half-hardy
FLOWERING SEASON: Summer/autumn

This popular plant has broadly oval, light green leaves and crimson drooping, rope-like flowers up to 18in (45cm) long. The stems of the plant often turn crimson in the autumn. *A. c.* 'Viridis' has attractive pale green tassels, while a very striking variety, *A. tricolor* var. *salicifolius* is grown for its drooping, willow-like leaves which are shades of orange, reddish-pink and bronze. This easy-going plant will grow in any light, from full sun through to partial shade. Propagation is by seeds sown in March.

Anemone × *hybrida* 'Königin Charlotte'

Japanese anemone
HEIGHT: 3ft (1m) • Hardy
FLOWERING SEASON: Late summer/early autumn

This vigorous branching plant thrives in moist soils, in a partially shaded situation. The mid to deep green leaves are deeply cut and almost trifoliate. The shallowly cup-shaped flowers, which range from white to deep rose-pink with a bright core of yellow stamens, are carried on tall, thin, green stems. Among the cultivars are *A.* × *h.* 'Honorine Jobert' with white flowers, and the semi-double-flowered *A. hupehensis* var. *japonica* 'Bressingham Glow' with rosy-red blooms.

Aralia elata

Japanese angelica tree
HEIGHT: 25ft (8m) • Hardy
FLOWERING SEASON: Late summer

This large suckering shrub has sparse, angular branches clad with short, broad-based prickles. It is grown for the beauty of its large clusters of dark green leaves which are arranged in a whorl on the end of each branch. Large spikes of small white flowers are carried on the tip of each branch from late August. A very attractive cultivar, *A.e.* 'Aureovariegata', has irregular, golden-yellow edged leaves. Propagate by root cuttings taken in February.

Aronia arbutifolia

Chokeberry
HEIGHT: 8ft (2.5m) • Hardy
FLOWERING SEASON: Spring

A colorful, deciduous shrub which has a rather erect habit when young, but becomes lax and spreading with age. It is grown for its flowers, fruits and autumn color. The leaves are narrowly oval, dark green with a gray-green underside, and turn shades of brilliant orange, crimson and purple in autumn. In spring, small, white, hawthorn-like flowers are produced in flat clusters, followed by small red berries. It prefers sun or semi-shade and moist well-drained soil. Propagation is by semi-ripe cuttings in summer or seed sown in spring.

Aruncus dioicus

Goat's beard
HEIGHT: 5ft (1.5m) • Hardy
FLOWERING SEASON: Summer

This hummock-forming perennial has large, light green, deeply-veined leaves which are made up of several strap-like leaflets, held on tough sturdy stems. In the summer, large feathery plumes of creamy-white flowers are carried on strong thin reddish-green stems. In the autumn the female plants bear chestnut brown seed-heads, but it is the male plants that produce the best flowers. It will grow in any well-drained soil and likes full sun. Propagation is by division in winter.

Astilbe × arendsii

Goat's beard
HEIGHT: 3ft (1m) • Hardy
FLOWERING SEASON: Midsummer

This hardy herbaceous perennial has deep green, finely cut, fern-like foliage, carried on thin wiry reddish-green stems; some of the red-flowered cultivars have bronze-green foliage in the spring. In the summer large, pointed spikes of plume-like blooms appear. A large number of cultivars are now available: *A.* 'Bressingham Beauty' has spikes of rich pink flowers, and *A.* 'Feuer', has salmon-red blooms. They like moist rich soil and at least partial shade. Propagation is by division in the winter.

Berberis × stenophylla

Barberry
HEIGHT: 8ft (2.5m) • Hardy
FLOWERING SEASON: Late spring

This evergreen shrub has gracefully arching, slender branches, with small, orange-yellow flowers, which are followed by small, blue fruits. The small, glossy, dark green leaves are narrow and tipped with sharp spines. It is effective as an impenetrable, informal hedge, but also as an individual specimen plant. The dwarf cultivar *B.* × *s.* 'Crawley Gem', has a low, bushy habit and orange flowers which are red when in bud. They are soil tolerant and grow in sun or semi-shade. Propagation is by semi-ripe cuttings taken in summer.

Campsis radicans

Trumpet flower/Trumpet vine
HEIGHT: 30ft (9m) • Moderately hardy
FLOWERING SEASON: Late summer/early autumn

A fast-growing plant ideal for sunny walls and fences, pergolas and gazebos, or other, similar structures. Four to twelve trumpet-like orange/red flowers are carried in clusters on the shoot tips. There are also red- and yellow-flowered cultivars. The light to mid green foliage consists of oval leaflets which form pinnate leaves. Good yellow autumn color. Fast rate of growth. Likes sun and fertile, well-drained soil, water in the summer in dry spells. Propagation is by root cuttings taken in early spring.

Cardamine pratensis 'Flore Pleno'

Cuckoo flower/Lady's smock/Bitter cress
HEIGHT: 18in (45cm) • Hardy
FLOWERING SEASON: Late spring

This neat, clump-forming plant has mid
green leaves divided into many small, rounded leaflets arranged in neat basal rosettes.
C. p. 'Flore Pleno', produces loose, open
clusters of double lilac flowers in late spring.
This plant does not produce seed but is very
easy to propagate: leaves in contact with a
moist surface produce adventitious roots,
and later shoots which can be divided up
to produce more plants.

Celastrus orbiculatus

Oriental bittersweet/Staff vine
HEIGHT: 22ft (7m) • Hardy
FLOWERING SEASON: Summer

A large, vigorous, useful climber with oval,
mid green leaves on short stalks and tiny
greenish flowers carried on the female plant
in summer. The leaves turn a good yellow in
autumn. The twining stems are light gray-
green, changing to light creamy-brown with
age in early summer, followed by bright
orange capsules containing a scarlet-coated
seed if a male plant is available as a pollinator.
Prefers shade and grows in most soils.
Propagation is from seed sown in autumn.

Chaenomeles japonica

Japonica/Japanese quince
HEIGHT: 4ft (1.2m) • Hardy
FLOWERING SEASON: Spring

A colorful, slow-growing shrub with a lax
spreading habit. The single flowers, orange-
red with a golden center, are produced in
profusion along the older wood in spring,
followed by bright yellow quince fruits.
Elliptical leaves are green, changing to pale
yellow in autumn. Often grown on walls it
prefers sun and well-drained soil. Prune
after flowering. Propagation is by semi-ripe
cuttings taken with a heel in late summer.
Coral spot fungus can cause problems.

Crambe cordifolia

Ornamental sea kale
HEIGHT: 6ft (1.8m) • Hardy
FLOWERING SEASON: Summer

A large spreading plant which forms a great
clump when established and in the summer
is covered with masses of small white
fragrant flowers rather like a giant gypsophila. They are carried above large dark
green crinkled leaves. *C. maritima* is a smaller
plant more generally found in the kitchen
garden where it can be grown as a spring
vegetable. Kale is easy to cultivate in ordinary well-drained garden soil and tolerates
some shade. Propagate by dividing up the
clumps in the spring.

Darmera peltata

Umbrella plant
HEIGHT: 4ft (1.2m) • Hardy
FLOWERING SEASON: Spring

This is a spreading perennial with large,
disc-like leaves which turn an interesting
bronze-pink in the autumn. The pale pink
flowers, which have a white reverse to the
petals, are carried in large round clusters on
dark greenish-brown stems, which are
covered in fine white hairs. The flowers and
stems appear before the leaves. It needs
moist conditions and makes a fine water
plant beside a pool. Grows in sun or shade.
Propagation is by division of the rhizomes
in spring or by seed in autumn.

Digitalis grandiflora

Foxglove
HEIGHT: 3ft (1m) • Hardy
FLOWERING SEASON: Late summer

This superb perennial foxglove forms a
clump of strap-like leaves which are mid
green and covered with soft hairs particularly
on the underside. The clear, pale yellow
flowers have a pattern of brown, net-like
markings on the inside, and are carried on
tall flower spikes up to 3ft (1m) or more in
height. Foxgloves grow best in moist well-
drained soil and semi-shade. This plant is
relatively short-lived and must be replaced
every third or fourth year. Propagation is by
seed sown in late spring or early summer.

Dodecatheon pulchellum

Shooting star/American cowslip
HEIGHT: 18in (45cm) • Hardy
FLOWERING SEASON: Early summer

These clump-forming hardy herbaceous perennials have light green, elliptical leaves arranged in flat, spreading rosettes growing close to the ground. In the summer the nodding flowers appear on strong slender stems, each bloom is a circle of rose–purple petals which are swept back away from the bright yellow anthers in the center of the flower. They prefer a shady position in moist soil. Propagation is by seed sown in autumn, or by division in winter.

Filipendula palmata 'Alba'

Meadowsweet/Dropwort
HEIGHT: 3ft (1m) • Hardy
FLOWERING SEASON: Midsummer

This attractive perennial has mid green, deeply cut foliage, giving the leaves a fern-like appearance. There is a double-flowered cultivar F. vulgaris 'Multiplex' which produces large spikes of creamy-white, plumes of flowers in summer which remain attractive for a long period. They grow best in a cool, moist situation with partial shade, and do not like too much disturbance. F. rubra has pink flowers and will grow in boggy ground. Propagation is by division in the winter.

Ginkgo biloba

Maidenhair tree
HEIGHT: 70ft (21m) • Hardy
FLOWERING SEASON: Spring

A most interesting and ornamental deciduous tree it has peculiarly shaped leaves with crinkled edges. They turn brilliant yellow and gold before falling in the autumn. The tree also carries fruits in the autumn, but it requires both male and female trees to be grown together for the flowers to become fertile. It prefers well-drained soil and tolerates some shade. The tree has been found in fossil beds millions of years old. It was often planted near temples.

Hemerocallis 'Burning Daylight'

Day lily
HEIGHT: 3ft (1m) • Hardy
FLOWERING SEASON: Summer

These are colorful, clump-forming plants, with leaves that are pale to mid green, strap-shaped, ending in a point at the tip. The brightly colored, lily-like flowers only last for a day, but are produced in such abundance that this is hardly noticeable. The popular Kwanso cultivars include the orange, double-flowered H. fulva 'Flore Pleno' and the variegated H. f. 'Kwanso Variegata'. They like full sun and moist soil. Propagation is by division in early spring.

Hosta 'Spinners'

Plantain lily
HEIGHT: 2ft (60cm) • Hardy
FLOWERING SEASON: Late summer/early autumn

These hardy herbaceous perennials are grown for their attractive foliage. Leaf shapes range from long and narrow to oval with a pointed tip. Leaf colors can vary from blue to rich combinations of silver or golden variegations. The flowers are carried on spikes above the leaves. H. sieboldiana var. elegans has broadly spear-shaped, glossy, bluish-green leaves with prominent veins, and soft lilac-blue flowers. Propagation is by division in early spring, but replant immediately. The leaves are very prone to slug and snail damage.

Houttuynia cordata 'Chameleon'

HEIGHT: 18in (45cm) • Hardy
FLOWERING SEASON: Spring

This is a vigorous, spreading perennial with dark blue-green, aromatic, heart-shaped leaves, carried on reddish-green leaf stalks, and fleshy erect stems. This plant spreads rapidly by means of underground runners just below the soil surface. The white flowers are carried on the tips of erect stems just above the leaves. There is a double white cultivar H. c. 'Flore Pleno'. H. c. 'Chameleon' has leaves splashed with yellow and red on a dark green base. Propagation is by division in late autumn or early spring.

Humulus lupulus 'Aureus'

Golden hop
HEIGHT: 25ft (8m) • Hardy
FLOWERING SEASON: Late summer

An attractive self-supporting, perennial climber with thin bristly twining stems. The bristly leaves are toothed around the margins and are deeply lobed. The flowers are inconspicuous, but the fruit clusters are quite attractive in the autumn. *H. l.* 'Aureus' has soft, golden-yellow leaves, stems and fruits. There is a less vigorous variegated sort with creamy-white and green variegated leaves. Propagation is by semi-ripe cuttings taken in June and July.

Iris pseudacorus

Yellow flag
HEIGHT: 3ft (1m) • Hardy
FLOWERING SEASON: Spring/summer

This popular hardy herbaceous perennial known as yellow flag has buttercup yellow flowers and broad, strap-like, bluish-green foliage arranged in a fan. A very striking plant is *I. p.* 'Variegata', with its gold and green striped foliage. It will grow in a range of conditions but it really thrives in semi-shade, heavy soil and waterlogged conditions, and even in water up to 18in (45cm) deep. Propagation is by division immediately after the plant has flowered.

Lathyrus grandiflorus

Everlasting pea
HEIGHT: 10ft (3m) • Hardy
FLOWERING SEASON: Summer/autumn

Originally from Italy, this tall, self-supporting climber has curling tendrils at the tip of each of the mid green leaflets. The flowers are scented (especially in the evening) and come in a variety of colors, with pink, white and deep purple being the most popular. The cultivar *L. latifolius* 'White Pearl' gives a lovely cottage garden effect. Propagation is by seed sown in September or March. Harden off before planting out. New growth is very prone to slug damage in wet seasons.

Leucanthemum × *superbum*

Shasta daisy
HEIGHT: 3ft (1m) • Hardy
FLOWERING SEASON: Mid/late summer

Formerly known as *Chrysanthemum* × *superbum*, this is a valued **perennial**, with strap-shaped, dark green leaves. The single flowers are white with a golden center, carried on tall green stems. The species is rarely grown, as cultivars with improved flowers have been introduced. These include *L.* × *s.* 'Snowcap', with a dwarfing habit and white daisy-like flowers, and *L.* × *s.* 'Wirral Supreme', with large double flowers with a golden center. Propagation is by division in winter or by basal cuttings taken in spring.

Mimulus × *burnetii*

Musk/Monkey flower
HEIGHT: 12in (30cm) • Hardy
FLOWERING SEASON: Early/late summer

This low, spreading plant thrives in cool, damp soil, but likes to have its head in the sunshine. They can be good plants for the bog garden and waterside. The elliptical, mid green leaves are carried on square stems and often have a green bract-like leaf at the point where the leaf stalk is attached to the stem. Yellow, snapdragon-like flowers open to reveal a throat mottled with brown and purple markings. Propagation is by division in the spring or seed sown in the autumn or spring, but it will often layer itself in wet soil.

Myosotis scorpioides

Water forget-me-not
HEIGHT: 10in (25cm) • Hardy
FLOWERING SEASON: Late spring/midsummer

This is a moisture-loving evergreen perennial with a long flowering period in summer when it produces branching green stems of minute blue flowers with a yellow-orange 'eye'. Spoon-shaped leaves are carried on thin green stems and covered with fine hairs when young. It is often grown as a marginal water plant. A cultivar with larger flowers is *M. s.* 'Mermaid', which has a sprawling habit and forms a loose mound. These plants last only for three or four years. Propagate by semi-ripe basal cuttings taken in spring.

Persicaria bistorta 'Superba'

Knotweed/Snakeweed
HEIGHT: 4ft (1.2m) • Hardy
FLOWERING SEASON: Summer

Persicarias were formerly known as polygonums and have the common name of knotweed. *P .b.* 'Superba' which is some-times called snakeweed, can be invasive, but makes an attractive drift beside a water feature. It forms large clumps of arrow-shaped, centrally ribbed, mid green leaves and spires of soft pink flowers throughout the summer. It will cope with sun or partial shade, but needs moist soil. Propagate by division in spring or autumn or raise from seed.

Phlox paniculata 'Fujiyama'

HEIGHT: 3ft (1m) • Hardy
FLOWERING SEASON: Late summer

Essential perennials for all herbaceous borders *P. paniculata* cultivars have tubular, five-lobed flowers, generally pink in color, carried on conical heads: among the best known are 'Amethyst', violet, 'Norah Leigh', pale lilac, and 'Franz Schubert', pink. They prefer deep rich soil that does not dry out and semi-shade. Cut down to soil level after flowering and propagate by division in spring or semi-ripe cuttings in summer.

Phormium tenax

New Zealand flax
HEIGHT: 4ft (1.2m) • Moderately hardy
FLOWERING SEASON: Summer

This clump-forming, evergreen perennial has bold, sword-shaped leaves which have a tough, leathery texture and are deep green in color. When the plant has established, dull orange flowers are borne on large, erect spikes. These are followed by scimitar-shaped seed capsules. Among the cultivars with variegated foliage, *P.* 'Dazzler' has leaves with shades of yellow, salmon-pink, orange-red and bronze. Propagation is by seed sown in the spring or division in spring.

Populus × candicans 'Aurora'

Ontario poplar/Balm of Gilead
HEIGHT: 80ft (25m) • Hardy
FLOWERING SEASON: Spring

A large tree with a broad crown and broad, almost heart-shaped, leaves which have a strong scent of balsam in the spring. The attractive *P. × c.* 'Aurora' has variegated foliage, the dark green leaves being splashed with pale green, creamy-white and pink. It must be pruned very hard each spring to maintain this striking effect. Poplars prefer full sun and deep moist well-drained soil. They have extensive root systems and are not suitable for planting close to buildings. Propagation is by hardwood cuttings taken in autumn.

Pterocarya fraxinifolia

Caucasian wing nut
HEIGHT: 80ft (25m) • Hardy
FLOWERING SEASON: Summer

A moisture-loving, spreading, deciduous tree, with a characteristic short trunk and deeply grooved bark. The glossy, dark green ash-like leaves are made up of many finely toothed leaflets and turn yellow in autumn. The flowers consist of long green catkins up to 18in (45cm) long, which are followed by greenish-brown winged fruits in autumn. It likes a sunny position and moist well-drained soil. Propagation is by softwood cuttings in summer, by seed sown outdoors in spring or by removing the suckers.

Pyracantha 'Orange Glow'

Firethorn
HEIGHT: 10ft (3m) • Hardy
FLOWERING SEASON: Early summer

Versatile evergreen shrubs, with attractive foliage, fruit and flowers, these are useful for hedging, as wall shrubs or free-standing specimens. The large clusters of small white, or pale pink blooms are followed by clusters of round fruits in autumn, colored yellow, orange or red depending upon the cultivar. Oval, glossy, dark evergreen leaves with a finely toothed margin, are carried on brown stems with sharp spines. Propagation is by semi-ripe cuttings taken in summer. Pyra-cantha scab may cause premature leaf drop.

Pyrus calleryana

Callery pear
HEIGHT: 50ft (15m) • Hardy
FLOWERING SEASON: Mid/late spring

This is a medium-sized, deciduous tree with
a broadly conical habit and slightly erect
thorny branches. The glossy green leaves are
broadly oval. Clusters of single white, cup-
shaped flowers are produced in spring, and
are followed by small brown fruits in
autumn. The cultivar *P. c.* 'Chanticleer' has a
narrow conical habit and is particularly
attractive in autumn when the leaves turn a
reddish-purple. Propagation is by budding in
summer or by grafting in winter.

Quercus palustris

Pin oak
HEIGHT: 50ft (15m) • Hardy
FLOWERING SEASON: Late spring/early summer

A fast-growing, dense-headed, deciduous tree
with a spreading habit and slender branches
that droop gracefully at the tips. As this tree
ages, the bark becomes purplish-gray and
deeply grooved. The leaves, which are a shining dark green on the upper surface and pale
green below, have deeply lobed margins, turn
a rich scarlet in autumn. The small flowers are
produced in late spring, and greenish-brown
'acorns' follow in autumn. Propagation is by
seed sown outdoors in spring.

Rheum palmatum

Rhubarb
HEIGHT: 6ft (1.8m) • Hardy
FLOWERING SEASON: Summer

Most ornamental rhubarbs have large, glossy,
mid green leaves which are held above the
crown on thick fleshy stalks. The small flowers are carried above the leaves on tall spikes.
R. alexandrae is grown for its 3ft (1m) flower
spikes. These have large papery bracts like
drooping tongues covering the small, inconspicuous flowers. *R. palmatum* has deeply
cut, hand-shaped leaves and greenish-yellow
flowers. They prefer moist conditions.
Propagation is by division in winter.

Rodgersia pinnata 'Superba'

HEIGHT: 3ft (1m) • Moderately hardy
FLOWERING SEASON: Summer

This clump-forming herbaceous perennial
is usually grown for its foliage. The deeply-
veined leaves are made up of as many as
nine deep green leaflets joined together
by a thin, green, central leaf stalk. In the
summer plumes of small pinkish-red, star-
like flowers are produced on erect, bare,
multi-branched stalks. The bronze-leaved
R. p. 'Superba', is very good for autumn
color. It prefers some shade and a sheltered
site but will grow in sun as long as the soil
does not dry out. Propagation is by division
of the rhizomes in spring.

Salix babylonica var. pekinensis 'Tortuosa'

Dragon's claw willow
HEIGHT: 50ft (15m) • Hardy
FLOWERING SEASON: Spring

This large shrub or small tree has unusual,
corkscrew-shaped branches and green winter
bark. A vigorous plant, initially it has a narrow shape, but spreads from the center with
age. The bright green leaves are narrow and
strap-like, and may be quite straight or as
twisted and contorted as the branches, with
some leaves being curled up like a watch
spring. Propagation is by hardwood cuttings,
taken in November and December when the
plant is dormant.

Salix caprea

Goat willow/Pussy willow
HEIGHT: 30ft (9m) • Hardy
FLOWERING SEASON: Spring

This familiar large shrub or small tree is most
noticeable in spring when male trees produce
large, yellow catkins later becoming soft,
silvery-gray 'pussy-willow' catkins. The fluffy
seeds shed in early summer. The elliptical
leaves are dark green on the upper surface and
gray-green and hairy on the underside. As
the shrub ages the gray-brown bark becomes
deeply fissured. Propagation is by hardwood
cuttings taken in winter and planted outside.
The disease anthracnose often causes brown
spots on leaves and stem die-back.

Sorbaria aitchisonii

HEIGHT: 9ft (3m) • Hardy
FLOWERING SEASON: Late summer

This very hardy, deciduous shrub makes
a broad dome shape, with reddish-brown
shoots and long spreading branches. The
fern-like, mid green leaves are made up of
many small leaflets, evenly arranged along a
slender leaf stalk. In autumn the leaves turn
golden-yellow and orange. Small, creamy-
white blooms are produced in large flower
spikes in late summer. Prefers sun and deep
moist soil. This plant can be very invasive.
Propagation is by semi-ripe cuttings with a
heel taken in summer.

Tradescantia × andersoniana 'Purple Dome'

Spiderwort/Flower-of-a-day
HEIGHT: 2ft (60cm) • Hardy
FLOWERING SEASON: Summer/autumn

This herbaceous perennial is a popular plant
for the mixed border, as it requires very little
care and attention and flowers throughout
the summer. It is attractive with dull green,
strap-like leaves which taper to a narrow
point. The flowers consist of three petals and
are produced in small clusters. Among the
hybrids are 'Blue Stone', with deep blue
flowers, and 'Isis', with rich purple ones.
Propagate by division in March or April.

Viburnum opulus

Guelder rose
HEIGHT: 15ft (4.5m) • Hardy
FLOWERING SEASON: Mid/late summer

A large deciduous popular shrub which
has a vigorous, spreading habit. The dark
green, sycamore-like leaves, which are
carried on reddish-green leaf stalks, turn
orange and yellow in autumn. The large,
white, elder-like flowers are followed by
translucent red berries. Striking cultivars
include *V. o.* 'Xanthocarpum', which has
all the characteristics of the type but golden-
yellow berries, and the golden-leaved
V. o. 'Aureum'.

More Plants for Clay Soil

Gardening on very heavy clay can be
extremely difficult. If the sub-soil is
moderately porous then, through cultivation, clay can usually be transformed into
good garden soil on which most plants can
be grown. If the sub-soil is incapable of
carrying away water then the list of trees
and plants that will survive is limited. To
improve heavy clay the land should first be
drained and then it should be dug roughly
and the soil allowed to lie in clumps over
winter. Don't attempt to cultivate the soil
in wet periods and dig in grit, ashes and
leaf mold when planting. Choose plants
that have a vigorous constitution and which
can look after themselves. Roses do
particularly well on clay soil and a section
on roses has been included in this chapter.
Bulbs can be grown but they may not do so
well if the soil becomes waterlogged.

TREES

Acer (in variety)
Amelanchier canadensis
Arbutus × andrachnoides
Betula ermanii
Catalpa bignonioides

Cercidiphyllum japonicum
Chimonanthus praecox,
Corylus avellana 'Contorta'
Crataegus (in variety)
Ficus carica
Fraxinus angustifolia
Liquidambar styraciflua
Malus (in variety)
Pyrus (in variety)
Sambucus racemosa
Taxodium distichum

SHRUBS

Artemesia absinthium
Berberis (in variety)
Chaenomeles (in variety)
Choisya ternata
Cornus (in variety)
Cotinus coggygria
Exochorda × macrantha 'The Bride'
Forsythia suspensa
Lavandula (in variety)
Lavatera 'Barnsley'
Ligustrum ovalifolium
Mahonia (in variety)
Philadelphus (in variety)
Roses
Salvia officinalis
Santolina chamaecyparissus
Sarcococca hookeriana
Stepanandra tanakae
Syringa (in variety)
Viburnum (in variety)

PERENNIALS & GROUND COVER PLANTS

Alchemilla mollis
Amenone × hybrida
Aquilegia alpina
Aster novi-belgii
Astrantia major
Aucuba japonica
Bergenia (in variety)
Buddleja (in variety)
Campanula carpatica
Centhranthus ruber
Dianthus (in variety)
Dicentra (in variety)
Digitalis (in variety)
Echinops bannaticus
Erysimum cheiri
Geranium (in variety)
Gunnera manicata
Hemerocallis (in variety)
Inula magnifica
Iris laevigata
Lamium maculatum
Ligularia (in variety)
Nepeta × faassenii
Penstemon (in variety)
Polygonatum × hybridum
Primula florindae
Pulmonaria saccharata
Scabiosa (in variety)
Tradescantia (in variety)
Trollius europaeus
Veronica prostrata
Vinca minor

Roses

Roses are among the commonest and best loved of all garden plants. They are hardy, generally soil tolerant, many have glorious scent and, with care, some can be found which will grow in shade, even as climbers on a north wall. The choice and variety is confusing but it can be simplified if you decide on the job you want the rose to do. Rambler and climber roses are self-explicit, climbers should be grown up walls and fences while ramblers should be grown through another plant such as a tree. Ramblers are very vigorous and you can only grow them successfully if you have a fair amount of room.

If you to make a formal rose bed then you should choose a hybrid tea, floribunda or English rose. If you want a shrub, choose a shrub or bush rose and to create an old-fashioned look in your garden plant a selection from the numerous old roses available which are wonderful in scent and bloom but usually flower only once a year. Many roses are also grown as standards which can make a focal point in any border and there are also roses which can be planted as ground coverers.

Rosa 'Abraham Darby'

TYPE: English rose
HEIGHT: 5ft (1.5m) • Hardy
FLOWERING SEASON: Summer/autumn

One of the English roses bred by David Austin in the 1970s, *R.* 'Abraham Darby' has deeply cupped blooms, yellow and apricot in color, combined with a rich fragrance. English roses are a cross between certain old-fashioned roses and modern hybrid tea and floribunda roses. They combine the scent and form of the old-fashioned roses with the ability to repeat flower throughout the season. They can be grown in borders or as shrubs making a focal point in the garden.

Rosa 'Albéric Barbier'

TYPE: Rambler (Wichuriana hybrid)
HEIGHT: 25ft (8m) • Hardy
FLOWERING SEASON: Early summer

'Albéric Barbier' is one of the most popular ramblers, less vigorous than some but it has strong growth and thick foliage which is almost evergreen. It is an ideal rose for growing up an unsightly wall. It has yellow buds which open into fully double creamy white flowers with a fruity fragrance. There is often a good second crop of flowers. Other good roses of this type are, 'Albertine', pink and deliciously scented, 'Crimson Shower', red and 'May Queen', pale pink.

Rosa banksiae 'Lutea'

TYPE: Climber • The Banksian rose
HEIGHT: 30ft (9m) • Half-hardy
FLOWERING SEASON: Summer

The species rose, known as the Banksian rose or Banks's rose, is tender and best grown up a south or south-west wall in the warmer parts of the country. It can also be grown along the ground. It has very fragrant, pure white, single flowers about 2.5cm (1in). More commonly, the double yellow cultivar 'Lutea' is grown which is not fragrant or the single yellow 'Lutescens'. The rose is thornless and requires the removal of spent wood after flowering as it flowers on the wood made in the previous year.

Rosa 'Cottage Rose'

TYPE: English rose
HEIGHT: 3½ft (1m) • Hardy
FLOWERING SEASON: Summer

A rose of true character with medium-sized, fragrant, cupped blooms in a lovely warm pink color which repeat flowers through the summer. It is a good idea to give English roses a good mulch in the spring followed by another after the first flush of flowers. Do not prune them in the first year but in the second year and after cut back the shoots by a third or a half of their length. David Austin recommends that they are planted in groups of three, 18in (45cm) apart, and allowed to develop into one large shrub.

Rosa 'English Miss'

TYPE; Floribunda
HEIGHT: 2½ft (75cm) • Hardy
FLOWERING SEASON: Summer

Floribunda roses carry large sprays of flowers and then have repeat shows throughout the summer. The flowers may not be so large or perfectly formed as hybrid tea roses but they are more graceful. Among the best known are 'Evelyn Fison' and 'Glad Tidings', red, 'Paddy McGredy' and 'Pink Parfait', pink, 'Apricot Nectar' and 'Summer Dream', apricot-yellow, 'Korresia' and 'Mountbatten', yellow, 'Iceberg' and 'Margaret Merrill' white and 'Masquerade' multi-colored, yellow, pink, red.

Rosa filipes 'Kiftsgate'

TYPE: Rambler
HEIGHT: 30-50ft (9-15m) • Hardy
FLOWERING SEASON: Midsummer

This is one of the biggest, most vigorous of rambler roses. It is literally covered with trusses of single, white, scented flowers in midsummer, followed by small red hips in autumn. It makes an ideal climber to grow over banks or trees but beware once established it is almost impossible to control. To prune, cut about a third of any stems that have flowered down to ground level. Its near relative *R.* 'Rambling Rector' with a yellow eye in the flower is slightly less vigorous.

Rosa 'Fragrant Cloud'

TYPE: Hybrid tea
HEIGHT: 4ft (1.2m) • Hardy
FLOWERING SEASON: Summer

This is one of the highly scented hybrid tea roses. Its deep rich red flowers fade after opening. Hybrid tea roses have the advantage of a long flowering season from mid to late summer. They do well in sun or partial shade, and like all roses need plenty of well-rotted manure as feed. Prune in winter, taking back the current year's growth to about four buds. 'Pascali' and 'Polar Star' are good white roses while 'Peace', light-yellow flushed with pink is an old favorite.

Rosa 'Iceberg'

TYPE: Floribunda
HEIGHT: 4ft (1.2m) • Hardy
FLOWERING SEASON: Summer/autumn

One of the best of the floribundas, 'Iceberg' has medium-sized double flowers, pure white in the summer and often tinged with pink in the autumn. It often flowers on into the winter. It is sometimes grown as a standard where it can make a focal point in a herbaceous border and there is a climbing form. The flowers, as with many of the floribundas, are fragrant. Prune in the winter cutting back shoots by about a half and removing any weak shoots.

Rosa 'Königin von Dänemark'

TYPE: Alba
HEIGHT: 5ft (1.5m) • Hardy
FLOWERING SEASON: Midsummer

Alba roses date back to the Middle Ages. They are restricted in color to white and shades of pink but they are amongst the hardiest roses there are and will survive and flower in shade. The 'Queen of Denmark' is one of the finest, with beautifully formed quartered flowers and gray-green leaves. Other well known roses of this type are 'Félicité Parmentier', a very delicate pale pink , *R.* × *alba* 'Alba Maxima', the Jacobite rose, which is white, tinted pink and 'Maiden's Blush' which is pink.

Rosa 'L D Braithwaite'

TYPE: English rose
HEIGHT: 3½ft (1m) • Hardy
FLOWERING SEASON: Summer

An English rose of the most brilliant crimson color and form, the flowers are produced over a long period and are very fragrant. When planting all roses the ground should be well prepared, and thoroughly dug with the addition of a good amount of farmyard manure or compost. If this is not available incorporate plenty of peat and bonemeal. Do not plant roses when the soil is very wet heel them in and wait for a dry period and do not plant roses in soil where roses have been growing in the last two years.

Rosa 'Madame Legras de Saint Germain'

TYPE: Alba
HEIGHT: 6ft (1.8m) • Very hardy
FLOWERING SEASON: Summer

One of the best of the alba roses the flowers open flat and then fill out with petals giving a pompom effect. They are carried on long, lax branches and are beautifully fragrant. Two other groups of old roses, all grown as garden shrubs, are gallica roses, often deep red in color, which date back to Roman times and damask roses, a group supposedly brought back from the Middle East by the Crusaders. Nearly all of these are fragrant but they only flower once.

Rosa 'Maigold'

TYPE: Climber
HEIGHT: 12ft (4m) • Hardy
FLOWERING SEASON: Midsummer

This is one of the most attractive yellow-flowered climbers with double flowers and prominent golden stamens. It is a rose which tolerates poor conditions and will flower when grown as a climber on a north wall. A number of roses have been bred as modern climbers which repeat flower well and are often shorter in growth making them suitable for town gardens: among them are 'Compassion', pink, 'Schoolgirl', orange, 'White Cockade' and 'Golden Showers'.

Rosa 'Nevada'

TYPE: Shrub
HEIGHT: 7ft (2m) • Hardy
FLOWERING SEASON: Early summer

'Nevada' grows into a large shrub, 7ft (2m) across which is smothered in early summer with semi-double, 4in (10cm), creamy-white blooms carried on arching red-brown branches. The leaves are light green. It has smaller crops of flowers later in the year. A spectacular rose, it makes an ideal shrub grown in the center of a lawn. Other well-known shrub roses are 'Ballerina', pink, 'Frülingsgold', pale yellow, 'Scarlet Fire', red, and 'Zigeunerknabe', dark purple.

Rosa nitida

TYPE: Shrub
HEIGHT: 3ft (1m) • Hardy
FLOWERING SEASON: Summer

This is a low-growing, shrub rose with thin stems covered in small, hair-like thorns. The mid green leaves, which are small and almost fern-like are held on reddish-brown, erect stems, and turn crimson in autumn. Small, deep-pink, single flowers are followed by small, crimson fruits in the autumn. This rose spreads by rhizome-like roots and can be very invasive. It makes good ground cover. Propagation is by softwood cuttings in summer or by division in late winter.

Rosa 'Pascali'

TYPE: Hybrid tea
HEIGHT: 3ft (1m) • Hardy
FLOWERING SEASON: Summer

'Pascali' is a strong healthy rose which has beautifully shaped white flowers ideal for cutting. They have a slight fragrance. Prune in the winter by cutting back to an outer bud about 12in (30cm) from the ground, alternately cut through the whole bush regardless of the condition of the wood at that height. This rather drastic method has been adopted after trials by the Rose Society. Other well known hybrid tea roses are 'Elizabeth Harkness', buff-pink, 'Ophelia', pink, and 'Blue Moon', silver-lilac.

Rosa 'Paul's Himalayan Musk'

TYPE: Rambler
Height: 30ft (9m) • Hardy
Flowering Season: Summer

This rose has been called the most beautiful of the ramblers and makes an unforgettable sight when established, epitomising the best of an English summer. It carries hanging open sprays of blush-pink rosettes on long trailing branches and is an ideal rose for growing into a tree or over a pergola. Like all ramblers, once established it is difficult to control, and the sharp arched spines which many of these roses possess make any pruning a trial. Eventually some of the old growth will need thinning.

Rosa primula

TYPE: Shrub • The incense rose
HEIGHT: 8ft (2.5m) • Hardy
FLOWERING SEASON: Spring

This species rose, also known as the incense rose, is unusual in the rose family in having aromatic foliage which releases a strong, spicy scent when crushed. The pale yellow, single flowers, with prominent golden stamens, are borne in late spring, and are also fragrant. They will cope with most conditions and can be trained against a trellis. In a hard winter the foliage may die back but it will regenerate in the spring. Prune in early spring. Prone to black spot, rust and various mildews.

Rosa 'Roseraie de l'Haÿ'

Type: Rugosa
Height: 6ft (1.8m) • Hardy
Flowering Season: Summer

Rugosa roses have sturdy stems, prickly branches and fresh green foliage, glossy on top and downy beneath. They grow under poor conditions and most repeat flower with a vivid display of hips in the autumn. They make good hedges although some flowers may be lost if they are kept closely trimmed: 'Roseraie de l'Haÿ', wine-red, 'Blanche Double de Coubert', white, 'Sarah van Fleet', pink, and 'Mrs Anthony Waterer', deep-red are among the best known.

Rosa rugosa

Type: Rugosa
Height: 6ft (1.8m) • Hardy
Flowering Season: Summer/autumn

This is a very tough, vigorous rose with light gray-brown shoots densely covered in fine bristly thorns. The leathery, deeply veined, glossy dark green leaves turn yellow in autumn. It is one of the few wild roses which repeat flowers. The large, single, cup-shaped flowers are a deep pink with a golden-yellow center. These are followed, in autumn, by large, round, bright red hips. *R. r.* 'Alba' has white flowers and *R. r. rubra* has red ones. They all make good hedges.

Rosa 'Tour de Malakoff'

Type: Centifolia rose • The Rose of Provence
Height: 6ft (1.8m) • Hardy
Flowering Season: Summer

Centifolia roses make lax open shrubs with many thorns and rather coarse leaves. Often they carry so many flowers that they hang their heads facing towards the ground. Nearly all have large cabbage-like flowers and heavy fragrance. Among the best are: 'Tour de Malakoff', richly purple and often grown as a climber, × *centifolia* 'Cristata', pink, 'Fantin-Latour', blush-pink and 'Robert le Diable' a mixture of many colors, purple, scarlet and cerise.

Rosa 'Whisky Mac'

Type: Hybrid tea
Height: 4ft (1.2m) • Hardy
Flowering Season: Summer

One of the most striking of the hybrid tea roses with yellow flowers which open copper-orange and then fade to a clear pale yellow. The flowers are very fragrant and are carried on very upright stems. Hybrid tea and floribunda roses look best grown in a beds devoted to a single variety and a rose garden can be planned with varying colors passing from deep red to yellow, pale orange, white and pink. Ideas can be gathered by visiting some of the best rose gardens or consulting rose breeders for advice.

Rosa 'Winchester Cathedral'

Type: English rose
Height: 4ft (l.2m) • Hardy
Flowering Season: Summer

A brilliant white rose with multi-petalled flowers 'Winchester Cathedral' forms a robust bushy shrub which produces new branches throughout the summer carrying a succession of flowers. When deciding to plant any rose the most important thing is to consider the situation in your garden and the effect that you are trying to achieve. Three similar plants grouped together, or small beds planted with the same variety of rose make a better and more effective statement than a number of individual plants.

Rosa 'Zéphirine Drouhin'

Type: Climber
Height: 12ft (4m) • Hardy
Flowering Season: Summer and autumn

This rose is particularly renowned for the fact that it is thornless. It is a Bourbon climber, with bronze-red tinted foliage and bright pink, semi-double flowers that are sweetly scented. It will flower again in autumn if deadheaded. It is extremely hardy and is particularly suitable for growing on a north wall. It can also be planted as a hedge or shrub. Bourbon roses are a cross between China and Portland roses and other old roses. They were first bred in the 1840s and 'Zéphirine Drouhin' was bred in 1868.

MOISTURE-LOVING PLANTS

Many gardens have a damp, slightly waterlogged area or perhaps a small pond which can be turned to advantage to grow a wide range of moisture-loving plants. Some, such as bog plants, prefer just a moist soil, others, called aquatics, thrive with their roots actually in water or are grown fully submerged.

ABOVE: Ranunculus acris *'Flore Pleno', the meadow buttercup,* *growing beside water.*

OPPOSITE: *A shady pond crammed with variegated irises, water and arum lilies and surrounded by ferns, pulmonaria, alchemilla, clematis and hostas. Agapanthus grow in a pot beside the pool.*

ABOVE: *Some irises will grow in water, and some prefer damp soil. They are ideal pool and poolside plants, their tall strappy leaves as important a contribution as their delicate papery flowers. Large-leaved, lush-looking plants, like gunnera are spectacular, while, in this planting, ferns and ivy tumble down the brickwork.*

Moisture-loving plants have some special virtues. They are easily grown if you have a permanently damp corner in your garden or a small stream or pond, but for many they provide the incentive to make a pond in the garden or just a boggy area, to convert into a bog garden so that the range of plants in the garden can be extended.

These plants fall into different categories: those that thrive in moist soil, those that thrive in wet soil, and those that actually grow best in water. The plants listed in this section fall into all three categories, but where they actually do well in a depth of water, this is indicated in the entry.

If you already have a damp area of the garden, it is a question of choosing suitable plants for the existing conditions. Quite often, these damp corners are also shady, and any attempt on your part to grow the usual sun-loving perennials will be doomed to disappointment. Analyze the conditions in your garden, and try to learn some lessons from what naturally thrives. Very few bulbs like very wet soil (except those specifically listed here) and will simply rot if water-logged. Plants from dry, rocky areas or from the hot dry areas around the Mediterranean will also fail to grow. Foliage is a good indication of a plant's natural habitat and often plants with larger, greener, lusher leaves have acquired these characteristics from exposure to moist or shady conditions.

A damp garden or corner, therefore, is an opportunity to grow some exciting large foliage plants such as gunneras, rodgersias, rheums and ligularias. If you are making a pond, you can increase your range of plants to those that enjoy being in water, including some of the irises and marsh

LEFT: *This stream has a wealth of damp-loving plants surrounding it, including different kinds of primula (such as the unusual P. vialii with its poker-like flowers), irises, water buttercups, hostas, and the interestingly marked leaves of the* Houttuynia cordata *'Chameleon' with big-leaved ligularias planted behind.*

BELOW: *In a raised pool and bog garden, irises, primulas and the handsome white spathes of the arum lily (zantedeschia) make the most of a small space.*

marigolds, and if the water is deep enough, the exotic-looking water lilies as well.

Even if your garden is not naturally damp, you can create a small area of bog garden by digging out a section and lining it with black plastic liner, with a few perforations in it for drainage and returning the soil on top. This will act like a layer of natural clay, helping to retain the moisture in the soil for longer periods, and allowing you to grow those plants that enjoy wet soil. You will have to be prepared to keep the soil moist by watering in periods of drought.

Garden ponds do not have to be large, and even a 3ft x 3ft (lm x 1m) pond, created with a butyl liner, will provide the correct environment for a good selection of water-loving plants. It is also rewarding to encourage wildlife by providing a suitable ledge so that animals and birds can drink. Create more than one level in the pond, so that both marginal plants (those that like shallow water) such as marsh marigolds and rushes, as well as aquatics (those that float in deep water), including water lilies and the water hawthorn, can be grown successfully.

Acorus calamus 'Variegatus'

Sweet flag/Myrtle flag
HEIGHT: 2½ft (75cm) • Hardy
FLOWERING SEASON: Inconspicuous

This marginal water plant, commonly called
sweet or myrtle flag, grows at the water's
edge in water up to 10in (25cm) deep. It is
grown for its particularly handsome, sword-
shaped foliage, with its neatly cream-edged
border. The young leaves are flushed pink
in spring. It is sweetly scented, hence the
common name. This plant is fairly prolific
therefore to control its spread, divide the
clumps every few years. Propagation is by
division of the rhizomes.

Acorus gramineus 'Variegatus'

HEIGHT: 10in (25cm) • Hardy
FLOWERING SEASON: Inconspicuous

This is a much smaller plant than *A. calamus*.
A semi-evergreen perennial it grows at the
water's edge, or with its roots submerged in
shallow water. Its fine, grass-like leaves are
held stiffly upright. This particular form has
cream-edged foliage, and produces inconspicuous greenish yellow flowers in summer.
To propagate and to keep it under control,
divide the clumps every couple of years in
the spring or autumn.

Aponogeton distachyos

Cape pondweed/Water hawthorn
HEIGHT: 2in (5cm) • Half-hardy
FLOWERING SEASON: Late spring/autumn

The water hawthorn, as this deep-water
aquatic plant is known, originates in South
Africa and has large, oval, slender leaves that
float like a water lily's on the surface of the
water. They are deep green, occasionally
splashed with purple. The flowers, which
are white and waxy, are carried in a forked
spire and are hawthorn-scented. This plant
does best in a sunny position but will also
succeed in partial shade. Propagation is by
division of the tubers.

Asplenium scolopendrium

Hart's tongue fern
HEIGHT: 2ft (60cm) • Hardy
FLOWERING SEASON: Inconspicuous

The hart's tongue fern is so-called because
it produces long, curling leaves, which are
bright green and evergreen. *A. s.* Crispum
Group has wavy margins to the leaves while
cultivars of *A. s.* Cristatum Group have
crested tips to the fronds. *A. scolopendrium*
does best in moisture-retentive soil in shade,
and will seed itself from spores in the right
conditions. Propagate by sowing the spores
in spring, or divide plants at the same time of
year. Generally problem free, although rust
can develop on young fronds.

Astilboides tabularis

HEIGHT: 3ft (1m) • Hardy
FLOWERING SEASON: Midsummer

This plant was formerly known as *Rodgersia
tabularis*. It is a large-leaved perennial and
makes a handsome foliage plant for the
bog garden, with its huge, umbrella-shaped,
bright green leaves. It bears creamy panicles
of flowers in midsummer. Plant the crowns
about 1in (2.5cm) below the soil surface in
spring, ensuring that it contains plenty of
decayed vegetable matter. The plant will
grow in sun or semi-shade and is propagated
by division of the crowns in the spring. It
may require some protection in very hard
weather.

Butomus umbellatus

Flowering rush
HEIGHT: 3ft (1m) • Hardy
FLOWERING SEASON: Summer

Known as the flowering rush, *B. umbellatus*
is a most attractive deciduous perennial that
bears umbels of rose-pink flowers in
midsummer. It quickly makes large
spreading clumps of strappy foliage, which
is bronze-purple when young and becomes
green later, and it grows in depths of water
up to 10in (5cm). It prefers a sunny position
and is best suited to large ponds. Divide
the clumps in spring to keep its spread
under control. Propagation is also by
division in spring.

Calla palustris

Bog arum
HEIGHT: 10in (25cm) • Hardy
FLOWERING SEASON: Spring

Known as the bog arum, *C. palustris* is a deciduous or semi-evergreen perennial that makes a spreading clump at the water's edge. It has large, heart-shaped, bright green, glossy leaves, and the typical arum flowers with a white spathe, followed by a bright orange spire of fruits. Plant in full sun, either in the bog garden, or into water a few inches deep. It likes good soil enriched by leaf mold or compost. Propagate by division of the rhizomes in spring.

Caltha palustris

Marsh marigold
HEIGHT: 2ft (60cm) • Hardy
FLOWERING SEASON: Late spring

The marsh marigold or kingcup flourishes in water of up to 6in (15cm). It has attractively rounded rich green leaves and the profuse large yellow flowers are cup-shaped. There is a white variety with yellow stamens, *C. p.* var. *alba*, which is not as free-flowering. It does best as a marginal plant, in slightly acid soil with plenty of humus, in sun or light shade. Divide and replant after flowering.

Cornus alba 'Sibirica'

Red-barked dogwood
HEIGHT: 10ft (3m) • Hardy
FLOWERING SEASON: Summer

The dogwoods, to which this suckering deciduous shrub belongs, do well in moist soil in sun or partial shade, and look particularly good as the backdrop to a water feature. *C. a.* 'Sibirica' has coral-red stems in winter and small clusters of creamy white flowers in summer, followed by white berries. The leaves are green and turn a bright scarlet in autumn. Cut hard back in spring to promote the growth of colorful stems. Propagate from rooted suckers, or layer shoots in autumn.

Cyperus involucratus

Umbrella grass
HEIGHT: 2ft (60cm) • Tender
FLOWERING SEASON: Summer

Known as umbrella grass, this moisture-loving rush-like perennial carries umbrella spoke-like leaves at the top of long arching stems. Very small flowers are borne in summer. It will grow in shallow water or at the water's edge in mild climates, or in harsher ones can be grown in containers in shallow water and overwintered indoors. 'Variegatus' has white-striped leaves. Remove the dead stems from plants grown out of doors in the spring. Propagate by detaching and replanting young growths.

Filipendula palmata

Meadowsweet
HEIGHT: 3ft (1m) • Hardy
FLOWERING SEASON: Summer

F. palmata, which is related to the European wild meadowsweet, is a good subject for a bog garden, thriving in rich, moist soil in sun. The leaves are divided, with five lobes, dark green, and hairy underneath. The pale rose-pink flowers rise well above the leaves, in multi-branched heads. Grow it in a large garden in drifts, with lythrum and lysimachia. Cut the stems back hard in autumn. To propagate, divide and replant crowns in autumn or early spring. It is sometimes prone to mildews, but is usually pest-free.

Gunnera manicata

Prickly rhubarb
HEIGHT: 10ft (3m) • Half-hardy
FLOWERING SEASON: Spring

This huge bruiser of a herbaceous perennial hails from Brazil. It has massive, rhubarb-like leaves, up to 4ft (1.2m) across borne on tall prickly stems and bears conical, light green flower spikes in early summer. It needs moist soil with plenty of humus incorporated, and it is an admirable architectural plant for the bog garden. It dies down in autumn, and the remaining crown should be protected with sacking, straw or bubble plastic in frosts. Increase by removing small crowns and replanting in spring.

Hemerocallis dumortieri

Day lily
HEIGHT: 2ft (60cm) • Hardy
FLOWERING SEASON: Early summer

This robust day lily produces large numbers
of highly scented, yellow, typical lily flowers
which last only a day or two, but several
flowerheads are borne on one stem, set
among the strap-shaped leaves. A clump-
forming, spreading perennial, it will quickly
establish a large drift given the right conditions: preferably sun and moist soil.
H. lilioasphodelus has flowers of a brighter
yellow Propagate by division in autumn.
Slugs and snails may attack young foliage.

Hottonia palustris

Water violet
HEIGHT: Irrelevant • Hardy
FLOWERING SEASON: Summer

This submerged water plant, which is
known as the water violet, is an oxygenating
plant and does best in deep water in a sunny
pool. The leaves form a dense mass of
spreading foliage, from which the pinkish-
lilac or whitish flowers rise above the water's
surface in summer. It may be necessary to
divide the plant occasionally to control its
spread. Propagation is by division.

Hydrocharis morsus-ranae

Frogbit
HEIGHT: 2in (5cm) • Hardy
FLOWERING SEASON: Summer

This delightful floating water plant is known
sometimes as frogbit and has small water-
lily-like leaves that are waxy and pale olive
green. It bears small, white, flowers with
yellow stamens which rise slightly above the
water's surface and are produced in summer.
H. morsus-ranae is a plant which prefers to
be positioned in full sun. Propagate by
detaching any young plantlets from the
main plant in spring and then replanting
them immediately.

Inula magnifica

Fleabane
HEIGHT: 6ft (1.8m) • Hardy
FLOWERING SEASON: Late summer

This is the largest of the most commonly
grown species in this genus of daisy-like
herbaceous perennials. The smallest, which
is *I. acaulis*, is only about 6in (15cm) tall.
I. magnifica forms large clumps of lance-
shaped, hairy leaves above which rise tall
stems bearing bright yellow, daisy flowers
that are up to 4in (10cm) across. It does well
in large drifts in moisture-retentive soil in
sun but it will require staking. Plant in
autumn and spring, and divide plants from
autumn to spring.

Iris ensata

Bog iris/Japanese flag
HEIGHT: 12in (30cm) • Hardy
FLOWERING SEASON: Late spring

This is one of the beardless irises which
belongs to a sub-section known as Apogon
irises, popularly called bog irises. It does well
in sun in very moist soil and will succeed in
shallow water. It comes from Tibet and
China and is characterized by its fine, grass-
like leaves and delicate mauve flowers. There
are numerous cultivars in shades of white,
violet, pink, blue and red. 'Alba' is an elegant
white cultivar and 'Variegata' has handsomely striped leaves. Divide in autumn to
propagate. Prone to various viruses.

Iris laevigata

Japanese iris
HEIGHT: 2ft (60cm) • Hardy
FLOWERING SEASON: Early summer

This Japanese iris is a true water iris, thriving
in water up to 6in (15cm) deep. It has deciduous, pale green leaves and bears three deep
blue flowers, with a white streak on the falls,
on each stem. There are several named
cultivars, including the pure white 'Alba',
'Variegata' with striped leaves and pale blue
flowers which sometimes flowers for a
second time in the autumn, 'Atropurpurea'
with reddish-purple flowers and 'Regal'
with red flowers. It does best in sun or semi-
shade. Propagate by division in autumn.

Ligularia dentata 'Desdemona'

Giant groundsel
HEIGHT: 4ft (1.2m) • Hardy
FLOWERING SEASON: Mid/late summer

This big herbaceous perennial forms a hand-some mound of large, heart-shaped, deep green leaves, with rusty red undersides, borne on the end of long stalks. Big, bright orange, daisy flowers appear in late summer, making a striking contrast with the leaves. In addition to being suited to bog gardens, it makes a good container plant provided the soil is kept moist. It needs humus-rich retentive soil and a sunny or partially shaded site. Divide in spring. Prone to attacks by slugs and snails.

Ligularia stenocephala

Giant groundsel
HEIGHT: 6ft (1.8m) • Hardy
FLOWERING SEASON: Late summer

This cultivar forms similar clumps to *L. dentata* (left), but the leaves are rounded and toothed, and paler green. The yellow-orange daisy-like flowers are borne in long spires on purplish stems. It likes the same conditions as *L. dentata* and looks best when planted in groups of five to seven, in the moist soil around the edge of a water feature. It needs humus-rich retentive soil.

Lobelia cardinalis

Cardinal flower
HEIGHT: 3ft (1m) • Half hardy
FLOWERING SEASON: Summer

This unlikely-looking lobelia bears tall spires of bright red, five-lobed flowers in mid to late summer. The foliage is carried on erect, branching stems. It makes a good border plant in moist soil in partial shade but is not very long-lasting. Grows best in a mild, moist climate with shelter from cold winds and it will grow close to water. Cut down the dead spikes after flowering. Propagate by division in spring. Can be affected by a virus which causes the leaves to mottle and distort.

Lysimachia clethroides

Loosestrife
HEIGHT: 3ft (1m) • Hardy
FLOWERING SEASON: Mid to late summer

This native of China and Japan is a tall summer-flowering perennial with elongated green leaves that turn color in autumn. It carries small, starry, white flowers with pronounced eyes in long arching spires. It does well in moist soil in sun or partial shade and is most suitable for naturalising by the waterside or in a bog garden. The name comes from the Greek, *lusimachion*, *lysis* meaning concluding or ending, and *mache*, strife, from the reputedly soothing properties of the plant. Divide and replant in autumn.

Lysimachia nummularia

Creeping Jenny/Moneywort
HEIGHT: 2in (5cm) • Hardy
FLOWERING SEASON: Summer

This small creeping perennial, known as moneywort or creeping Jenny, has rounded soft leaves and bright yellow flowers that form in the leaf axils. A cultivar known as 'Aurea' has yellowish-green leaves. It prefers partial shade, and a moist, retentive soil but it is one of the easiest garden plants and can be grown in almost any soil or situation. It is ideal for planting near the borders of a garden pond. Propagate by division in spring or by planting short lengths of the stem in spring or autumn.

Lysimachia punctata

Garden loosestrife
HEIGHT: 3ft (1m) • Hardy
FLOWERING SEASON: Summer

This garden loosestrife is a rapidly spreading, clump-forming, herbaceous perennial. In summer it will produce large drifts of tall, bright golden-yellow flower spires, rising on erect stems above the oval, lance-shaped leaves. *L. punctata* blends well with ligularias in informal bog garden plantings. It prefers moist well-drained soil in partial shade although it will tolerate some sun. It may need staking occasionally. Propagate by division in spring or by seed sown in the open or in a cold frame.

Lysichiton americanus

Yellow skunk cabbage
HEIGHT: 4ft (1.2m) • Hardy
FLOWERING SEASON: Spring

This big-leaved perennial flourishes in the
very moist soil alongside streams and ponds.
It will spread rapidly in the right conditions,
making an eye-catching feature with its
huge, ribbed, mid green leaves and bright
yellow flower spathes about 18in (45cm) tall.
A smaller species, *L. camtschatcensis*, has white
flower spathes. Plant in wet soil or shallow
water, and ensure that the plants have plenty
of humus. Succeeds with sun or partial
shade. Propagate by division in early spring.

Mertensia pulmonarioides

Virginian cowslip
HEIGHT: 2ft (60cm) • Hardy
FLOWERING SEASON: Late spring

The Virginian cowslip has bluish-gray leaves
and attractive terminal clusters of hanging
purple-blue bells in late spring. It needs a
rich, moist soil in shade to do well. Cut the
plants back in autumn. These plants are
suitable for growing in the shady side of a
rock garden, under deciduous trees or at the
edge of a shrubbery. They do not like being
disturbed but when the clumps grow too
large they can be divided and the roots
replanted in autumn or spring.

Miscanthus sinensis

Zebra grass
HEIGHT: 5ft (1.5m) • Hardy
FLOWERING SEASON: Late summer/autumn

This attractive vigorous giant grass is a hardy
perennial that will serve as a windbreak, its
narrow bluish-green leaves arching over.
There are a number of different cultivars
'Zebrinus' has a yellow band on the leaves,
while 'Gracillimus' has particularly narrow
leaves. It may bear fan-shaped panicles of
hairy white spikelets in the autumn. Plant
in moist garden soil in sun. Cut down to
ground level in late spring. Divide and
replant roots in spring.

Nuphar lutea

Yellow water lily/Brandy bottle
HEIGHT: 2in (5cm) • Hardy
FLOWERING SEASON: Summer

This deep-water aquatic perennial is a good
subject for a large pool. It is vigorous and not
as fussy about sun as the real water lily, and
will grow in running water, which water
lilies will not. The flat, water lily-like leaves
float on the water's surface. In summer it
produces yellow flowers, which are bottle-
shaped, giving rise to the common name
of brandy bottle. Plant in good garden loam
in a sack which is then lowered into the
water. Divide in spring to control its spread.
Propagation is by division in spring.

Nymphaea alba

Water lily
HEIGHT: 2in (5cm) • Hardy
FLOWERING SEASON: Summer

A large water lily, *N. alba*, as the name
implies, has large, pure white flowers which
are semi-double and cup-shaped, with
bright gold stamens. They measure about
4in (10cm) across. Water lilies are deciduous,
perennial, deep water plants and generally
need a 3ft (90cm) depth of water, which
must be still and in sunshine, preferably away
from overhanging trees. It is necessary to
divide the plants every few years in spring or
summer to keep them under control.
Propagation is also by division of rhizomes.

Nymphaea × helvola

Water lily
HEIGHT: 2in (5cm) • Hardy
FLOWERING SEASON: Summer

This small water lily has dark green leaves
which are purple beneath and float on the
surface of the water. It will grow in 12in
(30cm) of water. It bears small, star-shaped,
semi-double yellow flowers in summer. For
best results plant in good loam in a wicker
basket or old-fashioned sack. Like all water
lilies it must be grown in still water and in
sunshine. It is best to remove the foliage of
all water lilies as it dies back. Propagate by
dividing and replanting the rhizomes every
few years.

Nymphaea 'James Brydon'

Water lily
HEIGHT: 2in (5cm) • Hardy
FLOWERING SEASON: Summer

Dark green leaves and fragrant, cup-shaped, rose-colored, semi-double flowers are the hallmarks of this water lily. White, pink, yellow and purple cultivars are also available, all with characteristically large, semi-double flowers. It needs about a 3ft (1m) depth of water, which must be still and in sunshine. If you want to grow water lilies in a concrete pool you need two barrow loads of soil for each plant. Divide every few years in spring or summer and to propagate.

Nymphoides peltata

Fringed water lily/Water fringe
HEIGHT: 2in (5cm) • Hardy
FLOWERING SEASON: Summer

This deciduous perennial deep-water plant is similar to the water lily, and has the common name fringed water lily. It has dark green, floating, rounded leaves with brown splashed markings and produces small, fringed, yellow flowers throughout the summer. It needs sun and a sheltered site and, like water lilies, likes deep, still water. To propagate, or control its spread, divide in spring or summer.

Osmunda regalis

Royal fern
HEIGHT: 5ft (1.5m) • Hardy
FLOWERING SEASON: Inconspicuous

This, the royal fern, is an extremely handsome fern, with large, yellowish-green fronds arching over gracefully, growing out of a crown that gradually becomes like a small trunk. There are a couple of interesting varieties, *O. r.* Cristata Group has crested pinnae, and *O. r. purpurascens* has young fronds which are bronzy-pink. The royal fern does well in very damp soil near pond margins. Propagate by dividing well-separated crowns in spring.

Polystichum setiferum

Soft shield fern
HEIGHT: 3ft (1m) • Hardy
FLOWERING SEASON: Inconspicuous

The soft shield fern, a native of temperate and tropical regions throughout the world, has large soft-textured fronds which are finely divided and mid green in color. It will naturalize in damp conditions. There are several named cultivars, including 'Divisilobum Laxum' which has huge fronds with white scales when young, these arch initially and become prostrate later. It is best to grow these ferns in shade in humus-rich, moisture-retentive soil. Propagate by dividing the crowns in spring.

Pontederia cordata

Pickerel weed
HEIGHT: 2ft (60cm) • Hardy
FLOWERING SEASON: Late summer

The pickerel weed, as it is commonly known, is a vigorous, aquatic perennial that will grow in up to 9in (23cm) of water. It has glossy green, heart-shaped leaves, rather like those of an arum lily, and produces small, bright blue flowers with a yellow eye in late summer. It needs full sun, and should be planted in loam. It is a good idea to remove the flower heads as they fade to encourage further flowering. Divide the plant in late spring and replant in shallow water until the plants are established.

Populus × canadensis 'Serotina'

Canadian poplar
HEIGHT: 36ft (11m) • Hardy
FLOWERING SEASON: Spring

This is a quick-growing tree with oval, pointed leaves that are coppery red when juvenile, turning dark green later. There is a golden-leaved cultivar, 'Aurea', which turns a very bright yellow in autumn. It bears long red catkins in the spring and should be planted well away from buildings as the branches are somewhat brittle and often break off in very strong winds. Propagate from hardwood cuttings in autumn. May be attacked by aphids and suffer various fungal disorders.

Primula florindae

Giant cowslip/Himalayan cowslip
HEIGHT: 6ft (1.8m) • Hardy
FLOWERING SEASON: Spring

This giant cowslip, also known as the Himalayan cowslip, originates in Tibet and China. It has large, heart-shaped leaves with serrated edges on a fairly long leaf stalk. In spring, tall stems bear umbels of scented, bell-shaped, pale lemon flowers on drooping stalks. Forms are also available with orange or red flowers. These primulas prefer sun or partial shade and moist soil but may require protection from winter wet. Divide to propagate. Prone to rots and molds.

Primula pulverulenta

Candelabra primula
HEIGHT: 3ft (1m) • Hardy
FLOWERING SEASON: Spring

These tall, candelabra-type primulas look attractive in large drifts near a pond or a stream. They have the typical oval, primrose-type leaves in pale green while the flowers are deep reddish-purple carried in a whorl at the top of long white stems. *P. p.* Bartley Hybrids and *P. p.* 'Bartley Pink' are soft pink in color with a deeper crimson eye. *P. pulverulenta* does best in sun or partial shade and prefers rich loamy soil. Propagate named forms by dividing crowns or by removing offsets in spring. They are prone to attacks by aphids and various molds.

Ranunculus acris 'Flore Pleno'

Double meadow buttercup
HEIGHT: 18in (45cm) • Hardy
FLOWERING SEASON: Summer

This is double-flowered buttercup is sometimes also known as yellow bachelor's buttons. It produces large, bright yellow, saucer-shaped flowers in sprays and has deeply cut, lobed, mid green leaves. This widely grown species is mat-forming but not invasive. It thrives in moist, well-drained soil and prefers to be in sun or partial shade. Once established, it needs little attention. To propagate, divide and replant the clumps in autumn or in spring.

Ranunculus aquatilis

Water crowfoot
HEIGHT: 2ft (60cm) • Hardy
FLOWERING SEASON: Spring/midsummer

This water crowfoot is an aquatic plant which can be grown in water up to 12in (30cm) deep and will grow in slow-moving streams. It has myriads of white blossoms in the spring which cover the surface of the water, looking like miniature water lilies. It has two types of leaf, floating leaves carried on long stems which are smooth and round and submerged leaves which are finely divided and hair-like. Plant in the sun. *R. aquatilis* is very vigorous and will need to be divided and thinned annually.

Rheum palmatum

Ornamental rhubarb
HEIGHT: 6ft (1.8m) • Hardy
FLOWERING SEASON: Summer

This ornamental rhubarb is an excellent large perennial for a bog garden and forms a huge and spectacular plant. It produces a pyramid-shaped clump of large, deeply cut, rhubarb-like leaves that open reddish purple and turn green. The flowers, which are rusty pink, are carried at the end of tall spires in midsummer. Plant in humus-rich soil in partial shade and mulch each autumn. Do not let the soil dry out in the growing season. Generally pest and disease-free, but can be prone to aphid attacks.

Sagittaria sagittifolia

Common arrowhead
HEIGHT: 3ft (1m) • Hardy
FLOWERING SEASON: Summer

The common arrowhead can be planted in water of depths up to 3ft (90cm). A hardy perennial, it has arrow-shaped, light green leaves and whorls of white flowers in summer. *S. s.* 'Flore Pleno' is a double-flowered variety. Plant in March or October in any good garden soil enriched with well-rotted manure. Put the soil in an old-fashioned sack or wicker basket, plant the tubers, weigh the soil down with a large stone and then drop it into the pool. It likes full sun. Thin in the summer.

Stratiotes aloides

Water soldier/Crab's claw
HEIGHT: 6in (15cm) • Hardy
FLOWERING SEASON: Summer

This semi-evergreen perennial, known as the water soldier, is a submerged aquatic, which floats freely in any depth of water. It has strappy, fleshy, olive-green leaves in a rosette formation, and produces small, cup-shaped, white flowers in summer. During winter the plants lie dormant on the pool bottom. The plant spreads quickly and may well need to be controlled in a garden pool. Propagation is by division of the plants in spring.

Trapa natans

Jesuit's nut/Water chestnut
HEIGHT: 1in (2.5cm) • Half-hardy
FLOWERING SEASON: Summer

This annual aquatic plant, which is sometimes known as the Jesuit's nut or water chestnut, has pretty triangular leaves, with serrated edges, that are marked with bronze-purple splashes. It produces white flowers in summer. It is not reliably frost-hardy so the young plants will require some degree of protection if planted in early spring, or plant when the last frosts have passed. Propagation is by division of the plants in spring or by seed.

Typha latifolia

Reed mace/Bulrush
HEIGHT: 6ft (1.8m) • Hardy
FLOWERING SEASON: Summer

This marginal reed is grown for its long, strappy, mid green leaves and its decorative dark brown cylinders of seed heads in autumn. The beige flowers which emerge in midsummer are not particularly significant but the seed heads are spectacular and a common sight, often used by flower arrangers. It is invasive, and is often used to colonize large ponds and lakes. To control its spread plant it in a tub. It will do well in sun or shade, and can be propagated by division in spring.

More Plants for Moisture

AQUATICS

Examples of the majority of aquatic plants, plants that like growing with their roots in water, have been included in this chapter. There is a wide choice of water lilies and if you plan to make a pond, it is best to visit a nursery which specializes in plants for the water garden. It is worth stressing that water lilies must be grown in deep, still water and a sunny position.

Other suitable aquatic plants worth considering include:

Alisma plantago-aquatica (Water plantain)
Azolla filiculoides (Water fern)
Lagarosiphon major
Myosotis scorpioides (Water forget-me-not)
Myriophyllum aquaticum (Parrot's feather)
  M. verticillatum (Water milfoil)
Orontium aquaticum (Golden club)
Potamogeton crispus (Curled pondweed)

PLANTS FOR MOISTURE

If you have a very wet area of your garden then you have to grown plants that will tolerate these conditions. All plants need water but a relatively small number will survive in conditions of constant moisture.

Bog garden plants are obvious examples. Plants that will survive in swampy sites are marked (S).

TREES

Abies (in variety)
Acer negundo
Alnus (in variety)
Amelanchier canadensis
Betula nigra
Crataegus (in variety)
Embothrium coccineum
Fraxinus angustifolia
Liquidambar styraciflua
Liriodendron tulipifera
Parrotia persica
Populus (in variety) (S)
Prunus padus
Pterocarya fraxinifolia (S)
Salix (in variety) (S)
Sambucus (in variety) (S)
Taxodium distichum (S)
Tsuga heterophylla

SHRUBS

Aucuba japonica
Camellia (in variety)
Clethra arborea
Cornus (in variety)
Desfontainia spinosa,
Elaeagnus × *ebbingei*
Fatsia japonica
Hydrangea (in variety)
Osmanthus (in variety)
Sarcococca hookeriana
Skimmia japonica
Symphoricarpus × *doorenbosii*
Viburnum davidii
Zenobia pulverulenta

PERENNIALS & GROUND COVER PLANTS

Ajuga reptans
Alchemilla mollis
Anemone × *hybrida* cvs
Aruncus dioicus
Astilbe (in variety)
Bergenia (in variety)
Campanula persicifolia
Cardamine pratensis
Convallaria majalis
Darmera peltata (S)
Dodecatheon pulchellum
Enkianthus campanulatus
Filipendula palmata
Helleborus orientalis
Hosta (in variety)
Houttuynia cordata (S)
Iris pseudacorus (S)
Kirengeshoma palmata
Mentha (in variety)
Menziesia ciliicalyx
Persicaria bistorta
Polypodium vulgare (S)
Rheum palmatum
Rodgersia pinnata (S)
Trillium grandiflorum

PLANTS *for* SHADE

Shade-loving plants are essential in most gardens as few are completely without a dark corner or spot under trees. In this selection you can find plants that like damp or dry shade, and also different degrees of shade, from heavy shade to only partial shade.

ABOVE: Alchemilla mollis, *lady's mantle, an invaluable standby for all gardens, was a plant much used by the great Gertrude Jekyll.*

OPPOSITE: *A shady corner is brightened with gold-splashed varieties of holly with the yellow flowers of the perennials like coreopsis and genista (broom) blending in with the yellow rose.*

ABOVE: *A small woodland garden has a handsome* Acer *palmatum var.* dissectum *'Ornatum' as a prominent feature which is underplanted with bluebells.*

RIGHT: Aucuba japonica, *with its yellow-splashed, evergreen leaves, on the right of the picture, will grow even in deep shade, as will the ivies covering the walls and steps. Camellias, on the left, are another plant that grows well in partial shade.*

Very few gardens are completely without shade in some form, but before planting you need to work out whether the shade is dry or damp, since not all plants that do well in damp shade will do well in dry shade and vice versa. Only a tiny number of plants will cope with almost total shade – ivies among them – since all plants require light in some form to create the food they need to survive.

On the whole, shade-loving plants appear rather different from sun-loving ones. They tend to have large foliage – nature's way of ensuring that the maximum amount of chlorophyll is exposed to the light to help photosynthesis (food manufacture) – and with smaller and paler flowers, quite often white. It is possible to create sophisticated and attractive shade gardens using only foliage and white-flowered plants.

This lack of color was at one time regarded as a disadvantage particularly by the Victorians and Edwardians who preferred the brightest, biggest flowers they could grow in rigidly controlled bedding formations. Gardens that are heavily shaded will not support a bright array of flowering plants – begonias and impatiens are among the very few flowering annuals that will survive in shade. They will, however, provide a successful home for many handsome architectural foliage plants and one of the best is *Fatsia japonica* with its big, glossy, evergreen, hand-shaped leaves. Another good performer in quite deep shade is the mottled, green-leaved *Aucuba japonica*. Rhododendrons and azaleas prefer partial shade (but they also like acid soil, so refer to this section as well). Remember that there are many varieties of ivy, with a whole range of different leaf colors and formations

that will grow in even the deepest
shade, as will some ferns.

Usually shady areas are to be
found under a tree, for example,
or beneath a wall. These, because
of the canopy of the tree or the
shelter of the wall, will also tend
to be dry and you must therefore
look for plants that like dry shade.
Ivies, of course, manage extremely well with dry shade, as do some
hostas, foxgloves, hellebores and
alchemilla (lady's mantle).

In moist soil in shade you can
grow many of the woodland
plants, as well as the Welsh poppy
(*Meconopsis cambrica*) and some
ferns, such as the
shuttlecock fern (*Matteuccia
struthiopteris*) and the soft shield
fern (*Polystichum setiferum*).

Ideally, when creating areas of
shade-loving foliage plants, try to
contrast the different types, colors
and forms of foliage, to make a
green tapestry of leaves. Tall, strappy leaves of irises can be
contrasted with soft feathery fronds of ferns and the big pleated leaves of
veratrums, for example. If you have a wide selection of different foliage
forms and colors, the garden will acquire just as much interest as a more colorful sunny flower border, and will last throughout the growing season, and
into winter if you select a few evergreens as well.

Among good evergreens for the shade garden are the ivies, aucuba and
fatsia, mahonia (some of which have the bonus of scented flowers), yew
(taxus) and skimmias (again with scented flowers), skimmias are particularly
good for town gardens as they grow slowly.

Many of the plants listed in other sections will flourish in partial shade as
well and a comprehensive cross index to the other plants in the book can be
found at the end of the chapter.

ABOVE: *A shady border, with the front edge in sun, provides a home for ligularias and aucuba, with nasturtiums* (tropaeolum) *providing front of the border color.* Anthemis tinctoria *with its yellow daisy-like heads is on the left.*

Aconitum 'Bressingham Spire'

Monkshood/Wolfbane
HEIGHT: 3-5ft (1-1.5m) • Hardy
FLOWERING SEASON: Summer

Known as monkshood or wolfbane, from
its hooded flowers, all parts of this plant,
from the tuberous roots to the finely divided
leaves, are very poisonous. Various aconitum
cultivars include: 'Blue Sceptre' and
'Bressingham Spire' which have straight spires
about 3ft (1m) tall with deep mauve blue
flowers in summer. Needs a moist soil. Cut
the flowers down after flowering to encourage flowering stems. Cut down all stems in
autumn. Propagate by division in autumn.

Adiantum pedatum

Northern maidenhair fern
HEIGHT: 12in (30cm) • Hardy
FLOWERING SEASON: None

This attractive small fern is native to North
America and Japan and is fully hardy in the
British Isles, although it dies down soon after
the first frosts. The light green fronds with
purple stalks arch gracefully from a central
rosette. There are several variants: *A. p.* var.
subpumilum, which is only 5in (12cm) high,
is ideal for a rock garden; *A. p.* Asiatic form
has copper-coloured fronds in spring, which
turn green as they mature. Propagate by
sowing the spores in spring, or by dividing
the rhizomes in spring. May be attacked by
woodlice and root mealy bugs.

Ajuga reptans

Bugle
HEIGHT: 5in (12cm) • Hardy
FLOWERING SEASON: Spring

Known as bugle, this small, vigorous
perennial likes shade, although it will grow
quite well in sun. It makes good ground
cover for damp soil. The dark-leaved cultivars,
such as 'Atropurpurea' and 'Braunherz', are
among the most attractive. The little spikes
of brilliant blue flowers rise above the leaves
in spring. It spreads by means of runners.
Another cultivar, 'Burgundy Glow', has light
blue flowers and cream-edged leaves.
Propagate by dividing clumps in winter.

Alchemilla mollis

Lady's mantle
HEIGHT: 18in (45cm) • Hardy
FLOWERING SEASON: Summer

Known as lady's mantle, this perennial has
rounded leaves about 5in (13cm) across, with
a serrated edge in a downy bluish-green, and
it is the foliage which is the plant's chief
glory. The lime-green flowers appear in tall
sprays in midsummer. It will normally self
seed easily, particularly in cracks in paving
and grows in all but very boggy soil. A
smaller species, *A. alpina*, grows to about
5in (13cm). To propagate, sow seeds under
cover in early spring, or divide clumps and
replant in autumn and winter.

Begonia rex hybrids

Begonia
HEIGHT: 18-24in (45-60cm) • Tender
FLOWERING SEASON: Insignificant

These evergreen begonias are grown principally for their attractive leaf forms. In general,
the leaves are heart-shaped with purple-
tinged edges, but different hybrids all have
particular characteristics: 'Merry Christmas'
has red leaves with an emerald green outer
band, while 'Princess of Hanover' has large
emerald green leaves with silver and dark red
bands. They are ideal for hanging baskets.
They require a minimum temperature of
13-15°C (55-59°F), humid conditions,
partial shade and moist, slightly acid soil.

Brunnera macrophylla

Siberian bugloss
HEIGHT: 18in (45cm) • Hardy
FLOWERING SEASON: Late spring

The Siberian bugloss bears delicate sprays
of small, brilliant, blue flowers, very similar
to forget-me-nots, in late spring. These are
followed by hairy, heart-shaped, green leaves.
The cultivar, *B. m.* 'Hadspen Cream' has
green and cream leaves, which tend to
colour best in the shady conditions which
the plant prefers. Divide the plants in autumn.
They are generally trouble-free, but do best
in soil that does not dry out in summer.
They are fully hardy and make good ground
cover plants.

Carex elata 'Aurea'

Bowles' golden sedge
HEIGHT: 3ft (1m) • Hardy
FLOWERING SEASON: Summer

Bowles' golden sedge is a selection of the
tufted sedge, a perennial needing very moist
soil or, ideally, its feet in water. It is one of
the most graceful sedges with very fine
golden-yellow leaves that arch attractively
and, if planted in the right position, reflect
the sunlight beautifully. Blackish-brown
flower spikes are borne in summer. Divide in
spring. *C. buchananii* from New Zealand has
reddish leaves and *C. pendula* likes moist
conditions and partial shade.

Choisya ternata

Mexican orange blossom
HEIGHT: 6ft (1.8m) or more • Hardy
FLOWERING SEASON: Early summer

This evergreen shrub, which is sometimes
known as Mexican orange blossom, with its
distinct foxy scent, is supposed to like sun,
but, in fact, does extremely well in partial
shade. The glossy evergreen leaves grow in
a whorl, and the plant naturally makes an
attractive dome-shaped bush. Many clusters
of small, white, scented flowers are borne in
late spring and early summer. It propagates
easily from semi-ripe cuttings simply struck
in ordinary garden soil in late summer.

Crataegus laevigata 'Punicea'

Hawthorn/May
HEIGHT: 20ft (6m) • Hardy
FLOWERING SEASON: Spring

This hawthorn is deciduous. In spring the
small, oval, dark green leaves provide a foil
for the clusters of deep crimson flowers,
which are then followed by round bright
red fruit. It copes well with urban pollution,
and partial shade, and makes an excellent
tree for a small garden. Some species of
hawthorn have very good autumn color,
notably *C. crus-galli, C. × lavalleei* and
C. persimilis 'Prunifolia'. Hawthorns make
very good hedging plants.

Dicentra spectabilis 'Alba'

Bleeding heart/Dutchman's trousers
HEIGHT: 2½ft (75cm) • Hardy
FLOWERING SEASON: Late spring/summer

Known as Dutchman's trousers, or bleeding
heart, this perennial has arching, pendant
sprays of clear white, heart-shaped flowers
with white inner petals, rather like a locket
on a necklace. The leaves are gray-green and
dissected, like those of ferns. *D. spectabilis* has
pinkish-red flowers. *D. formosa* is a much
smaller species with spreading blue-gray
foliage and heart shaped purple flowers held
aloft on stems 12in (30cm) high. It makes a
good ground cover plant. They like moist
soil, semi-shade and resent being moved.

Dicksonia antarctica

Australian tree fern
HEIGHT: 10ft (3m) or more • Half-hardy
FLOWERING SEASON: None

These handsome tree-like ferns come from
Australia and do best in partial shade and soil
which is moist and humus-rich. In temperate
climates they are usually grown in containers,
so that they can be overwintered indoors as
they require a minimum temperature of
41°F (5°C). The fern makes a stout trunk,
topped with huge, feathery, palm-like fronds
which arise from the center of the trunk in a
curled spear. Remove the external, brown
fronds as they fade. In its native state it will
reach a height of 30ft (10m) or more.

Digitalis purpurea

Foxglove
HEIGHT: 3ft (1m) • Hardy
FLOWERING SEASON: Summer

The native foxglove is biennial (although it
is sometimes perennial in ideal conditions).
Its distinctive spire of tubular flowers rises
high above a rosette of large, soft, green
leaves and the flowers are noticeably speckled
on the inside. There are many garden
varieties and colors, including cream and
pinkish-purple. Remove the main flower
spike after flowering to encourage secondary,
but smaller, flower spikes. Propagate by
sowing seed in early summer. The crowns
may rot in very damp or wet soil.

Dryopteris filix-mas

Male fern
HEIGHT: 3ft (1m) • Hardy
FLOWERING SEASON: None

The male fern, as it is commonly known, is the most common native fern and self-seeds itself freely, often popping up in crevices in pavings, but it is none the less welcome, having pretty, finely-divided, deep green fronds. It is unfussy as to soil but does best in plenty of shade – in the shadow of a wall for example – and looks best planted in small colonies, perhaps with other ferns, as a ribbon planting at the foot of a wall or under trees.

Elaeagnus × *ebbingei* 'Gilt Edge'

HEIGHT: 10ft (3m) or more • Hardy
FLOWERING SEASON: Autumn

This evergreen shrub is grown for its attractively silvered, small, oval leaves. It forms a large, densely covered, mounded shrub which makes a good screen and is also useful for hedging. The very small, bell-shaped and hard-to-spot flowers are very sweetly scented and fill the autumn air with unexpected fragrance. Small, egg-shaped, orange or red fruits follow the flowers. Plant in spring or early autumn, and prune by one-third after planting to promote bushy growth.

Epimedium grandiflorum

Barrenwort
HEIGHT: 9-12in (23-30cm) • Hardy
FLOWERING SEASON: Spring

This smallish perennial is native to Japan, and is grown for its foliage, which it retains throughout the winter, making good ground cover in partial shade. The leaves turn attractive shades of gold, scarlet and copper in autumn. The flowers come in shades of white, pink and yellow during a short season in spring. A cultivar known as 'Rose Queen' has bright pink flowers. It does best in a sandy soil with plenty of leaf-mold. To propagate, divide and replant in autumn.

Euphorbia amygdaloides var. *robbiae*

Milkwort/Wood spurge
HEIGHT: 18in (45cm) • Hardy
FLOWERING SEASON: Midsummer

There are more than 2,000 species in this genus. *E. amygdaloides* var. *robbiae* is a tough perennial that does particularly well in shade. It has the typical whorl-like euphorbia leaves in a dark glossy green, and the bright lime-yellow bracts are borne in quite large heads. Propagate by dividing clumps in autumn or by taking cuttings in early summer. May be subject to gray mold if damaged by frost. Note: the white sap is a skin irritant and care must be taken when handling the plants.

Fatsia japonica

Rice paper plant
HEIGHT: 15ft (4.5m) • Half-hardy
FLOWERING SEASON: Autumn

This plant, which hails from Japan, is grown principally for its handsome, glossy, evergreen leaves, which are hand-shaped with seven to nine lobes. It is particularly good for town gardens and it will grow under the shade of trees, where it will rapidly make a large spreading bush. It prefers fertile well-drained soil. In cold areas, give it the shelter of a south or west wall. There is also an autumn display of white panicles of flowers. Generally trouble-free, although young growth can be prey to blackfly.

Fuchsia 'Golden Dawn'

HEIGHT: 5ft (1.5m) • Half-hardy
FLOWERING SEASON: Summer/autumn

Fuchsia is a large genus with over 2000 plants in cultivation. These range from fully hardy to half-hardy and come in a bewildering range of colors and shapes mainly white, pink, red and purple. The flowers are variations on a bell-shaped theme and hang gracefully from the branches. They prefer a sheltered, shaded position and like moist well-drained soil. The top growth can often be damaged by frost and this can be cut back to ground level each spring. It is often necessary to cut back the hardiest varieties too, to keep them within their allotted bounds.

Gentiana asclepiadea

Willow gentian
HEIGHT: 2ft (60cm) • Hardy
FLOWERING SEASON: Mid/late summer

The willow gentian is not at all like its more
familiar Swiss cousin, the trumpet gentian.
This perennial also has blue, trumpet-shaped
flowers, but there the similarity ends, as the
willow gentian is a large perennial with
slender, arching stems along which small,
bright blue flowers are borne in mid to late
summer, a good plant will throw up twelve
or more shoots a year. It needs moist soil and
partial shade to thrive. Can be grown from
seed or cuttings, and is usually pest free.

Geranium phaeum

Mourning widow
HEIGHT: 18in (45cm) • Half-hardy
FLOWERING SEASON: Late spring/summer

This clump-forming geranium has lobed soft
green leaves and carries its single dark-purple
flowers on arching stems in late spring. In
the right conditions it will self-seed freely.
G. palmatum with its purplish-pink flowers,
is another good geranium for growing in
shade and has larger leaves than most geraniums with good autumn color. Hardy
geraniums or cranesbills are among the best
garden plants, flowering for long periods in
the summer and generally tolerant of a wide
range of soils and conditions. Propagate by
division in autumn or spring.

Hedera canariensis 'Gloire de Marengo'

Canary Island ivy
HEIGHT: 20ft (6m) • Half-hardy
FLOWERING SEASON: Insignificant

The Canary Island ivy is one of the less
hardy ivies, but will grow quickly against a
wall in a sheltered spot. If cut down by frost,
it will regrow. The leaves are oval and without the usual lobes. 'Gloire de Marengo' has
silver-splashed leaves; *H. algeriensis*
'Ravensholst' has large, mid green ones. To
propagate, grow from softwood cuttings or
rooted layers. Generally pest and disease free,
but may be attacked by red spider mite.

Helleborus orientalis

Christmas rose/Lenten rose
HEIGHT: 18in (45cm) • Hardy
FLOWERING SEASON: Early spring

This particular hellebore, known as the
Lenten rose because of its flowering time,
is a native of the eastern Mediterranean, and
in mild climates the leaves, which are broad
and dark green, are evergreen. The nodding
heads of cup-shaped flowers are the plant's
chief attraction. The flowers can be mauve,
purple, pink or white; all have prominent
central stamens. It prefers moist, well-
drained soil and partial shade. Grow from
seed or divide in spring after flowering.
Prone to aphid attacks in early summer.

Hepatica nobilis

Hepatica anemone
HEIGHT: 4in (10cm) • Hardy
FLOWERING SEASON: Spring

This little woodland plant, formerly
Anemone hepatica, is ideal for a shady corner
of a rock garden. The leaves which are mid
green have three lobes, and the anemone-
like flowers with their many petals come in
various shades of white through pale pink to
deep carmine, pale blue and purple to
mauve. There are also fully double forms.
It does best in partial shade in deep moist
soil to which plenty of leaf mold has been
added. The plants resent being disturbed.
Generally pest and disease free.

Hosta fortunei

Plantain lily
HEIGHT: 2ft (60cm) • Hardy
FLOWERING SEASON: Early summer

The plantain lily, as the hosta is sometimes
called, is particularly good for moist soil and
partial shade. *H. fortunei* is a robust, vigorous
hosta, that usually forms large clumps. Pale
violet flowers are carried in a spire above
the leaves. *H. f.* var. *aureomarginata* has
yellow-edged leaves and is widely available,
and *H. f.* var. *albopicta* has pale green leaves,
with a yellow center. Propagate by dividing
mature clumps in early spring. All hostas are
prone to attacks by slugs and snails and for
this reason are often grown in containers.

Hosta sieboldiana var. *elegans*

Plantain lily
HEIGHT: 3ft (1m) • Hardy
FLOWERING SEASON: Summer

This hosta has huge, thickly ribbed leaves in an unusual shade of gray-green, and forms an impressively large clump when fully grown. Off-white flowers are tinged with lilac, and are borne in a tall spire, appearing in late summer. The variety *H. s.* var. *elegans* has waxy leaves, and lilac-colored flowers in mid to late summer. Propagate by dividing mature clumps in early spring. If you don't use slug pellets, protect from slugs by circles of ash, or lime and soot around the plants.

Hydrangea anomala subsp. *petiolaris*

Climbing hydrangea
HEIGHT: 33ft (10m) or more • Hardy
FLOWERING SEASON: Summer

The climbing hydrangea is one of the few climbers that do well in shade; it climbs by means of aerial roots and will cling unaided. It is particularly useful for cool, north-facing walls. It has toothed green leaves and distinctive large flat heads of white flowers in summer. Like all hydrangeas, it needs a moisture-retentive soil and plenty of well-decayed manure. Prune out weak or damaged shoots in early spring and cut back to keep within bounds. Propagate it by tip cuttings taken after flowering.

Hypericum × *inodorum* 'Elstead'

St John's wort
HEIGHT: 4ft (1.2m) • Moderately hardy
FLOWERING SEASON: Summer

This particular species of St. John's wort comes from the Canary Islands. It is a semi-evergreen shrub with the typical golden yellow, cup-shaped flowers, borne on the ends of the branches right through the summer. These are followed by brilliant red large clusters of berries that are slightly oval in shape. It makes a good ground cover plant in the milder parts of the country. Take cuttings from non-flowering shoots in summer. Can be prone to rust.

Impatiens New Guinea Hybrids

Busy lizzies
HEIGHT: 12in (30cm) • Tender
FLOWERING SEASON: Summer

Busy lizzies, as they are often known, are an extremely popular tender plant, grown as an annual in cold climates, and used for hanging baskets, window boxes and summer bedding. They are one of the few brightly colored flowering plants that do well in shade. The New Guinea hybrids have handsome deep red leaves and strongly colored flowers, in pinks, reds and whites. Frequent watering is required in hot weather. Propagate named cultivars from cuttings or grow from seed sown in spring in warmth.

Mahonia aquifolium 'Atropurpurea'

Oregon grape
HEIGHT: 4ft (1.2m) • Hardy
FLOWERING SEASON: Spring

This evergreen shrub, known as the Oregon grape, has distinctive spiny, glossy, dark green foliage, each leaf composed of five to thirteen spiny leaflets. Richly scented bright yellow flowers are borne in dense clusters in spring, followed by blue berries. It has attractively colored leaves which turn wine-red in winter. Plant mahonias in spring or autumn, in a soil rich in leaf-mold, in partial shade. Take tip cuttings in summer. Troubled by rust, powdery mildew and leaf spot.

Matteuccia struthiopteris

Ostrich feather fern/Shuttlecock fern
HEIGHT: 3ft (1m) • Hardy
FLOWERING SEASON: Inconsequential

The shuttlecock fern, as it is often known, is one of the most elegant ferns, with an attractive arching habit. The name shuttle-cock fern describes the plant clearly with its crown of shorter, dark brown fronds surrounded by a circle of paler green ones. It needs moisture-retentive soil, with plenty of humus added to it, and does best in partial shade. It also requires plenty of room for the roots to expand. To increase the stock, remove any offsets in spring, and plant at least 4ft (1.2m) from the parent plant.

Meconopsis cambrica

Welsh poppy
HEIGHT: 12in (30cm) • Hardy
FLOWERING SEASON: Summer

This perennial, known as the Welsh poppy, produces large, bright, yellow or orange, papery flowers, rather like a large buttercup, all summer long. The plant grows 12-18in (30-45cm) tall and sends up a clump of fresh, green, fern-like foliage surmounted by a number of poppy-like flowers. It flourishes in shady places and needs a light rich soil, preferably neutral to acid, and plenty of water in summer but not very much in winter. It will usually seed itself.

Paeonia lactiflora hybrids

Peony
HEIGHT: 2ft (60cm) • Hardy
FLOWERING SEASON: Summer

There are both single and double-flowered forms of this herbaceous perennial and some are scented. Although the double cultivars are more showy, the single cultivars have a particular beauty, especially the pure white cultivars such as *P. l.* 'White Wings' and *P. l.* 'Whitleyi Major'. Grow peonies in a situation sheltered from morning sun, and humus-rich soil. Deadhead after flowering.

Paeonia mlokosewitschii

Peony
HEIGHT: 2ft (60cm) • Hardy
FLOWERING SEASON: Spring

This perennial peony has large, bright, lemon-yellow, single flowers with prominent stamens. The pale green leaves sometimes turn color in autumn. It also has attractive seedpods. Peonies can be grown in moist, well-drained, well-manured soil in partial shade, ideally sheltered from the morning sun. Plant in early autumn or spring, making sure the crowns are not planted too deep. Prone to some viral disorders and damage from dry soil conditions or root disturbance.

Phyllostachys viridiglaucescens

Bamboo
HEIGHT: 20-25ft (6-8m) • Moderately hardy
FLOWERING SEASON: None

Phyllostachys are useful clump-forming bamboos which come from East Asia and Himalaya. They like moist rich soil which is on the light side and they must have a sheltered position. They flower about once every 30-40 years and after planting the whole plant dies so it is important to save seed when it is available. Propagation is normally by division which should be done in May when the new shoots are only an inch or two long. Cut the old shoots right down to the ground in spring.

Polygonatum × hybridum

Solomon's seal
HEIGHT: 4ft (1.2m) • Hardy
FLOWERING SEASON: Late spring

Solomon's seal (or David's harp) is a large herbaceous perennial which is tough and very hardy. It will grow almost anywhere in both shade and sun. It makes an attractive arching plant with its thickly ribbed, mid green leaves and tubular white flowers dangling the length of the stems in late spring. Give it plenty of leaf-mold, and cut the stems down in autumn. Propagate by division in autumn or spring. Generally disease-free, but sawfly caterpillars may damage leaves.

Schizophragma integrifolium

Hydrangea vine
HEIGHT: 20ft (6m) • Hardy
FLOWERING SEASON: Summer/autumn

This climber will attach itself to a wall or tree trunk using its aerial roots, so it needs no tying in. Closely related to its more vigorous cousin, *S. hydrangeoides*, it has the same large, flat, white, hydrangea-like florets from summer through to autumn, and bright green leaves with silvery backs. The plant will grow against a north wall but does better with some sun. It prefers moist well-drained soil. Propagate by taking short cuttings of the side shoots made with a slight heel of old wood inserted in sandy soil in July.

Skimmia japonica

Skimmia
HEIGHT: 4ft (1.2m) • Hardy
FLOWERING SEASON: Early summer

This handsome, rounded, bushy shrub is an
excellent plant for a small urban garden. It
has the bonus not only of neat, glossy evergreen leaves, but of scented, creamy-white
flower panicles, followed by bright scarlet
berries. It does well in partial shade in good
garden soil. The cultivar *S. j.* 'Rubella' with
its red rimmed aromatic leaves and red
flower buds which open to white flowers in
spring is particularly popular. Propagate from
semi-ripe cuttings in late summer.

Smilacina racemosa

False spikenard/False Solomon's seal
HEIGHT: 3ft (1m) • Hardy
FLOWERING SEASON: Summer

Known as the false spikenard, or false
Solomon's seal, this herbaceous perennial
likes lightly shaded woodland and moist,
neutral to acid soil. The white scented
flowers are carried on the ends of the stems.
Cut back the plants in autumn. To
propagate, lift the plant in spring and divide
the rhizomatous rootstock once the plant
has been established for a few years.

Stewartia pseudocamellia

HEIGHT: 16ft (5m) • Hardy
FLOWERING SEASON: Late summer

S. pseudocamellia is a small tree that makes a
good subject for planting in part shade in
neutral to acid soil. It has single large white
cup-shaped flowers in summer and the mid
green ovate leaves turn attractive shades of
gold and scarlet in autumn, while in winter
the peeling bark is a bonus. *S. p.* Koreana
Group is similar with flowers that open out
flat. *S. sinensis*, has fragrant saucer-shaped
flowers. The plant will not flourish against
an east wall. Propagate from half-ripe cuttings in late summer.

Symphytum × uplandicum 'Variegatum'

Comfrey
HEIGHT: 10in (25cm) • Hardy
FLOWERING SEASON: Spring

This is a vigorous perennial, which does best
in partial shade and fairly moist conditions.
They are, perhaps, best suited to a wild
garden and generally will self-seed freely.
The leaves, which are lance-shaped, are
bristly and tough, cream and green splashed,
and the flowers are blue or pink.
S. grandiflorum has small creamy-white
flowers and makes good ground cover,
S. 'Hidcote Blue', is similar with pale blue
flowers. Propagate by division in autumn.

Tellima grandiflora

Fringe cup
HEIGHT: 2ft (60cm) • Hardy
FLOWERING SEASON: Early summer

This evergreen perennial is easy to grow and
a very good subject for shade. It is a
particularly good weed suppressor and
makes a good ground cover plant in a shrubbery. The leaves, which form a dense crown
close to the ground, are fairly large, maple-
like and rough in texture. The tall flower
spires carry rather inconspicuous greenish-
yellow flowers in early summer. The
Tellima grandiflora Rubra Group cultivars
have attractive bronze purple leaves.
Propagate by dividing the plants or by seed.

Thalictrum aquilegiifolium var. *album*

Meadow rue/Maidenhair fern
HEIGHT: 3-4 ft (1-1.2m) • Hardy
FLOWERING SEASON: Summer

This elegant, clump-forming perennial has
particularly attractive foliage, very similar to
that of the aquilegia. In summer it carries
branching heads of small, white, starry
flowers. There is another good white cultivar
called 'White Cloud'. *T. aquilegiifolium* has
attractive lilac-purple flowers. This plant
prefers moist soil, and flourishes in partial
shade, although it will also cope with sun. It
looks well grown at the edge of woodland.
Propagate by division in spring.

Trollius europaeus

Globe flower
HEIGHT: 2ft (60cm) • Hardy
FLOWERING SEASON: Early summer

The globe flower has attractive bright yellow or orange tightly petalled flowers, some 2in (5cm) across. The leaves are deeply divided, lobed and toothed. It does well as a marginal plant for streams or ponds or in any moist soil in sun or partial shade. Good hybrids include the pale yellow *T.* × *cultorum* 'Canary Bird', or the bright orange *T.* × *c.* 'Orange Princess'. Cut the flowers back after flowering to produce a second flush of blooms. Divide and replant fibrous roots in autumn.

Veratrum nigrum

Black false hellebore
HEIGHT: 4ft (1.2m) • Hardy
FLOWERING SEASON: Late summer

These big, hardy perennials make handsome spires of deep purple, star-shaped flowers above large, dark green, pleated leaves. They are good imposing plants for the back of a shady border. *V. nigrum* likes moist soil to which peat has been added, and benefits from being cut down in autumn. Propagate by dividing the clumps in autumn or spring. A greenish-white flowered species, *V. album*, makes a similar height and can be treated in the same way.

Viola riviniana Purpurea Group

Sweet violet
HEIGHT: 5in (12cm) • Hardy
FLOWERING SEASON: Spring

This small woodland plant formerly known as *V. labradorica purpurea* is ideal for shade. It has attractively colored purplish-bronze leaves and the typical small, mauve violet flowers in spring. It does well on any light fertile soil which does not dry out. Plant in autumn or spring, and deadhead the flowers as they fade, to encourage a longer flowering season. Can be grown from seed. Pest-free, but prone to a variety of viral disorders.

More Plants for Shade

All gardens have some shade and we have divided the plants that grow best in shade into three groups: plants that will grow in dry shade; plants that will grow in moist shade, of which a number are listed under moisture on page 69; and plants that will grow on a north wall. These lists are only a selection and there are a number of other plants that are suitable for these problem positions.

PLANTS FOR DRY SHADE

TREES

Acer campestre
  A. platanoides & cvs
Alnus (in variety)
Betula (in variety)
Gleditsia triacanthos
Ilex aquifolium
Robinia pseudoacacia & cvs
Sorbus aucuparia

SHRUBS

Aucuba japonica
Bashania syn. *Arundinaria* (in variety)
Berberis (in variety)
Buxus sempervirens
Cotoneaster horizontalis
Euonymus fortunei cvs

Hippophae rhamnoides
Lonicera pileata
Osmanthus (in variety)
Prunus laurocerasus

PERENNIALS & GROUND COVER PLANTS

Bergenia (in variety)
Iris foetidissima
Lamium maculatum
Pachysandra terminalis
Pulmonaria saccharata

PLANTS FOR MOIST SHADE

TREES

Acers (in variety)
Alnus incana
Betula nigra
  B. pendula
Crateagus (in variety)
Embothrium coccineum
Salix (in variety)
Sorbus aucuparia

SHRUBS

Aucuba japonica
Camellia (in variety)
Clethra arborea
Cornus (in variety)
Desfontainia spinosa
Gaultheria (in variety)
Kalmia latifolia
Leucothoe fontanesiana
Rhododendron (in variety)
Symphoricarpus × *doorenbosii*

PERENNIALS, GROUND COVER PLANTS & CLIMBERS

*Astilbe (*in variety)
Begonia rex Hybrids
Campanula lactiflora
Dicentra (in variety)
Dodecatheon pulchellum
Epimedium grandiflorum
Galium odoratum
Houttuynia cordata
Iris pseudoacorus
Mentha suavolens
Oxalis acetosella
Polypodium vulgare
Tradescantia (in variety)
Trillium grandiflorum
Tropaeolum speciosum

CLIMBERS & PLANTS FOR NORTH WALLS

Berberidopsis corallina
Clematis (large-flowered varieties)
Cotoneaster horizontalis
Forsythia suspensa
Garrya elliptica
Hydrangea petiolaris
Jasminum nudiflorum (Winter jasmine)
Kerria japonica
Parthenocissus (in variety)
Pyracantha (in variety)
Rosa 'Königin von Dänemark'
  R. 'Madame Legras de Saint German'
  R. 'Maigold'
Schizophragma hydrangeoides

PLANTS *for* DRY SUN

For sunny, dry areas in your garden, plants from the hotter areas of the world are a good choice because they thrive in these conditions. Many are distinguished by divided, waxy or felted leaves. Gray-leaved plants, such as lavender and senecio are typical examples.

ABOVE: Convolvulus cneorum, *a gray-leaved sub-shrub, thrives in hot dry conditions and produces a profusion of delicate white flowers.*

OPPOSITE: *A garden in summer with the climbing roses just coming into bloom. The roses give additional height to the border and the mixed colors of the herbaceous perennials provide a splendid contrast.*

ABOVE: *A mixed border, with the front edge in sun, provides a home for a cottage-garden style planting of opium poppies in the front, contrasting with the silvery-gray Miss Willmott's Ghost* (Eryngium giganteum) *with the spires of the purple form of the burning bush,* (Dictamnus albus *var.* purpureus) *behind.*

Anyone who has travelled abroad to the Mediterranean, California or Australia, especially in the spring, will realize that a hot and dry site is by no means a problem in a garden. If you select your plants carefully, you can create a fine display which will provide color and interest. Start with some of the best known plants from the Mediterranean; lavender, rosemary, sage, salvia and santolina, rock roses (cistus), helichrysum (the everlasting flower) and marigolds. These are just some of the plants that like a position in full sun and dry soil.

The plants which survive these conditions tend to have evolved and adapted in order to cope with high temperatures and low rainfall. These adaptations are often what make the plants so attractive. *Convolvulus cneorum*, with its silver and gray foliage, appears this color because it has developed a coating of fine hairs on the leaf surface, which has the effect of reducing moisture loss and reflecting sunlight or, conversely, to shed rain. Other plants, such as *Senecio* 'Sunshine' (now properly called *Brachyglottis*), have modified their leaves by thickening them to protect the inside, while the underside of the leaf remains felted. Brooms, such as *Genista aetnensis*, reduce moisture loss by having hardly any leaves at all, but thin tough stems.

The soil in which these plants grow in the wild is often poor and impoverished. It may be almost pure sand or gravel, which makes it very quick to drain, and in summer there is very little natural moisture. There is little organic matter too, as any fallen leaves burn up quickly, or there may be just a very shallow scraping of soil over solid rock, the roots clinging on for life by penetrating cracks and crevices.

In the garden, these conditions can exist naturally or can be created artifi-.cially; where the garden is of thin shallow soil overlying solid rock, for example, or where the subsoil is pure sand or gravel which has found its way to the surface, as can happen in a new garden if the topsoil has been removed during building work. Perhaps you have a south-facing border against a house wall, particularly if there is a path or patio to the other side, or a south-facing, sloping garden; these also tend towards dryness, and more so if the soil is also sandy.

The main problem with such soils is lack of moisture
for the plants. Improving the soil is difficult, as any
organic matter you try to incorporate is quickly burnt
up, and the plant nutrients you do apply will be washed
through the soil along with the water. On the positive
side, however, dry soils are quick to warm up in spring,
and if you can achieve a cover of plants that like this
environment, they will soon start to help themselves by
using their natural adaptations to conserve moisture.

RIGHT: *The brilliant white flowers of* Anthemis punctata *ssp.* cupaniana *with
their yellow eyes make it an ideal subject to plant at the edge of a gravel garden.*

BELOW: *A gravel garden provides a home for alpines that enjoy both sun and free
draining soil: here the yellow flowers of the helianthemum and the pink spreading
saponaria, tumbling Ted, provide a foil for the French lavender.*

Acantholimon glumaceum

Prickly thrift
HEIGHT: 6in (15cm) • Hardy
FLOWERING SEASON: Summer

An evergreen perennial with a low, cushion-forming habit; the stems often root into the soil as the plant spreads across the ground. The flowers are produced in small, short spikes of up to eight star-shaped, pink blooms which are carried above the spiny, spear-shaped, bluish-green leaves, and arranged in tight rosettes on the stems. Propagation is by softwood cuttings taken from non-flowering shoots in spring and summer and rooted in a cold frame.

Aethionema 'Warley Ruber'

Persian candytuft
HEIGHT: 6in (15cm) • Hardy
FLOWERING SEASON: Spring/summer

This colorful evergreen sub-shrub has tiny strap-like leaves which are a bluish-green color. It has a naturally spreading habit and forms a dense mat of foliage over the soil. The small cross-shaped flowers are a deep rose-pink and grow in loose clusters on the tips of the shoots. Often grown in the rock garden, this plant needs an open, free-draining soil to grow well. Trim the plants in July after the flowers are over and propagate by taking softwood cuttings from the new growth, either in the late summer, or in the spring.

Agapanthus Headbourne Hybrids

African lily
HEIGHT: 3ft (1m) • Moderately hardy
FLOWERING SEASON: Mid/late summer

A clump-forming herbaceous perennial with deep green strap-like leaves up to 2½ft (75cm) long and large clusters of deep blue flowers produced from July onwards. Cultivars, such as Headbourne Hybrids, are usually hardier than many of the species. They like full sun, and have thick fleshy roots which provide a good water store and drought tolerance. In northern areas they require winter protection. Propagate by division in spring.

Anthemis punctata ssp. *cupaniana*

Camomile/Dog fennel
HEIGHT: 12in (30cm) • Hardy
FLOWERING SEASON: Early summer

An evergreen herbaceous perennial that is invaluable for a dry sunny garden. It forms a loose cushion of finely cut silvery-gray, aromatic foliage, which turns green in winter. The white daisy-like flowers have a golden center, or 'eye', and are carried singly above the leaves on short erect stems. No regular pruning is required but the dead flower heads are usually removed in autumn. Propagation is by semi-ripe basal cuttings taken in summer.

Aster novi-belgii 'Jenny'

Michaelmas daisy
HEIGHT: 2½ft (75cm) • Hardy
FLOWERING SEASON: Early autumn

This popular herbaceous perennial has mid to deep green leaves carried on sturdy erect green stems, they are roughly elliptical but terminate in a sharp point. The colorful daisy-like flowers are produced in large quantities in autumn. Many reliable named cultivars are available: *A. n-b.* 'Royal Ruby' has deep red flowers, and 'White Ladies' has white flowers and dark foliage. They flourish in sun or part shade and are generally soil tolerant. Propagate by softwood cuttings in summer, or division in early spring.

Buddleja alternifolia

Butterfly bush
HEIGHT: 15ft (4.5m) • Hardy
FLOWERING SEASON: Summer

A large deciduous shrub with graceful arching stems covered in gray-green, narrow strap-like leaves, which have a bluish underside. Clusters of small, delicately fragrant, lilac-blue flowers are produced in June on the previous year's wood. Prune after flowering but if left unpruned the shrub develops into a sprawling plant with a semi-weeping habit. An interesting cultivar, *B. a.* 'Argentea', has hairy silver-gray leaves. This plant is easy to propagate by softwood cuttings in summer or hardwood cuttings in winter.

Campanula persicifolia

Peach-leaved bellflower
HEIGHT: 3ft (1m) • Hardy
FLOWERING SEASON: Mid-late summer

This clump-forming, evergreen, herbaceous perennial has long, narrow, mid green, leathery leaves which grow in tight rosettes. The bell-shaped flowers are produced close to the main stem, and range in color from bluish-purple to pure white. A number of cultivars are available: 'Telham Beauty' has deep blue flowers and *C. p.* var. *planiflora* f. *alba,* pure white ones. Propagate by seed sown in March and April, cuttings taken in April and May, or dividing the plants in October.

Catalpa bignonioides

Indian bean tree
HEIGHT: 50ft (15m) • Hardy
FLOWERING SEASON: Summer

This outstanding deciduous tree has an open, spreading habit and, in mature specimens, a deeply grooved bark. It is valued for its tolerance of urban pollution. The large, heart-shaped leaves are tinged with purple as they open, turning light-green as they mature.In summer white, bell-shaped flowers with yellow and purple markings are produced, followed by long hanging pods which stay throughout winter. There is a striking golden-leaved cultivar: *C. b.* 'Aurea'. Propagate in summer using softwood tip cuttings.

Catananche caerulea

Cupid's dart/Blue cupidone
HEIGHT: 2ft (60cm) • Hardy
FLOWERING SEASON: Summer

This clump forming perennial known as cupid's dart, has narrow, gray-green, strap-like leaves carried on tall erect mid green stems and masses of daisy-like, purple-blue flowers throughout the summer. They like a sunny, open position and light, well-drained soil. There are a number of named cultivars: *C. c.* 'Major', has lavender blue flowers, *C. c.* 'Perry's White', is the most popular white cultivar. Named cultivars must be propagated by root cuttings taken in winter.

Clarkia elegans

Clarkia
HEIGHT: 2ft (60cm) • Hardy
FLOWERING SEASON: Late summer/autumn

This popular annual is grown for its colorful display of summer flowers, the leaves are narrow, oval and mid green in color. The flowers are produced in bold spikes on erect green stems in colors which range through white, salmon, orange, purple, scarlet and lavender. In addition, double-flowered forms are also available; *C. e.* Love Affair, is a mixed color strain with large double flowers and compact growth. Propagation is by seed sown outdoors in early spring. Thin the seedlings to 9-12in (20-30cm) apart.

Convolvulus cneorum

HEIGHT: 2½ft (75cm) • Moderately hardy
FLOWERING SEASON: Late spring/early autumn

A rather surprising member of the same genus as the pernicious bindweed, this is a slightly tender evergreen shrub of compact and low-growing bushy habit, with silvery, silky, narrow pointed leaves, on silver hairy stems. The short-lived flowers, produced at the tips of the shoots from May to September, are a soft pink in tight bud, opening to pure white with a small golden-yellow eye in the center. It prefers a sheltered position in well-drained but nutrient-poor soil in full sun. Propagation is by semi-ripe cuttings, taken in July.

Cortaderia selloana 'Aureolineata'

Pampas grass
HEIGHT: 8ft (2.5m) • Moderately hardy
FLOWERING SEASON: Summer/autumn

A bold, showy, clump-forming ornamental grass, with narrow, pale to mid green, spear-shaped, evergreen leaves, which have razor sharp edges. The flowers, which are carried in majestic silvery-white plumes tinged red or purple in autumn, are held high above the arching leaves on erect almost white stems. A popular cultivar is *C. s.* 'Sunningdale Silver', which has long-lasting, large, silver flower-plumes. Propagation is by division in spring; select female plants for a better flower display.

Corylus avellana 'Contorta'

Cobnut/Hazelnut
HEIGHT: 10ft (3m) • Hardy
FLOWERING SEASON: Early spring

This large deciduous shrub is grown for its
curiously twisted branches and twigs. The
broadly oval, mid green leaves have a noticeably toothed margin and turn a deep gold in
autumn. The female flowers are very small,
but the long yellow male catkins are very
attractive in February. It likes well-drained
limy soil and mortar rubble may be added
before planting if the soil is lime-deficient. It
is best to propagate by layering one-year-old
shoots, but rooting will take up to a year.

Crataegus laciniata

Hawthorn
HEIGHT: 22ft (7m) • Hardy
FLOWERING SEASON: Spring

A beautiful small ornamental tree, with
sparsely thorned, lax branches covered in felt
when young. The deeply cut, downy leaves
are dark green above and gray-green
beneath. The large fruits are a pinkish-
yellow later turning red and hang on the
tree most of the winter. Propagation is by
budding in summer or grafting in early
spring. The bacterial disease fireblight
causes withering and progressive die-back
of young shoots.

Cytisus battandieri

Pineapple broom/Moroccan broom
HEIGHT: 12ft (4m) • Moderately hardy
FLOWERING SEASON: Early summer

A spectacular semi-evergreen open shrub
best grown against the shelter of a west- or
south-facing wall, the pineapple bush carries
large racemes of the pineapple-scented
flowers which give it its name from early to
midsummer. Like all brooms it prefers light
well-drained soil but it can be grown
successfully on heavier land provided plenty
of sand and leaf mold are worked into the
ground before planting. Propagate by
semi-ripe cuttings taken in late summer.

Cytisus × *kewensis*

Broom
HEIGHT: 2ft (60cm) • Hardy
FLOWERING SEASON: Late spring

This attractive, low-growing shrub was
raised at Kew Gardens in 1891 and has been
popular ever since. In spring, cascades of
creamy-yellow, sweet-pea-shaped blooms
cover the bush, obscuring the stems and
leaves. The mid green leaves are small, strap-
like, covered in fine hairs and grow sparsely
along the lax, twiggy, green stems. This plant
should be pruned after flowering but it does
not respond well to hard pruning or being
moved. Propagation is by semi-ripe cuttings
with a heel taken in summer.

Davidia involucrata

Dove tree/Handkerchief tree
HEIGHT: 50ft (15m) • Hardy
FLOWERING SEASON: Late spring

This beautiful tree is grown for the striking
display of large, white, modified leaf bracts,
from which it gets its common name 'hand-
kerchief tree'. The inconspicuous flowers
appear in small clusters on mature plants in
May. The mid green, heart-shaped leaves
have dense hairs on the underside, and in
autumn turn a bright golden-yellow with a
red tinge at the margin. It likes a sunny position and deep well-drained soil. Propagation
is by seed sown in autumn or semi-ripe
cuttings taken in early summer.

Diascia fetcaniensis

HEIGHT: 12in (30cm) • Half-hardy
FLOWERING SEASON: Summer

These plants are slender, low-growing annuals
or short-lived perennials with dark green,
glossy, broadly oval leaves, with a toothed
margin. The tube-shaped, rosy-pink, lilac
or apricot flowers open out into a shell-like
bloom with spotted throat. They are produced in large flushes on the tips of slender
green shoots. A popular cultivar, *D.* 'Ruby
Field', has salmon-pink flowers. They like
sun and rich, moist, well-drained soil that
does not dry out. Propagate by cuttings
taken in late summer. (This plant is often
mistakenly identified as nemesia.)

Dorotheanthus bellidiformis

Livingstone daisy/Ice plant/Fig marigold
HEIGHT: 4in (10cm) • Tender
FLOWERING SEASON: Summer/autumn

Some mesembryanthemums have become dorotheanthus, but this is still the Livingstone daisy, which is well adapted to surviving in dry, arid conditions. Low and spreading in habit, its narrow, light green, tube-like leaves have a glistening appearance. In a dry sunny position it produces masses of brightly colored, small, daisy-like flowers. The color range includes white, pink, carmine, salmon, apricot and orange. Propagate by sowing seeds indoors in March.

Echinops bannaticus 'Taplow Blue'

Globe thistle
HEIGHT: 4ft (1.2m) • Hardy
FLOWERING SEASON: Late summer

An attractive upright perennial with narrow leaves and palish-blue thistle-like heads carried on branching stems in late summer. Globe thistles flourish in ordinary garden soil and like a sunny position. They are useful plants for the herbaceous border as their pale, neutral color provides a good foil for brighter plants. Propagate by division in the autumn or by root cuttings taken in mild weather in winter.

Eryngium bourgatii

Sea holly
HEIGHT: 2½ft (75cm) • Hardy
FLOWERING SEASON: Summer/autumn

At first glance, these tough herbaceous perennials look like a cross between a holly and a thistle, but they are not related to either. The tough, spiny, coarsely toothed leaves vary in color from dark green to silvery-blue. The flowers, which often look very like teasel heads, are metallic silvery-blue, darkening with age, with a collar of broad spines at the base; they are held on strong wiry stems above the leaves. Propagation is by division or root cuttings in spring.

Escallonia 'Slieve Donard'

Escallonia
HEIGHT: 14ft (4.5m) • Not fully hardy
FLOWERING SEASON: Late spring/early summer

Escallonias are handsome evergreen shrubs which can be grown either as hedges, in the shrubbery, or against a wall. They have an attractive range of flower colors from white through pink to scarlet. The small, bell-shaped flowers are produced in clusters on short spur-like branches above the glossy oval leaves, dark green above and pale green beneath. They like sun and well-drained soil and are an excellent plant for southern coastal regions. Propagates very easily from softwood cuttings taken in midsummer.

Eucalyptus gunnii

Cider gum
HEIGHT: 35ft (10.5m) • Moderately hardy
FLOWERING SEASON: Autumn/winter

The cider gum is an evergreen tree that comes from Australia and is grown mainly for its blue-gray, leathery-textured leaves and stems. The leaf shape varies with the age of the plant: the juvenile leaves are almost circular and appear to clasp the short stems on which they are produced, but as the plant matures the new leaves are strap-like and hang down vertically. Young trees have a blue-gray bark. Eucalyptus can be cut to the ground each spring and grown as shrubs. Propagation is by seed sown in spring.

Galtonia candicans

Summer hyacinth
HEIGHT: 4ft (1.2m) • Moderately hardy
FLOWERING SEASON: Late summer/early autumn

These outstanding late-flowering bulbs have leaves which are a bluish gray-green, widely strap-shaped and quite thick and fleshy. Single stems carry a head of large, slightly scented, drooping, white bells, with pale green markings at the base of each petal. These bulbs make an attractive display at a time when many other plants are looking jaded. They like a sheltered sunny site. They produce seed very freely and may become invasive. Propagation is by seed sown in spring or bulblets in autumn.

Genista aetnensis

Mount Etna broom
HEIGHT: 25ft (8m) • Hardy
FLOWERING SEASON: Summer

This is a large elegant shrub, with many slender drooping, bright green branches, which are practically leafless. The tough, sparse leaves are mid green and strap-like, with fine, white, silky hairs. The golden-yellow, heavily scented, pea-like flowers are produced in large quantities at the tips of the shoots in midsummer. It likes full sun and will tolerate almost any soil conditions except waterlogging. Propagation is by seed sown in spring.

Gleditsia triacanthos 'Sunburst'

Honey locust
HEIGHT: 30ft (9m) • Moderately hardy
FLOWERING SEASON: Midsummer

A beautiful small tree ideal for giving light shade in the garden, provided the site is not exposed. The small, delicate leaflets are arranged in large numbers (up to 32) along a tough green leaf stalk, although a glossy mid green, the most popular cultivar is the golden-leaved *G. t.* 'Sunburst', and there is a purple-leaved cultivar, *G. t.* 'Rubylace'. Propagation is by seed sown under protection in spring or the named cultivars are increased by grafting in early spring.

Gypsophila repens 'Rosa Schönheit'

Chalk plant
HEIGHT: 3ft (1m) • Hardy
FLOWERING SEASON: Summer

These cottage garden favorites have thin, strap-like gray-green leaves very similar to those of the carnation, carried on thick, gray-green stems. Masses of very small, usually white, flowers are produced in large clusters. There are dwarf and pink-flowered forms. *G. repens* 'Rosea' is low-growing, 4–6in (10–15cm), and spreads to form a dense mat, with rose-pink flowers. Propagate by root cuttings taken when dormant.

× *Halimiocistus wintonensis*

HEIGHT: 2ft (60cm) • Not fully hardy
FLOWERING SEASON: Summer

This hybrid evergreen plant makes a low, spreading bush with small tough, slightly hairy, gray-green leaves supported on thin, gray-green, semi-prostrate stems. The small, saucer-shaped flowers are white with a red blotch at the base of each petal and a yellow center to the bloom. The flowers open early in the morning and die the same day, leaving a carpet of petals around the plant. It likes full sun and fertile well-drained soil but will require shelter if grown in colder areas. Propagation is by small semi-ripe cuttings taken in summer.

Helianthemum 'Amy Baring'

Rock rose/Sun rose
HEIGHT: 3–4in (7.5–10cm) • Hardy
FLOWERING SEASON: Late summer/autumn

A dwarf and very drought-resistant evergreen shrub with small, oval, pale green leaves covered in fine hairs. The small, saucer-shaped flowers are produced in massed flushes, close to the ground on short stems. Good cultivars are *H.* 'Rhodanthe Carneum' with pink flowers emerging through gray foliage, 'Wisley Primrose', soft golden-yellow flowers, and 'Wisley White', pure white flowers and gray foliage. Cut back lightly after flowering. Propagate by semi-ripe heel cuttings taken in August.

Helichrysum italicum

Curry plant
HEIGHT: 15in (35cm) • Moderately hardy
FLOWERING SEASON: Summer

This dwarf shrub has a dense, bushy habit and short, narrow silvery-gray, aromatic leaves which smell of curry when they are crushed or when the weather is very hot and sunny. The flowers grow in broad clusters of small, oblong, mustard-yellow flower-heads on long upright white shoots. It likes sun and well-drained soil. If not pruned with shears immediately after flowering, this shrub will spread, leaving an open, bare center. Propagation is by semi-ripe cuttings taken with a heel in summer.

Hibiscus syriacus 'Oiseau Bleu'

Hibiscus
HEIGHT: 10ft (3m) • Moderately hardy
FLOWERING SEASON: Late summer

A large upright deciduous shrub with deeply notched dark green leaves. *H. s.* 'Oiseau Blue' carries large lilac-blue flowers with a red center from late summer to mid autumn. Hibiscus come from the mallow family, *malvaceae*, and vary from hardy to frost tender. They like full sun and rich well-drained soil. Among the best garden plants are the species, *H. syriacus* which is white with a red center, and its cultivar *H. s.* 'Woodbridge' which is deep pink with a dark red center.

Hibiscus syriacus 'Red Heart'

Hibiscus
Height: 10ft (3m) • Moderately hardy
FLOWERING SEASON: Late summer

Another popular cultivar of *H. syriacus*, 'Red Heart' has large white flowers with conspicuous red centers. Hibiscus should be planted in March or November and are useful as background plants in a herbaceous border in the milder parts of the country. Little pruning is required but they can be thinned out in spring if the shrub is becoming overcrowded. Propagated by semi-ripe cuttings taken in summer and inserted in sandy soil in a cold frame.

Hypericum 'Hidcote'

St John's wort
HEIGHT: 4ft (1.2m) • Hardy
FLOWERING SEASON: Late summer/early autumn

This is a deciduous to semi-evergreen shrub with a dense bushy habit and thin, gray-green stems which turn pale-brown as they age. The small strap-like leaves are deep green on the upper surface with a slight blue-green sheen on the underside. The golden yellow saucer-shaped flowers are produced in clusters from late summer to early autumn. *H.* 'Hidcote Variegated' has a white margin to the leaf. Propagation is by semi-ripe cuttings taken with a heel in summer and autumn.

Ilex aquifolium 'Silver Queen'

Holly
HEIGHT: 15ft (4.5m) • Hardy
FLOWERING SEASON: Spring/summer

The hollies, the evergreen shrubs associated with Christmas, all have small, white, star-shaped flowers, with red, orange, yellow or even white berries produced on the female plants in winter. The leaves vary in color but have sharp spines around the margin. Popular cultivars are *I. aquifolium* 'Silver Queen' with dark green leaves and a silver margin and *I.* × *altaclerensis* 'Golden King', with a golden margin. All of them prefer well-drained soil. Propagation is by semi-ripe cuttings taken in summer.

Kniphofia 'Royal Standard'

Red-hot poker/Torch lily
HEIGHT: 3ft (1m) • Moderately hardy
FLOWERING SEASON: Late summer

A familiar sight in many borders in late summer red-hot pokers carry their spears of red-tipped buds opening to yellow flowers above grass-like tufts of leaves. They prefer full sun and fertile well-drained soil and they do not do well in soil that becomes water-logged. The crowns may need protection in winter in hard weather. *K.* 'Little Maid' carries pale creamy-yellow, whitish flowers and *K.* 'Samuel's Sensation' deep orange ones. The plants resent being disturbed. Propagate by division in spring.

Laburnum × *watereri* 'Vossii'

Voss's laburnum
HEIGHT: 28ft (9m) • Hardy
FLOWERING SEASON: Late spring

A well-known flowering tree which produces large quantities of long, trailing clusters (racemes) of deep golden-yellow, pea-like flowers in late spring. In autumn the small, gray-brown pods split open to release small black seeds, which are poisonous. The gray-green leaves, which have a glossy upper surface and paler underside, are made up of three small leaflets. Laburnums grow in any but waterlogged soil but have a brittle root system and must be permanently staked. Propagate by grafting in spring.

Lavandula angustifolia

Lavender
HEIGHT: 3ft (1m) • Hardy
FLOWERING SEASON: Mid/late summer

This evergreen perennial has long, narrow, aromatic, silver-gray leaves covered with fine, felt-like hairs which are very effective in reducing moisture loss. The small, tube-like flowers are carried in narrow clusters, on tough, square stems. The most commonly grown cultivar, *L. a.* 'Hidcote', has strongly scented, deep purple-blue flowers and a compact bushy habit. *L. a.* 'Alba' is white and *L. a.* 'Rosea', pink. Propagation is by semi-ripe cuttings with a heel in summer.

Liriope muscari

Lilyturf
HEIGHT: 18in (45cm) • Hardy
FLOWERING SEASON: Late summer/late autumn

This clump-forming perennial has glossy, deep green, grass-like leaves. A network of rhizomes below ground provides a spreading habit which makes it ideal for ground cover. The thick clusters of flower spikes bear violet-blue, bell-shaped flowers.
L. m. 'Curly Twist' has lilac flowers flushed with burgundy and spirally twisting leaves.
L. m. 'Variegata' has a bold yellow stripe along the leaf margin. Propagation is by division in early spring.

Lithodora diffusa 'Heavenly Blue'

Gromwell
HEIGHT: 4in (10cm) • Hardy • pH
FLOWERING SEASON: Summer/late autumn

This prostrate, spreading plant is perfect for a hot, dry position, the slender stems are covered with small, dull green leaves which are spear-shaped and covered with fine hairs to reduce moisture loss. Small, deep-blue, funnel-shaped flowers are produced in vast quantities from early June onwards. Hard pruning in spring will prevent the plant becoming straggly. Propagation is by semi-ripe cuttings taken in midsummer.

Lychnis chalcedonica

Jerusalem cross/Maltese cross
HEIGHT: 3ft (1m) • Hardy
FLOWERING SEASON: Summer

A neat clump-forming perennial which bears large clustered heads of flowers of an intense pure scarlet color in early summer. It is easily grown and does best in full sun in fertile well-drained soil but it prefers soil which does not dry out. The cultivar *L. c.* 'Alba' is white. Other species include *L. flos-cuculi*, the ragged robin or cuckoo flower, which grows wild in Europe and Great Britain, its rose-pink flowers are extremely showy. Propagate by division of the roots in March.

Macleaya microcarpa

Plume poppy
HEIGHT: 6ft (1.8m) • Hardy
FLOWERING SEASON: Summer

Known as the plume poppy, this is an invasive herbaceous perennial which is particulary useful for the back of the border or for areas of woodland garden, since it does well in dappled shade as well as sun. The leaves are handsome, gray-green in color, large and deeply lobed, the rather inconspicuous flowers are carried in tall plumes, in a soft bronze-pink shade. It grows in any soil but prefers soil that is well-manured and does not dry out. Divide and replant in autumn.

Nepeta × faassenii

Catmint
HEIGHT: 18in (45cm) • Hardy
FLOWERING SEASON: Late spring/autumn

This low-growing, bushy perennial is used for ground cover or as an edging plant for borders. The mounds of narrowly oval, gray-green leaves are arranged on short, square, gray stems, the tips terminating in tubular lavender-blue, salvia-like flowers which are held above the foliage. The cultivar *N.* 'Six Hills Giant', which is generally grown, is larger, with flower spikes up to 3ft (1m) high. It prefers a light soil and sunny position. Propagate by division in winter or by stem cutting in spring.

Oenothera missouriensis

Evening primrose
HEIGHT: 8in (20cm) • Hardy
FLOWERING SEASON: Mid/late summer

An excellent perennial for a hot, sunny spot. The spear-shaped, mid green leaves are carried on reddish-green, prostrate stems with upward-turning growing tips. The large, golden-yellow, bell-shaped flowers which open in the evening are produced continuously from June until August. It prefers a well-drained soil in sun or light shade. Cut the plant down to ground level in autumn. Propagation is by seed sown in spring or by division in late winter.

Osteospermum 'Buttermilk'

HEIGHT: 2ft (60cm) • Half hardy
FLOWERING SEASON: Summer/autumn

Evergreen semi-woody perennials which will require protection in cold areas, osteospermums flower continually from midsummer through to the autumn carrying their daisy-like flowers on single stems above narrow deep green foliage. The most popular cultivars are 'Buttermilk', 'Cannington Roy', pink with dark eyes, 'Silver Sparkler', 'Tresco Purple', deep purple-red, and 'Whirligig', bluish-white with flower heads that look like the spokes of a wheel with drops on the end. They prefer sun and well-drained soil. Propagate by cuttings of non-flowering shoots in midsummer.

Papaver orientale 'Mrs Perry'

Oriental poppy
HEIGHT: 3ft (1m) • Hardy
FLOWERING SEASON: Summer

The oriental poppy bears large cup-shaped flowers in a variety of brilliant colors in early summer and is one of the most striking border plants. The species plant has deep orange flowers and good cultivars are 'Black and White' and 'Mrs Perry'. Poppies like sun and deep rich soil although they will flower in semi-shade. They are unruly plants and need careful siting. Propagate by taking root cuttings in mild weather in winter although they will all self-seed freely.

Parrotia persica

Persian ironwood
HEIGHT: 15ft (4.5m) • Hardy
FLOWERING SEASON: Late winter/early spring

A small deciduous tree with a wide-spreading habit and attractive autumn leaf colors. The leaves, which are roughly oval with a rounded base, are mid green until turning crimson-red and gold in the autumn. Small crimson flowers appear before the leaves, and the bark of mature plants flakes off in patches to reveal interesting patterns in the winter. The flowers may be killed by late frosts. There is also a weeping cultivar, *P. p.* 'Pendula'. Propagation is by softwood cuttings taken in summer or by seed sown in autumn.

Penstemon 'Apple Blossom'

Beard tongue
HEIGHT: 18in (45cm) • Moderately hardy
FLOWERING SEASON: Midsummer

A large genus of annuals, perennials, sub-shrubs and shrubs, the most popular are the semi-evergreen perennials which carry sprays of flowers above narrow green foliage throughout the summer. Among the best known cultivars are 'Alice Hindley', 'Apple Blossom' and 'Andenken an Friedrich Hahn' syn. 'Garnet'. They must have a sunny position in rich well-drained soil and will not flourish in poor conditions. Propagate by taking semi-ripe cuttings in summer or division in spring.

Perovskia atriplicifolia

Azure sage/Russian sage
HEIGHT: 4ft (1.2m) • Hardy
FLOWERING SEASON: Late summer/mid autumn

This deciduous shrub has thin gray-white stems which carry the narrowly oval, coarsely toothed, gray-green, aromatic foliage. The violet-blue, salvia-like flowers are produced in long slender spikes at the tips of the shoots. The best-known hybrid is *P.* 'Blue Spire', which has larger blue flowers and deeply cut gray-green leaves. Average winter frosts will cut the plant down to the ground, but it grows up again from the base in spring. Propagation is by softwood cuttings taken in late spring.

Ruta graveolens 'Jackman's Blue'

Rue
HEIGHT: 4ft (1.2m) • Hardy
FLOWERING SEASON: Summer/autumn

This is a bushy sub-shrub with leaves which are blue-green, oval and deeply divided to give a fern-like appearance with small, mustard-yellow flowers on the tip of each shoot. *R. g.* 'Jackman's Blue' has a more compact habit and brighter, blue-gray foliage. *R. g.* 'Variegata' has creamy-white and green variegated leaves. Propagation is by semi-ripe cuttings taken in late summer. This plant has sap which is a skin irritant.

Salvia officinalis Purpurascens Group

Sage
HEIGHT: 4ft (1.2m) • Hardy perennial
FLOWERING SEASON: Late summer/autumn

The true sage has dull green leaves with a roughly textured surface, arranged in pairs on erect, square stems, which often have a reddish tinge to them. The tubular flowers open into a funnel shape, and are produced in clusters at the tips of the stems or from the leaf joints. The Purpurascens Group have purple leaves and *S. o.* 'Icterina' variegated yellow ones. Propagation is by semi-ripe cuttings taken in May or August.

Senecio 'Sunshine'

Daisy bush
HEIGHT: 3ft (1m) • Hardy
FLOWERING SEASON: Summer

The correct name for this shrub is now *Brachyglottis* Dunedin Hybrids Group 'Sunshine'. It forms a dense, broad-based mound and the leaves are silvery-gray at first, turning gray-green on the upper surface as they age. Sprays of silvery buds open to reveal yellow daisy-like flowers which are arranged in broad flat clusters. Prune after flowering to prevent the plant becoming straggly. Propagation is by semi-ripe cuttings taken with a heel in summer.

Sophora tetraptera

New Zealand laburnum
HEIGHT: 10ft (3m) • Not fully hardy
FLOWERING SEASON: Late spring

This large evergreen shrub or small tree will only grow well in a sheltered location. The foliage consists of rows of small, oblong, light green leaves which are held together by a tough, greenish-brown leafstalk. In spring a profusion of small, yellow, tubular flowers are produced in pendant clusters on the shoot tips, followed by winged fruits containing the seeds. The cultivar *S. microphylla* 'Early Gold' has pale yellow flowers and fern-like foliage. Propagation is by semi-ripe cuttings taken in early summer.

Spartium junceum

Spanish broom
HEIGHT: 10ft (3m) • Hardy
FLOWERING SEASON: Summer/early autumn

This deciduous flowering shrub has thin, tubular straggling branches which have a weeping appearance, the green stems make the plant seem evergreen. The small, inconspicuous leaves are short-lived, oval, mid green and covered in fine hairs. The large, pea-like flowers are bright golden-yellow and fragrant, they are carried at the tips of the new growth. It likes fairly poor soil and should be trimmed in early spring but does not respond well to hard pruning into old wood. Propagation is by seed sown in spring.

Stachys byzantina

Rabbit's ears/Lamb's tongue
HEIGHT: 16in (40cm) • Hardy
FLOWERING SEASON: Summer

This low growing, evergreen perennial is one of the most attractive and useful ground-cover plants for light soil and a hot sunny position. Its furry leaves which are covered in silvery hairs, give the plant a silver, gray or blue appearance, according to the light. The small, mauve flowers appear on white fluffy spikes up to about 16in (40cm) high. The cultivar *S. b.* 'Silver Carpet' is excellent ground cover. Propagation is by division in spring, although in summer it may be possible to find stems that have already rooted.

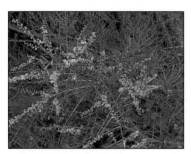

Tamarix ramosissima

Tamarisk
HEIGHT: 15ft (4.5m) • Hardy
FLOWERING SEASON: Late summer

An excellent plant for hot exposed sites, or coastal regions because it tolerates salt spray. The slender, gracefully arching, reddish-brown branches carry plumes of narrow, conifer-like foliage. The pink flowers are produced on long thin spikes during the summer. There are cultivars with darker flowers: the rose-pink, *T. r.* 'Rosea', the pale red *T. r.* 'Rubra'. Propagation is by semi-ripe cuttings taken with a heel in summer or hardwood cuttings in winter.

Yucca filamentosa

Adam's needle
HEIGHT: 2-3ft (60-90cm) • Moderately hardy
FLOWERING SEASON: Late summer

A striking evergreen shrub, generally grown as an architectural plant that thrives in poor, sandy conditions. The long, strap-like, bluish-green leaves are usually dried and brown at the tip, forming a sharp spine-like point and they are edged with white threads. The reddish-brown flower spikes are often 5-6ft (1.5-1.8m) high and covered with white, bell-shaped blooms. *Y. f.* 'Bright Edge' has a narrow golden margin to the leaf edges, and *Y. f.* 'Variegata' has creamy white ones. Propagate by division, removing and planting rooted suckers in spring.

Zauschneria californica

Californian fuchsia
HEIGHT: 18in (45cm) • Half-hardy
FLOWERING SEASON: Summer/autumn

This clump-forming perennial with a dense, bushy habit, produces an attractive display of bright scarlet, funnel-shaped flowers in clusters at the tips of slender green shoots from August onwards. The gray-green leaves are narrow, strap-like and end in a sharp point. The cultivar *Z. c.* ssp. *cana* 'Dublin' has deep, orange-scarlet flowers. Propagation is by division in the spring or semi-ripe cuttings in the summer. Prone to attack by aphids, which cause distorted growth.

More Plants for Dry Sun

There is a wide choice of plants that will thrive in hot dry conditions, particularly those plants which come from the Mediterranean. If you have a south-facing aspect and dry beds in your garden the main problem will be moisture loss during the hot summer months. It is a good idea to dig plenty of garden compost and leaf mold into the soil and it is also a help to mulch the bed in summer with wood bark or shavings. Both these measures help the soil to retain moisture and the mulch also suppresses the weeds.

TREES

Carpinus betulus
Juniperus communis
Populus alba

SHRUBS

Abelia × *grandiflora*
Berberis (in variety)
Buxus sempervirens
Carpentaria califorrnica
Caryopteris × *clandonensis*
Ceanothus (in variety)
Ceratostigma willmottiana
Cistus × *cyprius*

Coronilla valentina ssp. *glauca*
Cotoneaster horizontalis
Euonymus fortunei cvs
Fremontodendron 'California Glory'
Hebe pinguifolia 'Pagei'
Hippophae rhamnoides
Indigofera heterantha
Myrtus communis
Olearia × *haastii*
Philadelphus (in variety)
Phlomis fruticosa
Phygelius capensis (Cape figwort)
Potentilla fruticosa
Rhus typhina
Rosmarinus officinalis
Sambucus (in variety)
Santolina chamaecyparissus
Spirea (in variety)
Symphoricarpus × *doorenbosii*
Teucrium fruticans

PERENNIALS, GROUND COVER PLANTS & CLIMBERS

Acanthus spinosus
Achillea filipendulina
Anchusa azurea
Artemesia absinthium
Campsis radicans
Carex elata
Catananche centaurea
Centhranthus ruber
Centaurea cyanus (Cornflower)
Clematis tangutica

Crambe cordifolia
Crocosmia 'Lucifer'
Dianthus (in variety)
Eccremocarpus scaber
Euphorbia (in variety)
Geranium (in variety)
Gypsophila (in variety)
Ipomea hederacea
Iris germanica
Kniphofia 'Sunningdale Yellow'
Lamium maculatum
Lonicera japonica 'Halliana'
Lysimachia punctata
Nepeta 'Six Hills Giant'
Nerine (in variety)
Parthenocissus tricuspidata
Phlox paniculata
Phormium tenax
Osteospermum (in variety)
Romneya coulteri
Saponaria ocymoides
Sisyrinchium striatum
Stipa gigantea (Golden Oats)
Thymus herba-barona
Verbascum nigrum
Veronica prostrata
Viola (in variety)
Vitis coignetiae

CLIMBERS, WALL SHRUBS & HEDGES

To get the best from your garden, do not overlook the potential of walls, which can be used to provide a home for a wide range of colorful flowering climbers and wall shrubs, and plants with attractive foliage. Climbers and hedges with dense foliage also provide screening and a much-needed shelter in the garden.

ABOVE: Carpenteria californica, *with its attractive glossy green leaves and scented white flowers, is one of the best wall shrubs for a south- or west-facing wall.*

OPPOSITE: *This little walled garden has a rich array of perennials including lavender, rock roses, agapanthus, Canterbury bells and pansies in the borders with clematis and roses on the walls.*

ABOVE: *Clematis, both species and hybrids, are among the best climbing plants, and can be grown either over a trellis or scr*
ambling through other plants.

The plants used for hedges or as wall shrubs either define or decorate the boundaries of a garden and, if they are used within the garden in this way, they provide areas of privacy or shelter.

Choose the right plants for its purpose. If you want, for example, to create a boundary hedge, then you will almost certainly want plants that provide an impenetrable, permanent barrier. Some of the evergreen, spiny plants are ideal; tough berberis, for example, or Rugosa roses and beech, yew and hawthorn are excellent choices. Ideally, plants for hedges should be fairly easy to maintain, not being so fast growing that they need constant clipping, as well as resistant to pests, diseases and pollution. In another situation, you may be looking for quick cover of an unsightly fence or wall or an unattractive view, and then you will want a really rampant grower that will put on several feet in one season, and, for permanent cover, choose an evergreen.

In small gardens, it is good sense to include climbing plants and wall shrubs, since they will display their assets at a high level, effectively leaving the ground space for small perennials and annuals. You can get a lot of flower power from a relatively small number of flowering climbers trained up a wall. Plants such as clematis and climbing roses are invaluable for this, although bear in mind that their flowering season is relatively short, and that it pays to choose several with different flowering seasons, to prolong the period of attraction. A couple of handsome foliage plants, such as an ornamental vine (*Vitis coignetiae*), or an attractive ivy such as *Hedera canariensis*, will help lengthen the season. Always pay attention to the foliage attributes of any climber because a few have more than one virtue to their name, and are particularly valuable as a result. Take a good look first at the site and the kind of soil you have, since many climbers are fussy and require a particular soil or situation.

If you wish, you can use some of the evergreen hedging plants to create ornamental shapes, known as topiary. This simply involves clipping an evergreen, small-leaved shrub or perennial into a shaped structure – at its simplest, a ball, pyramid or cone. It provides a growing form of garden sculpture, and when combined in matched pairs, for example, at the entrance to an area of the garden, or on a doorstep in containers, it gives the garden the equivalent of a punctuation mark in a sentence. Box (*Buxus sempervirens*), yew (*Taxus baccata*) and privet (*Ligustrum*) are among the best subjects for topiary.

Hedges can also be used at a low level to section off parts of the garden; you can opt for informal, loose tapestry-type hedging of mixed plants, perhaps flowering ones such as Rugosa roses, or much more geometric, clipped forms, from small-leaved evergreens, again the box, yew or privet. If you opt for the latter, bear in mind that they must be kept in good condition by regular feeding and watering so they grow well, and clipped regularly to maintain a neat appearance.

BELOW: *A corner of a small walled garden uses climbing plants to good effect, mixing roses and clematis to provide both color and scent behind a classic wrought-iron bench.*

Bear in mind that when creating a hedge, the plants must be closely planted to form a solid, dense mass of foliage. Pinching out the growing tips of young plants will encourage bushiness, and although the hedge will take longer to reach the required height, it will form an appropriately impenetrable barrier. Normally, planting at about 12in (30cm) apart is the right spacing.

The plants listed in this section are a selection of large and small, evergreen and deciduous, flowering and foliage plants for a variety of situations: sun and shade, damp and dry, acid and alkaline soil. There are many, many others and the cross reference section at the end of the chapter lists other plants in the book which are suitable for these purposes.

Abutilon megapotamicum

HEIGHT: 10ft (3m) • Half-hardy
FLOWERING SEASON: Late spring/autumn

This is an attractive evergreen shrub, suitable for sheltered sites in mild climates, that should be trained on wires for support. It has dark green, oval leaves, heart-shaped at the base, and bell-shaped, drooping, yellow and red flowers. It does best in humus-enriched, well-drained soil with plenty of water during the growing season and likes full sun or partial shade. Prune the tips of young plants to promote a more bushy shape. Propagate by semi-ripe cuttings in summer. May be attacked by whitefly and red spider mite.

Acca sellowiana

Pineapple guava
HEIGHT: 10ft (3m) • Half-hardy
FLOWERING SEASON: Midsummer

The pineapple guava is not particularly common, but is a valuable evergreen shrub, with dark green leaves, white felted on the undersides. The dark red flowers have silvery edges and are followed (if male and female plants are grown) by reddish-green, edible fruits. Plant in full sun in light, well-drained soil. Propagate by softwood cuttings in summer.

Actinidia deliciosa

Chinese gooseberry/Kiwi fruit
HEIGHT: 30ft (9m) • Moderately hardy
FLOWERING SEASON: Summer

The kiwi fruit, or Chinese gooseberry, is grown in warmer climates for its fruits, but in colder climates it can be grown for its foliage and flowers. It has large, heart-shaped leaves which are attractive in their own right, and cup-shaped, white flowers, borne in clusters, followed by the fruit (if both male and female plants are grown). Plant in partial shade and moist soil but it may need protection in the winter. Propagate by semi-ripe cuttings in summer or by layering in autumn.

Akebia quinata

Chocolate vine
HEIGHT: 30ft (9m) • Half-hardy
FLOWERING SEASON: Late spring/early summer

Known as the chocolate vine, on account of its small, brownish, vanilla-scented flowers, this twining climber is a good subject for a sheltered east- or north-facing position in good, well-drained soil but it does prefer a sunnier position. Sausage-shaped fruits follow the flowers if both male and female plants are grown. It is semi-evergreen in mild winters or sheltered areas. Propagate by seed sown in autumn or spring, from semi-ripe cuttings taken after flowering or by layering in the autumn.

Bignonia capreolata

Cross vine/Trumpet flower
HEIGHT: 30ft (9m) • Half-hardy
FLOWERING SEASON: Summer

An evergreen tendril climber, each leaf has two oblong leaflets and a tendril. In the summer large reddish-orange trumpet-shaped flowers emerge in clusters held on the leaf axis. The fruits appear in the autumn and are rather like long pea-pods about 6in (15cm) long. It is best grown against a south wall in the milder parts of the country and it flourishes in any well-drained garden soil. Prune in early spring by cutting back weak shoots. Propagate by cuttings taken from new growth with three buds in spring.

Buxus sempervirens

Box
HEIGHT: 13ft (4m) • Hardy
FLOWERING SEASON: Inconspicuous

This is one of the most popular shrubs for low hedges, such as those in knot gardens and parterres, as it is very dense, with small evergreen leaves, and very slow growing. It can be clipped into formal shapes (topiary) which need trimming about twice a year. Does best in sun but tolerates semi-shade (but beware of the shade being on one side of the plant – it will become lopsided) and in most soils except waterlogged. It will adapt well to dry conditions. Propagate by semi-ripe cuttings in spring, summer or autumn.

Carpenteria californica

Californian mock orange
HEIGHT: 10ft (3m) • Half-hardy
FLOWERING SEASON: Summer

This evergreen shrub is one of the best wall shrubs for a south- or west-facing wall. It has attractive, glossy green leaves all year round and its pristine white, anemone-like flowers are deliciously scented. It prefers a sunny site and moist, well-drained soil enriched with compost or leaf mold. No pruning is usually needed, except for trimming any straggly shoots after flowering. Propagate by green-wood cuttings of the non-flowering shoots in summer or layering the lower branches.

Carpinus betulus

Hornbeam
HEIGHT: 80ft (25m) in wild • Hardy
FLOWERING SEASON: Late spring

The common hornbeam, which makes a huge spreading tree in the wild, can also be used to create good hedging. Produces catkins in late spring. Although deciduous, it will form a tightly twisted mass of branches, and it retains its leaves through the winter. For a hedge, plant 12in (30cm) apart and feed well while establishing. Trim or clip to shape it in early summer.

Ceanothus 'Autumnal Blue'

Californian lilac
HEIGHT: 8ft (2.5m) • Hardy
FLOWERING SEASON: Summer/autumn

This is a spreading, evergreen shrub with small, glossy, dark green leaves. Long panicles of little, powder blue flowers are carried for a long flowering season, from summer through to autumn. Will grow against a sheltered wall in colder climates, although it does best in a sunny site in good garden soil that is free from lime. Prune in March by thinning out the weak shoots. Propagate from cuttings taken from lateral shoots in midsummer. Can be prone to attacks by scale insects.

Ceanothus 'Gloire de Versailles'

Californian lilac
HEIGHT: 6ft (1.8m) • Hardy
FLOWERING SEASON: Summer/autumn

This deciduous ceanothus is smaller than *C.* 'Autumnal Blue' and makes a good specimen for formal plantings, if kept hard pruned in early spring. The flowers, which are borne in long panicles, are similarly soft blue but are also fragrant and the leaves are larger and a paler green than most of the other forms. It does best in a sunny site in good garden soil that is free from lime but it may require some protection in cold spells. Propagate from cuttings taken from lateral shoots in midsummer.

Chaenomeles speciosa

Flowering quince/Japonica
HEIGHT: 6ft (1.8m) • Hardy
FLOWERING SEASON: Late winter/early spring

A vigorous deciduous shrub with spiky thorns, it has dark green, glossy leaves and small clusters of bowl-shaped red flowers, followed by yellow quince fruits. There is a wide range of different cultivars, with flowers that range from white, through pink, to scarlet, some with double flowers. *C. s.* 'Moerloosei' has pale, pinkish-white flowers and *C. s.* 'Crimson and Gold' has deep red flowers with bright yellow stamens. Plant in sun against a wall or fence. Propagate by cuttings taken in summer.

Clematis 'Comtesse de Bouchaud'

Large late-flowering clematis
HEIGHT: 10ft (3m) • Moderately hardy
FLOWERING SEASON: Midsummer

Clematis are divided into three groups: the early flowering species, alpina, macropetala and montana types, all of which should be pruned after flowering; early large-flowering cultivars which should be pruned in early spring, and the late-flowering cultivars. *C.* 'Comtesse de Bouchaud' belongs to the third group. It carries large pinkish-purple flowers with yellow anthers in late summer. All clematis like their feet in the shade and prefer moist well-drained soil.

Clematis 'Etoile Violette'

Late-flowering clematis (viticella)
HEIGHT: 13ft (4m) • Hardy
FLOWERING SEASON: Late summer

Late-flowering clematis are divided into
three sub-groups: the large-flowering cultivars, the late-flowering species and
small-flowered cultivars, and the herbaceous
types. The species, *C. viticella* has purple-
mauve flowers. Its cultivars are among the
most delicate-looking of all clematis, with
small hanging, open, bell-shaped flowers,
that are also fragrant. 'Abundance' is rose-
pink, 'Alba Luxurians' is white, flushed with
mauve and 'Etoile Violette' is deep purple.

Clematis 'Jackmanii'

Large late-flowering clematis
HEIGHT: 10ft (3m) • Moderately hardy
FLOWERING SEASON: Midsummer

The epitome of the large late-flowering
types, C. 'Jackmanii' carries large violet-
purple flowers which fade slightly as they
age. They have light brown anthers and the
flowers appear from midsummer onwards.
Other good late-flowering cultivars are 'Star
of India', purple-blue, 'Hagley Hybrid',
rosy-mauve, 'Perle d'Azur' blue, amd 'John
Huxtable', white. All these should be pruned
hard in February to within 12in (30cm), or
three buds, of the ground.

Clematis montana var. rubens

Early-flowering clematis (montana)
HEIGHT: 40ft (12m) • Hardy
FLOWERING SEASON: Late spring

C. montana is one of the easiest clematis to
grow, being vigorous and unfussy as to
aspect. It is one of the few that does well on
a north-facing wall. It is deciduous, with trifoliate, dark green leaves and four-petalled
white flowers with prominent stamens.
There are various named forms, including
C. m. var. *rubens* which has bronze-colored
leaves and *C. m.* var. *wilsonii* which is later-
flowering and has large white flowers. Plant
in alkaline soil with the roots in shade.

Clematis 'Nelly Moser'

Early large-flowered clematis
HEIGHT: 12ft (4m) • Moderately hardy
FLOWERING SEASON: Early summer

One of the best-known of all clematis,
'Nelly Moser' has large single mauvy-pink
flowers in early summer. The flowers are
fully 6in (15cm) across and have a prominent
red stripe down the center of each petal.
They do not like too much sun and do better
in a reasonably shady position. Other well
known cultivars in the same group are
'Marie Boisselet', white, 'Mrs Cholmondley',
pale-blue, and 'The President', purple.
Propagate from softwood or semi-ripe
cuttings taken in summer.

Clematis tangutica

Late-flowering clematis
HEIGHT: 16ft (5m) • Hardy
FLOWERING SEASON: Late summer/autumn

This autumn flowering clematis, carries
small, yellow bell-shaped flowers. It is
deciduous, with a slender habit and is best
grown scrambling over a low wall or tree
stump. The leaves are grayish-green, and the
bright yellow flowers are followed by silvery
seed heads. Train the young shoots horizon-
tally so that the flowering shoots grow
vertically. In spring prune back to a pair of
buds near the base of the vertical shoots.
Aphids, mildew and clematis wilt may give
problems with all clematis plants.

Cobaea scandens

Cup-and-saucer vine
HEIGHT: 20ft (6m) • Half-hardy
FLOWERING SEASON: Summer/autumn

The cup and saucer plant, as this is commonly known, is a vigorous climber, treated as an
annual in colder climates. It produces large
flowers (the cup) set in a green calyx (the
saucer). The flowers open green and change
via pink to purple. It supports itself with
tendrils growing from the ends of leaf stalks.
There is a white-flowered form, *C. s. alba*.
Plant in a sunny site in well-drained soil.
Sow seeds in spring. May be attacked by a
variety of pests, including aphids and red
spider mite, but it is usually disease-free.

Euonymus japonicus 'Ovatus Aureus'

Japanese spindle/Spindle tree
HEIGHT: 12ft (4m) • Moderately hardy
FLOWERING SEASON: Summer

An excellent evergreen shrub grown mainly for its variegated foliage, often used for hedging in the milder parts of the country. It is popular in coastal districts as it tolerates poor soil conditions. It carries clusters of small greenish-white flowers in spring followed by small fruits. *E.j.* 'Latifolius Albomarginatus' has leaves edged with white. If grown as a hedge clip in midsummer and again in autumn.

Fagus sylvatica

Beech
HEIGHT: 20ft (6m) (As a hedge) • Hardy
FLOWERING SEASON: Insignificant

Beech trees are among the most graceful of the hardy deciduous native trees, growing to a height of 100ft (30m) or more. They make one of the best hedges, retaining the old leaves throughout the winter, and as such should be planted about 2ft (60cm) apart in soil that has been well dug and enriched by manure and compost. They will grow in any soil but do not like waterlogged conditions. A beech hedge can be almost any height and width but 6-12ft (1.8-4m) high and 2ft (60cm) wide is usually enough. Clip in midsummer and again in early autumn.

Fagus sylvatica Atropurpurea Group

Copper beech
HEIGHT: 38ft (12m) • Hardy
FLOWERING SEASON: Insignificant

A purple-leaved form of the beech, this beautiful tree can be used effectively for hedging and some gardeners plant mixed groups of copper and ordinary beech to give the hedge added variety. There is no difference in cultivation. Remove the upper shoots after planting to encourage branching and mulch the hedge in the spring to encourage growth. Prone to scale insects and aphids and sometimes to coral spot.

Fallopia baldschuanica

Russian vine
HEIGHT: 33ft (10m) • Hardy
FLOWERING SEASON: Summer/autumn

Formerly known as *Polygonum baldschuanicum* this is a singularly rampant, tough climber, generally called the Russian vine. It is not easy to eradicate once planted, and will grow very fast, up to 15ft (4.5m) a year, so beware of planting it in restricted situations. It is ideal for covering an unsightly wall or fence but it is deciduous so dies down in winter. The leaves are mid green, pointed ovals. The flowers, borne in long fluffy panicles, are creamy white. Plant in sun or partial shade in any soil.

Fremontodendron 'California Glory'

Flannel flower
HEIGHT: 20ft (6m) • Half-hardy
FLOWERING SEASON: Spring/autumn

This is a tall, fairly upright, vigorous evergreen or semi-evergreen shrub. Its chief glory is the profusion of large, brilliant yellow flowers borne from late spring to early autumn. The leaves are dark green, rounded and lobed. It makes an excellent wall shrub on a south- or west-facing wall in full sun in well-drained soil, to which humus has been added. Propagate by semi-ripe cuttings in summer. Generally trouble-free, but dislikes being moved.

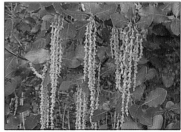

Garrya elliptica

Silk-tassel bush
HEIGHT: 8ft (2.5m) • Hardy
FLOWERING SEASON: Late spring

An ideal wall shrub, *G. elliptica* has thick, oval evergreen leaves with a slightly crinkled margin, dark green, with a glossy upper surface, and a slightly blue sheen on the underside. In spring long strands of small bell-like flowers on the male plants form attractive catkins. Tolerates poor soil but likes a sunny position and may require protection in prolonged cold spells. The cultivar *G. e.* 'James Roof', has the longest, most colourful catkins. Propagate by semi-ripe cuttings taken in midsummer.

Griselinia littoralis 'Variegata'

HEIGHT: 25ft (8m) • Half-hardy
FLOWERING SEASON: Inconspicuous

This evergreen shrub, a native of New Zealand, makes an excellent hedging plant, especially for the milder coastal areas of the country as it is both wind and salt resistant. It has leathery, glossy, white-variegated leaves. The species plant, *G. littoralis,* is the hardier and has yellow-green leaves. Plant in sun or shade in any well-drained garden soil but protect young plants from frost. Remove tips to encourage bushiness and trim hedges with secateurs to avoid damaging the leaves. Propagate from heel cuttings in autumn.

Hedera colchica 'Sulphur Heart'

Ivy/Paddy's pride
HEIGHT: Unlimited • Hardy
FLOWERING SEASON: Inconspicuous

This particular ivy, also known as 'Paddy's Pride', has unusually large leaves with strongly marked yellow and green coloring and a slightly drooping habit. It is a self-clinging climber and will succeed in partial shade and dry soil, but the variegated cultivars of ivy are less shade-tolerant than the green cultivars. It can be propagated from rooted layers or softwood cuttings.

Hedera helix 'Königer's Auslese'

Common English ivy
HEIGHT: 4ft (1.2m) • Hardy
FLOWERING SEASON: Inconspicuous

This is a particularly pretty ivy with the usual three-lobed leaf formation, but with finger-like, deeply cut leaves. Another cultivar of *H. helix*, 'Pedata', known as the bird's foot ivy, is similar with narrow leaves of which the central lobe forms a long finger. It is more vigorous, growing to 10ft (3m) or more. Ivies will grow in poor soil, in shade. Propagate from softwood cuttings or rooted layers. Generally pest- and disease-free but may be attacked by red spider mite.

Hippophae rhamnoides

Sea buckthorn
HEIGHT: 8ft (2.5m) • Hardy
FLOWERING SEASON: Inconspicuous

The sea buckthorn is an excellent subject for hedges in coastal areas as it will withstand seaspray and makes a good windbreak. It is deciduous with thin, silvery leaves and sharp spines on the branches. Very small yellow flowers appear before the leaves in April and if both male and female plants are planted, small orange berries will ripen along the branches in the autumn and hang all through the winter to the spring. Grow in any good garden soil in sunny or part-shaded situations. Trim hedges in late summer.

Ipomoea hederacea

Morning glory
HEIGHT: 13ft (4m) • Tender
FLOWERING SEASON: Summer

Morning glory, as this tender twining climber is known, has three-lobed, mid green leaves and showy, funnel-shaped flowers in shades from white through pink and blue to purple, from summer through to early autumn. It needs a sunny site and well-drained soil to which plenty of leaf mold has been added. Grow it up a trellis or let it scramble through a shrub. Propagate from seed sown in spring or from semi-ripe cuttings in summer. Red spider mite and whitefly can be a problem.

Jasminum officinale

Common jasmine
HEIGHT: 40ft (12m) • Hardy
FLOWERING SEASON: Summer/autumn

The common jasmine is one of the most attractive climbing plants. It has prettily divided leaves and clusters of highly fragrant, small, white flowers, with pink buds, over a long season. It is semi-evergreen and supports itself by twining. The cultivar known as 'Aureum' has yellow-splashed leaves and *J. o.* f. *affine* has larger flowers. It needs full sun and a rich, well-drained soil. It is very vigorous and must be pruned after flowering. Propagate from semi-ripe cuttings in summer. May be attacked by aphids.

Lapageria rosea

Chilean bellflower
HEIGHT: 15ft (4.5m) • Half-hardy
FLOWERING SEASON: Summer/autumn

The Chilean bellflower is a climber that will twine itself around a support. Its dark green, slightly pointed, oval leaves are evergreen, and throughout the summer hanging bells of rosy red flowers, about 3in (7.5cm) long, are carried either singly or in small clusters. There is also a white-flowered variety, *L. r.* var. *albiflora*. It likes a slightly acid soil and a warm sheltered wall. Protect the roots in winter in colder climates. Propagate by layering in spring or autumn.

Lathyrus latifolius

Everlasting pea/Perennial pea
HEIGHT: 6ft (1.8m) • Hardy
FLOWERING SEASON: Summer/autumn

This everlasting pea is another perennial sweet pea, which grows vigorously and can be trained over a support like a climber. It has rather dull green leaves but a profusion of flowers in shades of red or pink. There is also a white-flowered cultivar 'White Pearl'. Grow in good garden soil, preferably slightly limy, but put in lots of manure as the plants are very greedy. Pinch out tips of young plants to promote bushiness. Deadhead to encourage a longer flowering season and cut down the plants in late autumn. Sow from chipped seed in spring.

Ligustrum ovalifolium

Privet
HEIGHT: 12ft (4m) • Hardy
FLOWERING SEASON: Midsummer

This privet comes from Japan, and has evergreen, glossy, oval leaves and is very good for hedging or clipping into topiary shapes. The white flowers are attractive to bees. Black berries follow the flowers in autumn. There is a golden-leaved cultivar, 'Aureum', known as the golden privet. Grow in sun or shade in any soil. For hedging, prune hard in the first year to encourage bushy growth. Propagate from hardwood cuttings in autumn. Can be attacked by honey fungus.

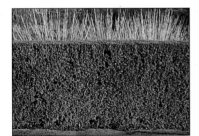

Lonicera nitida

Honeysuckle
HEIGHT: 5ft (1.5m) • Hardy
FLOWERING SEASON: Inconspicuous

This dense evergreen shrub is a native of China. It makes excellent hedging, or can be used for topiary, and is a good subject for shade. The leaves are small, glossy and dark green. There is also a golden-leaved cultivar, 'Baggesen's Gold', which must be planted in sun. For a hedge, plant in rich soil about 12in (30cm) apart. Cut new hedges hard back in the first year and pinch out growing tips to establish bushy plants. Clip in late spring and early autumn to maintain. Prone to aphid attacks and to leaf spot.

Lonicera periclymenum 'Belgica'

Early Dutch honeysuckle
HEIGHT: 12ft (4m) • Hardy
FLOWERING SEASON: Summer

L. p. 'Belgica' is a cultivar of the common honeysuckle or woodbine, *L. periclymenum*, whose orangy yellow–white flowers are a common sight in hedges in summer. It has reddish-yellow fragrant flowers and is one of the best garden forms. Other good cultivars are 'Graham Thomas', whitish-yellow and 'Serotina', deeper red. All honeysuckles like moist well-drained soil and full sun to moderate shade. Cut back hard in the spring to prevent them becoming straggly.

Lonicera × tellmanniana

Honeysuckle
HEIGHT: 15ft (4.5m) • Moderately hardy
FLOWERING SEASON: Summer

A favourite deciduous woody-stemmed climber which bears a profusion of fragrant orange-yellow flowers from late spring through the summer. As all honeysuckles tend to be unkempt it is a good idea to grow them as climbers over an old tree or a large fence as they do not appear at their best if they are confined to a trellis or a wall. They do not like very wet or very dry conditions. Propagate by taking semi-ripe suttings in summer but some varieties are difficult to strike. Layering is often successful.

Malus domestica

Apple
HEIGHT: 10ft (3m) • Hardy
FLOWERING SEASON: Spring

Apples make good wall shrubs if trained as
espaliers or cordons. 'Egremont Russet' is a
good garden variety which keeps reasonably
well, is hardy, and has compact growth.
Espalier apples should be planted about 10ft
(3m) apart; cordons about 6ft (1.8m) apart,
against a supporting network of posts and
wires, and the young plants are then pruned
to develop fruiting branches along the wires.
They need enriched garden soil and plenty
of watering while setting fruit.

Olearia × haastii

Daisy bush
HEIGHT: 5ft (1.5m) • Hardy
FLOWERING SEASON: Summer

An evergreen dense shrub with thick leathery leaves, dark green above and silvery
beneath. The branches and undersides of the
leaves are covered with a thick grayish down.
It has numerous clusters of fragrant star-like
daisy flowers in late summer. It makes a good
hedge in milder parts of the country and by
the seaside. It should be trimmed as soon as
the flowers fade. Dislikes soil which contains
a lot of lime. Propagate by semi-ripe cuttings
taken in late summer.

Parthenocissus henryana

HEIGHT: 30ft (9m) • Hardy
FLOWERING SEASON: Spring/summer

An attractive self-clinging climber closely
related to *P. quinquefolia*, the Virginia creeper. It has five-parted leaves which are a deep
velvety-green marked with white and pink
along the midrib and veins. The leaves turn a
brilliant red in the autumn and the color is
best if it is grown on a north- or east-facing
wall. Likes well-drained soil. Do not let the
tendrils of the climber get into gutters or
under slates or tiles on the roof. It has bluish-
black berries in the autumn. Propagate by
softwood cuttings in summer.

Parthenocissus tricuspidata

Boston ivy/Japanese ivy
HEIGHT: 40ft (12m) • Hardy
FLOWERING SEASON: Summer

The Boston ivy is a hardy deciduous climber
that clings by means of aerial roots, so needs
no tying in. It is grown primarily for its
brilliantly colored autumn foliage, the three-
lobed leaves of which turn a rich, bronze-red
in autumn. Small, yellowish flowers are
borne in summer, followed by dark blue
fruits in some years. Grow in any good garden soil in sun or partial shade. Propagate by
layering or by half-ripe
cuttings taken in late summer. Prone to
scale insects and to aphids.

Passiflora caerulea

Common passion flower
HEIGHT: 20ft (6m) • Not fully hardy
FLOWERING SEASON: Mid/late summer

The passion flower is really a climbing
perennial, but although frequently dying
down in winter, it will emerge as vigorous
as ever the following spring. The large,
beautiful flowers are fragrant, and have big
pinky-white sepals and petals, with spiky
blue filaments tinged white and purple in the
center of the bloom. The palm shaped-leaves
are mid green and carried on square, green
stems which are supported by thin green
tendrils. Propagation is by semi-ripe cuttings
taken in summer or by seed.

Passiflora caerulea 'Constance Elliott'

White passion flower
HEIGHT: 25ft (8m) • Half hardy
FLOWERING SEASON: Early summer/autumn

The best known white passion flower *P. c.*
'Constance Elliott' is a tough, vigorous
evergreen climber, with palmate, mid green
leaves. It produces quite extraordinary flowers with a surrounding saucer of petals and
prominent corolla and stamens in clear
white. Oval yellow fruits are sometimes
borne after the flowers. Will grow in sun or
partial shade. Protect young plants in winter.
Thin out overgrown plants in early spring.
Propagate from stem sections in late summer.

Pyracantha 'Mohave'

Firethorn
HEIGHT: 8ft (2.5m) • Hardy
FLOWERING SEASON: Midsummer

Pyracantha 'Watereri'

Firethorn
HEIGHT: 10ft (3m) • Hardy
FLOWERING SEASON: Early summer

Prunus laurocerasus 'Otto Luyken'

Cherry laurel/Laurel
HEIGHT: 6ft (1.8m) • Hardy
FLOWERING SEASON: Summer

This ornamental cherry laurel makes a good specimen for a low hedge. It has the usual glossy, evergreen, dark green leaves that are oval and slender and borne slightly upright. Long spires of white flowers are borne in summer, followed by small black fruits. Grows in shade or sun. *P. l.* 'Zabeliana' is almost prostrate, making good ground cover. Plant in autumn in alkaline soil. Propagate from half-ripe cuttings in summer.

This hybrid firethorn, as it is known, is a tough, evergreen shrub that is grown either as a wall shrub or as hedging. It has spiny branches, small, glossy, dark green leaves, and clusters of small white five-petalled flowers in summer followed by bright orange-red berries in autumn. Grow in any well-drained garden soil in sun or partial shade, against wires, to which it should be tied. For hedging, pinch out young plants to encourage bushiness and clip in summer. Take cuttings of new shoots in summer to propagate. Can be troubled by scale insects.

This particular hybrid firethorn makes a tallish evergreen shrub, with arching, spiny branches and dense, glossy, bright green leaves. The flowers are white, cup-shaped, and borne in fattish clusters, followed by big clusters of bright red berries in autumn. For hedging, pinch out young plants to encourage bushiness and clip once a year in summer. Take cuttings of current year's shoots in summer to propagate. Can be troubled by scale insects.

Pyrus 'Conference'

Conference pear
HEIGHT: 24ft (7.5m) • Hardy
FLOWERING SEASON: Spring

Pear trees are slightly easier to grow than apple trees, provided the situation is fairly warm and sheltered. They grow best in full sun, in fertile loam with adequate moisture. They can be trained against a wall either as cordons or espaliers. Pears must be planted with or near a cross-pollinator to produce fruit. Two which do this are 'Conference' and 'Williams' Bon Chrétien'. Plant in autumn, about 6ft (1.8m) apart for cordons, and 8ft (2.5m) for espaliers and tie in to supports. Prone to the usual pests and diseases.

Schizophragma hydrangeoides

Japanese hydrangea vine
HEIGHT: 25ft (8m) • Hardy
FLOWERING SEASON: Summer

This deciduous climber is very similar to *Hydrangea anomala* ssp. *petiolaris* and will attach itself to a support by means of aerial roots. It has broad, hairy leaves almost 5in (12cm) long that are deep green above and silvery beneath. The large, flat flowerheads are small, creamy flowers surrounded by pale lemon-colored bracts in summer. Does best in semi-shade in a soil with plenty of leaf mold. Deadhead after flowering. Propagate by half-ripe cuttings in late summer or layering in autumn.

Solanum crispum 'Glasnevin'

Chilean potato tree
HEIGHT: 19ft (6m) • Almost hardy
FLOWERING SEASON: Summer/autumn

Known as the Chilean potato tree (the edible potato belongs to the same genus), this semi-evergreen, almost hardy scrambler has dark green, oval, pointed leaves and produces trusses of star-shaped, violet-blue flowers with bright yellow centers throughout the summer. 'Glasnevin' has a longer flowering season than the species. Grow in any good garden soil against a south- or west-facing wall, and tie in to trellis or wires. Propagate from cuttings of side shoots in late summer. Can be prone to attacks by aphids or mold.

Solanum jasminoides 'Album'

Jasmine nightshade/Potato vine
HEIGHT: 10ft (3m) • Half-hardy
FLOWERING SEASON: Summer/autumn

Known as the jasmine nightshade, the species of this almost hardy climber has clear blue star-shaped flowers with golden anthers, but this variety is a white-flowered form that has a yellow eye. The leaves are evergreen, and a glossy pale green. Unlike *S. crispum* this plant is usually self-clinging, but it may need support occasionally. Propagate from cuttings of side shoots taken in late summer. Can be prone to attacks by aphids and to various molds.

Taxus baccata

Common yew
HEIGHT: 16ft (5m) • Hardy
FLOWERING SEASON: Inconspicuous

This yew is one of the best, if slow growing, hedging and topiary plants, its dark green, needle-like leaves forming a dense, impenetrable thicket. It copes well with wind, pollution and drought, and makes a good boundary hedge. The flowers are barely visible, and are followed by small, cup-shaped, red fruits. All parts of the plant are highly poisonous. It grows in any good well-drained garden soil in sun or deep shade. Plant hedging plants about 2ft (60cm) apart and mulch each spring. Pinch out leading shoots to encourage bushiness.

Thuja plicata 'Atrovirens'

Arbor-vitae/Red cedar
HEIGHT: 20ft (6m) • Hardy
FLOWERING SEASON: Inconspicuous

A cultivar of the giant red cedar, *T.p.* 'Atrovirens' makes a quick growing, dark green hedge which will grow well in any soil and tolerates full shade when established. The leaves give off a tansy-like aroma when crushed. If grown as a hedge, thujas should not be clipped hard in the same way as a yew hedge. They should be looked over carefully and long branches shortened with secateurs. Other useful cultivars are *T. p.* 'Aurea' and *T. p.* 'Stoneham Gold'.

Thunbergia alata

Black-eyed Susan
HEIGHT: 10ft (3m) • Half-hardy
FLOWERING SEASON: Summer/autumn

Known as black-eyed Susan, this is one of the few orange-yellow flowered climbers. The flowers have flat heads and a long purplish tube, with a dark brown eye, hence the common name. It flowers from early summer until the autumn. In sheltered areas it can be grown out of doors, but in colder regions it must be overwintered indoors, so grow it in a container with its own support system in normal potting soil mix or against a sunny wall in a sheltered spot. It will twine around a trellis. Sow seed in spring.

Trachelospermum jasminoides

Confederate jasmine/Chinese jasmine
HEIGHT: 10ft (3m) • Hardy • pH
FLOWERING SEASON: Summer

This is a handsome evergreen, self-clinging, twining climber, with dark green, oval, leathery leaves and very fragrant white, five-petalled, starry flowers with a yellow eye, profusely borne in summer, followed by seed pods up to 6in (15cm) long. The cultivar *T. j.* 'Variegatum', has cream-splashed leaves. Plant it against a south or west wall in acid soil. Deadhead after flowering. Propagate from cuttings taken from side shoots, or by layering in autumn. Generally disease-free, but may be subject to attacks by aphids.

Tropaeolum speciosum

Flame creeper/Scottish flame flower
HEIGHT: 10ft (3m) • Hardy
FLOWERING SEASON: Summer/autumn

This perennial nasturtium is a twining climber with apple-green, lobed, waxy leaves and bright scarlet flowers, held erect on long, reddish stems. It flowers from late summer onwards and the flowers are followed by dull red seed capsules exposing lovely turquoise blue seeds as large as peas. It should be planted in peaty soil in at least partial shade preferably on the north side of a yew hedge. Once established it will scramble over trees and shrubs although in some gardens it can prove difficult.

Vitis coignetiae

Crimson glory vine
HEIGHT: 70ft (21m) • Hardy
FLOWERING SEASON: Spring

This Japanese crimson glory vine is one of the best foliage climbers, clinging by means of tendrils. It is deciduous and in autumn the large, heart-shaped leaves turn a glorious mixture of orange, crimson and gold. The greenish flowers are borne in spring in panicles, followed by inedible black 'grapes'. Grow in sun or partial shade in limy, moist soil. Prune back hard after planting and tie in young shoots. Propagate by layering in autumn. Prone to attacks by scale insects.

Vitis vinifera 'Purpurea'

Grape vine
HEIGHT: 20ft (6m) • Hardy
FLOWERING SEASON: Summer

This ornamental form of the grape vine is known as the Teinturier grape. It is grown for its handsome, dark foliage which turns purple in autumn. The leaves are large, serrated and lobed. Tiny green flowers are borne in summer in short panicles, followed by blue-black fruits. Grow in moist loamy soil in sun or partial shade. Grow in sun or partial shade in limy, moist soil. Prune back hard after planting and tie in young shoots. Propagate by layering in autumn.

Wisteria floribunda

Japanese wisteria
HEIGHT: 22ft (7m) • Hardy
FLOWERING SEASON: Early summer

This vigorous climber, which will twine around a support, has attractive, light green leaves, composed of many small leaflets, and scented, blue-mauve flowers, in long, drooping racemes. There is a white cultivar, 'Alba', and one with very long, lilac-blue flowers, 'Macrobotrys'. Plant in sun in rich, moist soil, ideally against a south- or west-facing wall. Tie it in to supports until established. Propagate from heel cuttings of current growth in late summer.

More Climbers, Wall Shrubs and Hedging Plants

We have divided the additional plants for this section into the three groups and sub-divided the climbers and wall shrubs into those which are suitable for north- and east-facing walls and those which should be grown on south- or west-facing walls. A letter after the plant means that where there is a choice it should only be grown on that wall.

CLIMBERS FOR NORTH- AND EAST-FACING WALLS

Aristolochia durior (N)
Berberidopsis corallina
Celastrus scandens
Clematis armandii
  C. texensis
Hedera helix 'Buttercup'
Holboella coriacea (N or W)
Hydrangea petiolaris
Kerria japonica
Rosa 'Gloire de Dijon'
  R. Golden Showers
  R. 'Guinée'
  R. 'Madame Alfred Carrière'
  R. 'Madame Grégoire Staechelin'
  R. 'Maigold'

  R. 'New Dawn'
  R. 'Zéphirine Drouhin'
Schizophragma integrifolium (N or W)
(see also *Climbers for North Walls* on page 81)

SHRUBS FOR NORTH- AND EAST-FACING WALLS

Cotoneaster horizontalis
Escallonia (in variety)(N)
Elaeagnus × ebbingei 'Gilt Edge'
Euonymus fortunei cvs
Forsythia suspensa
Pyracantha (in variety)

CLIMBERS FOR SOUTH- AND WEST-FACING WALLS

Abeliophyllum distichum
Actinidia kolomikta
Ampelopsis glandulosa
Campsis radicans
  C. × tagliabuana 'Mme Galen'
Clematis (in variety)
Cytisus battandieri
Dregea sinensis
Eccremocarpus scaber
Hedera canariensis 'Gloire de Marengo'
  H. colchica 'Dentata'
Humulus lupulus 'Aureus'
Hydrangea petiolaris
Lathyrus odoratus
Lonicera (in variety)
Rosa 'Albéric Barbier'
  R. *banksiae* 'Lutea'
  R. 'Mermaid'

  R. 'Paul's Himalayan Musk'
Wisteria sinensis

SHRUBS FOR SOUTH- AND WEST-FACING WALLS

Berberis darwinii
Ceanothus (in variety)
Chaenomeles japonica
Chimonanthus praecox
Magnolia grandiflora
Osmanthus × burkwoodii
Prunus incisa
Tamarix ramosissima

HEDGES

Berberis (in variety)
Chamaecyparis lawsoniana
Crataegus (in variety)
Cupressocyparis × leylandii
Escallonia (in variety)
Ilex aquifolium
Juniperus communis
Lavandula (in variety)
Laurus nobilis
Osmanthus × burkwoodii
Pittosporum tenuifolium
Potentilla fruticosa
Pseudotsuga menziesii
Pyracantha (in variety)
Rosa 'Roseraie de l'Haÿ'
  R. *rugosa*
Rosmarinus officinalis
Symphoricarpus (in variety)
Syringa (in variety)
Thuja occidentalis 'Sunkist'

PLANTS *for* GROUND COVER

In large gardens, or where gardening time is at a premium, ground-cover plants are a valuable asset because they suppress weeds while creating an attractive carpet of color and texture. This selection includes spreading plants and those that self-seed to make large drifts.

ABOVE: Myosotis alpestris, *the Alpine forget-me-not, makes a spreading mound covered with light blue flowers.*

OPPOSITE: *The silver-splashed leaves of lungwort (Pulmonaria longifolia) with its purple-blue flowers held erect on stems are one of the loveliest sights in a spring garden.*

For many gardeners, particularly those with large gardens or who are too busy to spend a great deal of time looking after their plants, ground-covering plants are essential. They come in various forms – those that spread to create large areas of weed-suppressing cover and those, by virtue of their habit of growth, create enough shade to make it difficult for weeds to grow under their canopy.

Removal of light is one of the most effective means of controlling weeds, and if you do not want to do it with plants,

ABOVE: *Ground cover plants can be allowed to encroach onto a gravel path to soften the edges and provide an informality that would otherwise be lacking. There is a wide choice available: alchemilla, geraniums, forget-me-nots, pansies and stachys (lamb's ears) can all be used to break up the edge of a path or lawn.*

you can, of course, use black plastic covered with bark chippings instead – a system now often used by gardeners for public parks. This is often a useful means of covering the ground while waiting for your ground cover plants to do their job and is also useful while establishing larger plants or a shrub border, for example.

As with all plants, the natural habitat determines how successfully they will perform in any given situation. If your garden has a shady area that gets very little moisture, then you will have to pick ground-cover plants that thrive naturally in these conditions – ivy is an obvious choice. If, on the other hand, your garden is open and sunny, then the ground cover you seek must be able to withstand heat and drought. This is a bit more difficult, since ground-covering plants in nature tend to be woodland carpeting plants, that romp away under the shade of a taller canopy of leaves, so for dry sunny sites, you are better picking perennials with a mound-forming habits, such as geraniums, which fan out to cover quite a large area of ground. If you pick plants that can be propagated easily, you can soon build up a sizable collection of plants for these situations without spending a fortune.

Plants that spread by runners or layering will quickly create large drifts of ground cover, but be aware that they will not necessarily confine themselves to the areas you have chosen, so that some measure of control will be necessary to prevent invasive behavior. This may mean simply uprooting any additional growth in autumn. Plants that spread by root runners, however, can be more difficult to control – mint is one example – and these are sometimes best situated in a controlled space. You could use slates sunk into the soil to stop any such unwanted spread.

Try to pick ground-cover plants that look appropriate for the situation and, for interest, avoid very large expanses of the same plant, unless covering a bank, or creating ground cover in a small woodland area. To provide variation in color and texture, use several different mound-forming plants that will gradually spread and knit together to make an interesting tapestry of foliage.

Although evergreen plants will cover the ground throughout the year, most weed growth is in the growing season, so even deciduous plants can make effective ground cover.

BELOW: *A dense cottage-style planting of herbaceous perennials many of which will self-seed. Prominent in these borders is the purple knapweed (centaurea) with its thistle-like head.*

Acaena microphylla

New Zealand burr
HEIGHT: 2in (5cm) • Hardy
FLOWERING SEASON: Inconspicuous

This herbaceous carpeting perennial, which comes from New Zealand, makes good ground cover for growing between paving stones in patios or terraces and in rockeries. It forms dense mats of gray-green leaves, and russet-colored 'burrs' from early to late summer. It does well in sun or partial shade and likes well-drained soil. It will spread rapidly in the right conditions. Propagate by sowing seed in spring, or by dividing the plants in the autumn.

Adiantum venustum

Maidenhair fern
HEIGHT: 6in (15cm) • Hardy
FLOWERING SEASON: None

This little fern, which hails from the Himalayas, has delicately formed fronds which change color over the year. Pink when they first appear in spring, they change to pale green, becoming a russet brown after the first frosts. Does well in soil rich in leaf mold in partial shade. Propagate in autumn from rhizomes cut into pieces with a growing point on each piece. Prone to attacks by wood lice and root mealy bugs, but generally disease-free.

Aegopodium podagraria 'Variegatum'

Variegated bishop's weed/Variegated gout weed
HEIGHT: 4in (10cm) • Hardy
FLOWERING SEASON: Summer (inconspicuous)

This vigorous, creeping perennial, which is known as variegated bishop's weed, or variegated gout weed, is a fast-growing plant that is useful for ground cover. It has creamy-white splashed green leaves that are lobed and inconspicuous flowers in summer. It does well in either a sunny or a shady site with well-drained soil. Its spread may need restricting occasionally. Propagate by division of the rhizomes in spring or in autumn.

Anaphalis triplinervis

Pearl everlasting/Immortelle
HEIGHT: 12in (30cm) • Hardy
FLOWERING SEASON: Late summer

A. triplinervis makes an attractive mound of silvery-green divided foliage, topped with tightly packed heads of white flowers in late summer. They are known as pearl everlasting flowers or immortelle, and are popular with flower arrangers as the heads can be both dried and dyed. They are used for winter decoration. Plant in the autumn in well-drained soil in sun or dry shade. Cut the plants back in autumn if they start to sprawl too much. Propagate from cuttings of basal shoots in spring or sow seed in spring.

Aurinia saxatile var. citrina

Gold dust/Gold tuft
HEIGHT: 12in (30cm) • Hardy
FLOWERING SEASON: Late spring/early summer

This clump-forming shrubby perennial which was formerly known as *Alyssum saxatile* provides excellent cover on terraces and rockeries. Densely packed heads of yellow flowers create a golden carpet of color from late spring to summer. There are many different varieties with flowers varying in color from lemon to gold. Grow in a sunny site in well-drained soil. Propagate from cuttings in summer or from seed in spring. Prone to attacks by slugs and to downy mildew.

Bergenia cordifolia

Elephant's ears
HEIGHT: 12in (30cm) • Hardy
FLOWERING SEASON: Spring

Bergenia, sometimes known as elephant's ears, makes extremely good ground cover, its huge, leathery, evergreen leaves effectively suppressing any weeds beneath their canopy. *B. cordifolia* has pinkish-purple flower spires in spring, and *B. c.* 'Purpurea' has leaves that are purple-tinged. *B.* 'Silberlicht' has white flowers, and the leaves turn an attractive bronzy-red in autumn. The leaf color is often best in poorer soils. It is soil tolerant, and grows in sun or partial shade. Propagate by division in autumn. Prone to leaf spot.

Campanula carpatica

Carpathian bellflower
HEIGHT: 9in (23cm) • Hardy
FLOWERING SEASON: Summer

This little bellflower comes from the Carpathian mountains of eastern Europe. It makes clumps of toothed green leaves, surmounted with a sea of large, bright blue, cup-shaped flowers in summer. It self-seeds freely. There are a number of named cultivars in shades from deep indigo to white. *C. carpatica* will thrive in sun or partial shade, and does particularly well in crevices in pavings. Sow seed in spring or divide crowns in autumn. Prone to attacks by slugs and also leaf spot and rust.

Cotoneaster horizontalis

Wall-spray
HEIGHT: 2ft (60cm) • Hardy
FLOWERING SEASON: Summer

This widely spreading deciduous shrub has long slender branches which grow laterally from the main stem. The small, glossy, dark green leaves turn scarlet in autumn, and the small pinkish flowers in early summer are followed by clusters of bright red berries in autumn. It makes good ground cover for banks but it can also be trained as a wall shrub. Likes a sunny site and well-drained soil.

Epilobium glabellum

Willow herb
HEIGHT: 9in (23cm) • Hardy
FLOWERING SEASON: Summer/autumn

This little perennial, which is a form of willow herb, forms attractive low mounds of small, mid green, oval leaves and produces cup-shaped, white flowers on taller stems throughout the summer. It does best when grown in a sunny position or in partial shade in moist well-drained soil. *E. fleischeri* is taller – about 12in (30cm) – with narrow grayish leaves and rosy-pink flowers. Propagate from seed sown in spring, or from cuttings taken from basal shoots in spring.

Epimedium × youngianum 'Niveum'

Barrenwort/Bishop's hat
HEIGHT: 8in (20cm) • Hardy
FLOWERING SEASON: Spring

This little woodland plant, with the common name of barrenwort or bishop's hat, makes excellent ground cover in the partial shade provided by deciduous trees. The leaves turn an attractive bronze-red in autumn. The flowers of the species, appearing in spring, are pink, but 'Niveum' is a white cultivar. *E.* × *warleyense* is another carpeting hybrid, about 12in (30cm) high, with heart-shaped, chocolate-tinted leaves and orange flowers in spring.

Erigeron karvinskianus

Fleabane/Summer starwort
HEIGHT: 9in (23cm) • Hardy
FLOWERING SEASON: Summer

This herbaceous perennial self-seeds freely, particularly in cracks in pavings, and is therefore suitable for softening hard surfaces. It prefers a sunny site and grows in any well-drained soil but it must not be allowed to dry out in the growing season. Its sprawling stems bear narrow, lance-shaped leaves and clouds of small daisy-like flowers that open white, turn pink, then fade to a deepening purple. It can scramble up to 2ft (60cm) or more with support. Propagate by division in autumn or sow seed in spring.

Euphorbia characias ssp. *wulfenii*

Spurge
HEIGHT: 4ft (1.2m) • Moderately hardy
FLOWERING SEASON: Early summer

This is one of the largest euphorbias, with bluish-gray glaucous leaves that are evergreen in mild climates. The sulfur yellow, bottlebrush-like flowerheads rise above the leaves in early summer. Grow within the shelter of a wall to protect from cool easterly winds in spring. Cutting flowering stems down after flowering will help to promote bushiness. Propagate from cuttings of basal shoots in spring. Pest-free, but susceptible to molds. The sap is an irritant.

Galium odoratum

Bedstraw/Woodruff
HEIGHT: 6in (15cm) • Hardy
FLOWERING SEASON: Spring

The little woodruff is a carpeting perennial
with attractive lupine-like leaves and small,
starry, white flowers that stud the plant in
summer. All parts of the plant are aromatic
and the leaves used to be picked and dried
to scent clothes. It grows very well in partial
shade, making excellent ground cover in the
right conditions. It prefers well-drained
slightly acid soil with plenty of leaf mold.
Propagate by lifting and dividing the plants
in early spring or autumn.

Geranium × oxonianum 'Winscombe'

Cranesbill
HEIGHT: 18in (45cm) • Hardy
FLOWERING SEASON: Summer/autumn

Known as cranesbill, hardy geraniums
(not to be confused with pelargoniums,
commonly called geraniums) often make
good ground cover. *G. endressii* does so in
lightly shaded situations. There are many
hybrids, of which *G. × o.* 'Wargrave Pink'
has particularly bright pink flowers.
G. × o. 'Winscombe' has mauve flowers. Cut
back the old flowering stems to
encourage new growth. Propagate by
division in autumn. May be attacked by
slugs and prone to rust.

Glechoma hederacea 'Variegata'

Ground ivy
HEIGHT: 6in (15cm) • Hardy
FLOWERING SEASON: Inconspicuous

This variegated ground ivy is a rapidly
spreading, carpeting perennial that has small,
rounded leaves with lobed edges that are
marbled with white. *G. hederacea* does well
grown in sun or in partial shade so it can be
planted under trees but does not like deep
shade. It prefers moist well-drained soil. It
can be invasive so it is best planted where its
spread can be controlled. Propagate by
division in autumn or from cuttings taken
in spring.

Hebe pinguifolia 'Pagei'

Disc-leaved hebe
HEIGHT: 9in (23cm) • Hardy
FLOWERING SEASON: Early summer

This little hebe, which forms a spreading
mound up to 3ft (90cm) across, has small,
gray-green, waxy leaves and spires of pure-
white, star-shaped flowers in late spring or
early summer. It does best in full sun and
flourishes in most garden soils. Propagate
from cuttings taken in late summer or by
layering. If the plant suffers frost damage cut
right down almost to soil level in the spring.
This hebe is usually pest-free, but it is sometimes prone to downy mildew or leaf spot in
wetter areas.

Hedera colchica 'Dentata'

Persian ivy/Elephant's ears
HEIGHT: 20ft (6m) • Hardy
FLOWERING SEASON: Inconspicuous

This large-leaved ivy grows vigorously in
sun or shade. The leaves, which are dark
green, have toothed edges. Another cultivar,
'Dentata Variegata', has yellow-splashed,
lighter green leaves. Ivies are not fussy about
soil or situation, and climb by aerial roots
over any surface. Take cuttings of runners
for climbing ivies and from adult growth
for bushes. Prune back hard in the spring to
prevent it becoming unruly. Prone to attack
by scale insects and to leaf spot, red spider
mite may also be a problem.

× Heucherella tiarelloides

HEIGHT: 18in (45cm) • Hardy
FLOWERING SEASON: Early summer

From a hybrid genus (*Heuchera × Tiarella*), this
evergreen perennial makes good ground
cover, with the advantage of attractive spires
of small, rose-pink, bell-shaped little flowers
in early summer. The leaves form a dense
mound of heart-shaped leaves from which
the flower spires rise. This plant prefers semi-
shade and must have fertile well-drained soil.
It will not flourish in hot dry conditions.
× *H. alba* 'Bridget Bloom' has taller, lighter-
pink flower spikes which last for many
weeks. Divide the crowns in early autumn to
propagate or take basal cuttings in spring.

Hypericum calycinum

Aaron's beard/Rose of Sharon
HEIGHT: 18in (45cm) • Hardy
FLOWERING SEASON: Summer

The rose of Sharon, as this is sometimes known, is a vigorous sub-shrub that forms widely spreading mounds, making good ground cover via its spreading stolons. The leaves are bright green and oval and the brilliant gold flowers are borne on the end of the flowering shoots all summer long. It will succeed in dry shade, but flowers better in sun. Propagate by division of roots in autumn. Cut back hard every couple of years to keep it in shape. Sometimes prone to rust.

Juniperus communis 'Prostrata'

Common juniper
HEIGHT: 8in (20cm) • Hardy
FLOWERING SEASON: Inconspicuous

A carpeting form of the common juniper, *J. c.* 'Prostrata' is a conifer that spreads across the ground to about 5ft (1.5m). It has typical, needle-like, aromatic foliage and bears small berries that ripen from blue to black. It thrives in sun or light shade and in any garden soil although it will do better in soil that is not too heavy or alkaline. Prone to attacks by scale insects and to rust.

Lamium maculatum

Dead nettle
HEIGHT: 12in (30cm) • Hardy
FLOWERING SEASON: Early summer

This dead nettle has typical, small, nettle-like leaves but with a broad silver stripe running down the center rib. The pinkish-purple flowers are borne in spikes in early summer. There is a white-flowered form, *L. m. album*, and a cultivar with golden foliage, 'Aureum', which is not as vigorous and also needs shade and moist soil. Shear the plants after flowering to increase the ground-covering capacity of the leaves. Propagation is by division in autumn.

Leptospermum rupestre

HEIGHT: 6in (15cm) • Half-hardy
FLOWERING SEASON: Early summer

An evergreen flowering shrub, formerly known as *L. humifusum*, this particular species is semi-prostrate with arching branches and therefore makes good ground cover in a sunny sheltered spot, spreading up to 5ft (1.5m) across. The dark green leaves are narrow and oblong and turn bronze in winter, and the white flowers, flushed with red when in bud, are borne in great profusion in summer. It likes well-drained loamy soil to which some peat and sand have been added. Propagate from half-ripe cuttings in late summer, take care not to overwater.

Lonicera pileata

Honeysuckle
HEIGHT: 2ft (60cm) • Hardy
FLOWERING SEASON: Spring

An evergreen low dense shrub, this is by no means the prettiest of honeysuckles, but this particular lonicera has the advantage of a spreading habit even in heavy shade that makes it a good ground-cover plant. The leaves are pale green and narrowly oval, and the small, yellowish-green flowers are followed by small violet-blue fruits. Propagate from hardwood cuttings in autumn or by layering in autumn. Prone to attacks by aphids and to suffer from leaf spot and powdery mildew.

Myosotis sylvestris

Forget-me-not
HEIGHT: 12in (30cm) • Hardy
FLOWERING SEASON: Spring/early summer

This woodland herbaceous biennial will self-seed easily and quickly in the right conditions – partial shade and plenty of leaf mold, plus adequate moisture – to create useful ground cover. It makes bushy clumps of mid green, hairy leaves, surmounted by a profusion of tiny blue flowers carried in open sprays. To propagate, sow the seeds in spring and transfer young plants into their flowering position in autumn. Generally pest- and trouble-free free, but sometimes prone to molds and mildews.

Oxalis acetosella f. rosea

Wood sorrel/Shamrock
HEIGHT: 4in (10cm) • Hardy
FLOWERING SEASON: Mid/late spring

The little wood sorrel will naturalize well
in a shady area of the garden, it is very
invasive and self-seeds freely. It makes small
clumps of pale green shamrock-like leaves
with five-petalled pink flowers with a white
center and golden eye. The species plant,
O. acetosella has white flowers with purple
veined leaves. This plant prefers a moist well-
drained soil that contains plenty of leaf mold.
Propagate by dividing and replanting in
spring.

Pachysandra terminalis

Allegheny spruce
HEIGHT: 12in (30cm) • Hardy
FLOWERING SEASON: Spring

This sub-shrub spreads vigorously and is
excellent for ground cover in the shade,
since it is one of the few plants that will
thrive even in deep dry shade beneath trees.
It has neat, oval, shiny evergreen leaves and
tiny greenish-white flowers with prominent
purple-tinged stamens. *P. s.* 'Variegata' has
creamy edges to the leaves, and is slightly less
vigorous than the species. Divide in spring.

Petasites japonicus

Japanese butter burr
HEIGHT: 18in (45cm) • Hardy
FLOWERING SEASON: Early spring

This spreading perennial can be invasive, but
it makes an excellent ground-cover plant and
weed suppressor thanks to its huge dinner-
plate-like leaves. Cones of yellowish-white,
star-shaped flowers are produced in early
spring before the leaves appear. *P. japonicus*
does best in partial shade, and in moist but
well-drained soil. *P. fragrans*, the winter
heliotrope, has small vanilla-scented pinkish-
white flowers. Propagate by division of the
roots in autumn.

Phlomis russeliana

Jerusalem sage
HEIGHT: 4ft (1.2m) • Half-hardy
FLOWERING SEASON: Summer

One of a genus of more than 100 perennials,
shrubs and sub-shrubs, this particular species
originates in Syria. It has large, hairy, heart-
shaped leaves and tiers of yellow, hooded
flowers in summer. It does best in sun and in
any good garden soil. It is a good idea to
transplant the herbaceous kinds of phlomis
every two or three years. Cut the flowers
down after flowering is finished unless seeds
are wanted and cut back quite hard in
autumn. To propagate, divide the roots in
autumn or spring.

Phlox stolonifera

Creeping phlox
HEIGHT: 6in (15cm) • Hardy
FLOWERING SEASON: Early summer

This little phlox spreads to about 12in
(30cm). It is evergreen and more or less
prostrate, producing a profusion of small,
cup-shaped, azure blue flowers in early
summer. It prefers moist rather acid soil with
plenty of peat and is a good plant for a peat
bed. There are cultivars with different colored flowers: 'Ariane' has pure white ones
and 'Blue Ridge' pale mauve ones. Cut back
after flowering. Take cuttings of non-flowering shoots in summer. Prone to attacks by
powdery mildew.

Polypodium vulgare 'Bifidocristatum'

Polypody fern/Oak fern
HEIGHT: 6in (15cm) • Hardy
FLOWERING SEASON: None

This little fern spreads by means of creeping
rhizomes. Being hardy, evergreen and easy
to grow, it is ideal for ground cover in a
partially shaded spot such as under trees.
Plant with the rhizomes more or less on the
surface of the soil to which plenty of humus
has been added as it likes soil that is fertile
but well-drained. The cultivar
P. v. 'Cornubiense' is a particularly pretty
form and has deeply divided fronds. Divide
in spring to propagate. Generally pest-free.

Pulmonaria saccharata

Lungwort/Blue cowslip
HEIGHT: 12in (30cm) • Hardy
FLOWERING SEASON: Spring

This early-flowering, semi-evergreen, clump-forming perennial has long, broadly oval leaves, which are flecked with silvery-white on a dark green base. The small, tubular flowers are borne in clusters on the ends of short, erect stems just above the leaves. The flowers open pink but change to purple after pollination. *P. officinalis* 'Sissinghurst White' has large white blooms, and *P. rubra* 'Bowles' Red' has red ones. These plants are good for ground cover, but must have some shade.

Raoulia australis

HEIGHT: 2in (5cm) • Hardy
FLOWERING SEASON: Spring/summer

A small, carpeting evergreen perennial originating in New Zealand, which spreads to about 10in (25cm), this is a good subject for a sunny rock garden. Tiny greenish-yellow flowerheads, with a fluffy appearance, are borne in early summer. *R. glabra* is similarly mat-forming with bright green leaves and white flowers. and *R. haastii* has minute leaves that change from pale green in spring to brown in winter. It does well in sun or partial shade, but needs free-draining peaty soil. Propagate by division in late summer.

Ribes laurifolium

Currant
HEIGHT: 2ft (60cm) • Hardy
FLOWERING SEASON: Early spring

This attractive evergreen shrub will spread up to 4ft (1.2m). It has small, tough, leathery, dark green leaves and dangling racemes of greenish-yellow flowers in early spring. It does well in both shade and sun in well-drained soil. If both male and female plants are grown, the female plants will bear edible black berries. Propagate by cuttings in autumn. Prune out any old wood after flowering. Occasionally subject to aphid attacks and leaf spot.

Salix repens

Creeping willow
HEIGHT: up to 6ft (1.8m) • Hardy
FLOWERING SEASON: Inconspicuous

Known appropriately enough as the creeping willow, this deciduous prostrate shrub bears attractive silvery-gray leaves which gradually darken to mid green by summer. The catkins, which are about 1in (2.5cm) long and also silvery-gray, are produced in spring. On dry soil, it is smaller and less vigorous than in moist loam. It does best in a sunny position. Take hardwood cuttings in autumn. Like all willows it is prone to several pests, including scale insects, and to a variety of fungal disorders.

Sarcococca humilis

Christmas box/Sweet box
HEIGHT: 3ft (1m) • Hardy
FLOWERING SEASON: Late winter

Christmas box, or sweet box, as it is sometimes known, is grown both for its elegant, glossy, evergreen foliage and for its fragrant flowers which appear in winter. *S. humilis* grows in neat clumps, but because it spreads by underground stems it provides good ground cover. The tiny, white, scented flowers are followed by spherical fruits. This plant does well in sun or in partial shade, in good soil that does not dry out. It can be propagated by semi-ripe cuttings taken in summer.

Saxifraga cuneifolia

Saxifrage
HEIGHT: 8in (20cm) • Hardy
FLOWERING SEASON: Late spring

This evergreen perennial makes a good carpeting plant, the rosettes of rounded leaves covering the soil surface. Rising high above them in late spring and early summer are clouds of white flowers borne on delicate stems. It is rather like a small 'London pride', *S. × urbium,* and is a charming little plant for shady places in a rock garden. Does best in moist soil in partial shade and belongs to the group of saxifrages which needs protection from the midday sun. Propagate by sowing seed in autumn or division in winter.

Soleirolia soleirolii

Mind-your-own-business/Baby's tears
HEIGHT: 2in (5cm) • Half-hardy
FLOWERING SEASON: Inconspicuous

Known as mother of thousands, mind-your-own-business or baby's tears, this little carpeting plant spreads very rapidly in sun or partial shade. Its leaves are killed by frost but it grows again quickly in spring. It is ideal ground cover for patios and terrace but may need fairly ruthless control for it spreads rapidly. It has inconspicuous flowers in summer. It used to be grown in formal greenhouses as edging to the stagings. Propagate by division.

Tiarella cordifolia

Foam flower/False mitrewort
HEIGHT: 8in (20cm) • Hardy
FLOWERING SEASON: Early summer

The foam flower, so-called because it produces clouds of tiny white flowers on tallish stems in early spring, does well even in deep shade, provided the soil is moist. It spreads vigorously by runners. The evergreen leaves are heart-shaped, bright green and serrated and they have darker veins which turn red in winter. The plant is easy to grow and may be divided at almost any time in the year.

Tolmiea menziesii 'Taff's Gold'

Pick-a-back or piggyback plant
HEIGHT: 18in (45cm) • Hardy
FLOWERING SEASON: Spring

This is known as the pick-a-back plant or youth-on-age from its habit of producing plantlets where the leaves join the stem. It is semi-evergreen and has ivy-shaped leaves with crinkled edges. Small, bell-shaped, green and brown flowers appear in spring. *T. menziesii* is fully hardy and does well in shade and well-drained, neutral to acid soil. It is a suitable plant for the woodland area in any garden. Propagate by removing young plantlets and replanting.

Trifolium repens 'Purpurascens Quadrifolium'

Clover trefoil/Dutch clover
HEIGHT: 5in (12cm) • Hardy
FLOWERING SEASON: All summer

This little clover has very attractively marked leaves, bright green on the edge with purplish-bronze centers, the leaves on this cultivar are held in groups of four, hence the name. Small, white, typical pea flowers are borne in summer. *T. r.* 'Purpurascens' often does duty as the shamrock on St Patrick's Day but the true shamrock is the wood sorrel (page 118). It does well in sun and well-drained soil, and is ideal for covering a bank, because it can spread to about 12in (30cm).

Vaccinium glaucoalbum

Ornamental blueberry
HEIGHT: 4ft (1.2m) • Moderately hardy • pH
FLOWERING SEASON: Early summer

This is an ornamental form of the common bilberry or blueberry which hails from the Himalayas. An evergreen, it makes a good spreading bush about 5ft (1.5m) wide. It has dark green leaves that are paler when young and whitish underneath. The short racemes of white-tinted pink flowers are borne in early summer, followed by fine blue-black edible fruits. It should be planted in an acid, peaty soil in a sunny position or in partial shade. Propagate by layering, division in autumn, or half-ripe cuttings in summer.

Veronica prostrata

Prostrate speedwell
HEIGHT: 12in (30cm) • Hardy
FLOWERING SEASON: Early summer

This speedwell forms a dense mat of narrow green leaves, above which are borne a profusion of saucer-shaped, bright blue flowers in early summer. Two cultivars, 'Spode Blue' and 'Trehane', have taller spires of blue flowers. They do best in full sun and well-drained soil. Other good ground covering speedwells are *V. austriaca*, *V. pectinata* and *V. reptans*. Propagate by division in spring or by semi-ripe cuttings in late summer. It is pest-free, but prone to mildew.

Viburnum davidii

HEIGHT: 4ft (1.2m) • Hardy
FLOWERING SEASON: Summer

This evergreen viburnum makes good
ground cover, because its spreading, neat
mound of foliage which forms a dome
effectively blankets out any weeds. It is also
grown for its decorative leaves. Flat white
flowerheads, about 3in (7.5cm) across are
produced in summer, followed by greenish-
blue berries if both male and female plants
are grown. It prefers a moist soil and full sun.
Prune in late summer if necessary. Propagate
by taking cuttings in late summer or by
layering in autumn.

Vinca minor '*Argenteovariegata*'

Lesser periwinkle
HEIGHT: 4in (10cm) • Hardy
FLOWERING SEASON: Spring/autumn

This vigorously spreading sub-shrub makes
ideal ground cover and is slightly less
invasive than the larger, but similar, *V. major.*
V. minor 'Argenteovariegata' has leaves
attractively splashed with white and the
typical pale blue periwinkle flowers. It grows
in any soil that does not dry out completely
and will grown in shade but it prefers some
sun. Propagate by semi-ripe cuttings in
summer or division in autumn. It is pest-
free, but sometimes prone to cucumber
mosaic virus.

Waldsteinia ternata

HEIGHT: 4in (10cm) • Hardy
FLOWERING SEASON: Early summer

This spreading semi-evergreen perennial has
attractive three-lobed, bright green leaves
and small, yellow, saucer-shaped, five-
petalled flowers in late spring to early
summer. It spreads via runners, making good
ground cover. It grows best in sun although
it will tolerate some shade and does best in
well-drained soil. It will not flourish in
heavy soils. Another species, *W. fragarioides*
has similar characteristics and carries yellow
flowers in spring to late summer. Propagate
by division in early spring.

More Ground Cover Plants

Good ground cover plants are essential to
any garden both for their own sake and to
help suppress the weeds, the bigger the
garden the more important they become.
Take care to choose plants to fit the
situation, be it dry or moist, sunny or shady,
and remember that many clump-forming
perennial plants spread, so that a vigorous
hardy perennial like one of the geraniums
or *Alchemilla mollis,* makes a good ground
cover plant over a period and the same
applies to low-growing, prostrate shrubs.

There are also a number of roses available
which have been bred specifically to
provide ground cover. Generally these are
in two forms, the prostrate creeping
varieties, *Rosa* 'Max Graf' and *R.* Partridge
are good varieties, and the low growing
shrubs up to 3ft (1m) in height with a
spread wider than their height, *R.* Bonica
and *R.* Fiona are two of these.

If you are creating a new garden and have
largish areas of soil where you need to
control the weeds, you can buy or hire one
of the chipper/shredder machines. They
produce an instant fine mulch of wood or
leaves which can be spread on the garden.
This not only suppresses the weeds but
helps to improve the soil. Mulching with
garden compost is even more beneficial to
the soil but is not quite so good at
suppressing the weeds.

Evergreen plants are marked (E) and semi-
evergreen, (S-E).

SHRUBS

Arctostaphylos uva-ursi (E)
Calluna vulgaris (E)
Cassiope 'Muirhead' (E)
Cornus canadensis
Daboecia cantabrica (E)
Erica carnea 'Springwood White' (E)
    E. × *darleyensis* 'Darley Dale' (E)
Euonymus fortunei cvs (E)
Gaultheria shallon (E)
Gypsophila repens 'Rosa Schönheit' (S-E)
Hebe pinguifolia 'Pagei'
Hypericum 'Hidcote' (S-E)
Hypericum × *inodorum* 'Elstead' (S-E)
Juniperus virginiana 'Sulphur Spray' (E)
Leucothoe fontanesiana (E)
Lithodora diffusa 'Heavenly Blue' (E)
Rosmarinus officinalis 'Jackman's Prostrate' (E)
Rubus tricolor (E)
Senecio (syn. *Brachyglottis*) 'Sunshine' (E)
Stephanandra tanakae
Zauschneria californica

PERENNIALS

Acantholimon glumaceum (E)
Ajuga reptans (E)
Alchemilla mollis
Aubrieta (in variety)
Brunnera macrophylla
Cardamine pratensis 'Flore Pleno'
Convallaria majalis (in variety)
Corydalis cheilanthifolia
    C. lutea
Darmera peltata
Dryas octopetala
Epimedium grandiflorum
Geranium (in variety) (S-E)
Hosta fortunei
Iberis sempervirens
Lysimachia nummularia
Mertensia pulmonarioides
Mimulus × *burnetii*
Nepeta × *faassenii*
Ourisia macrophylla (E)
Persicaria affinis (E)
Stachys byzantina (E)
Symphytum grandiflorum
Tellima grandiflora (S-E)
Thalictrum aquilegiifolium
Veronica prostrata

AUTUMN &
WINTER FOLIAGE

Even after the main flowering season is over in summer, gardens retain much interest. Many shrubs and trees are grown for their autumn color and often it is the most beautiful time of the year. Trees and shrubs native to the eastern states of the US and to China, especially the maples, are particularly striking.

ABOVE: *The buff colored bark of* Acer griseum *rolls off in large pieces to reveal striking orange-brown new bark beneath.*

OPPOSITE: *The red maple* (Acer rubrum) *in the autumn sunlight. If you have room in your garden it is worth planting some fall foliage trees: maples, cherries, hawthorn and rowans are all good choices.*

ABOVE: *Autumn color can be found in perennials and shrubs as well as trees — in fact any plants that lose their leaves in winter. The deep purple of* Cotinus coggygria *Purpureus Group make an excellent foil for the winter-flowering heather below.*

Autumn is a time of year when many deciduous plants, and a few evergreen ones, will make you appreciate their presence. Their brilliant and dramatic hues are highly prized and many gardeners select them to extend the season of interest. Among the most popular plants for small gardens are the Japanese maples (*Acer palmatum*), some of which have brilliant autumn color, as well as several climbers, including various creepers and ornamental vines.

The vivid color changes of autumn foliage are part of the natural processes which begin well before the leaves fall and are usually a response to the shortening autumn days, rather than to lower temperatures or frost. The brilliance of autumn color differs considerably in any one area from year to year and there can be marked differences in the intensity of the color. This is usually owing to the prevailing weather conditions. The ideal conditions for a good autumn display are a cool wet autumn, with very little wind and no frost, as these give slow color changes, with the leaves hanging on the trees for the longest possible time. Autumn color is, therefore, somewhat elusive.

The chemistry of autumn leaf color is mainly concerned with the irregular rate at which aging takes place in different parts of the leaf. Natural pigments within the leaf of the carotene (red/orange) group persist after the chlorophyll (green) has almost gone. This is augmented in some plants by the presence of tannins which account for the brilliant yellow characteristic of birches, ginkgos, the tulip tree (*Liriodendron tulipifera*) and poplars. The red or purple colors of acers (maples), liquidambar and many others are caused by anthocyanins, a result of accumulations of sugars in the leaves caused by photosynthesis continuing after the transportation of sugars to other parts of the plant has stopped.

When considering where to position trees that are to be grown for the beauty of their autumn foliage, choose a site which is well drained, but not too dry, especially in late summer or this may result in premature coloring and early leaf-drop. Exposure to full sun, however, especially in the second half of the day, will give you the best effect, and contribute to the production of the brightest colors.

A number of the best plants for autumn color are illustrated in this chapter and in a sense it is invidious to single out out one rather than another. Much will depend on the situation, soil and the weather in any particular year but, for the connoisseur, *Fothergilla major* (page 19) has particularly striking autumn color, as has *Parrotia persica* (page 93) and many of the maples while the Virginia creepers (parthenocissus) make a brilliant if rather short-lived splash of color against the wall of a house. Everyone will have their own favorites. There is a comprehensive list of all plants that provide good color at the end of this chapter and one or two suggestions of other plants that there was not room for in this book which can be found in most well-stocked nurseries and garden centres.

ABOVE: *Perennial borders assume attractive tints before they die down at which point the plants can be cut right back, and the debris cleared away. Many gardeners prefer to leave this task until early spring as the form of the foliage is often attractive in winter particularly in a hard frost.*

LEFT: *The tinted leaves of a golden hop (Humulus lupulus 'Aureus') and Virginia creeper, turning rusty red, combined with the variegated evergreen leaves of ivy make an attractive picture in the fall.*

Acer cappadocicum

Cappadocian maple
HEIGHT: 30ft (9m) • Hardy
FLOWERING SEASON: Spring

This exquisite tree has very striking five- to
seven-lobed palmate leaves held by scarlet-
red leaf stalks. A glossy dark green in spring
and summer, the leaves turn a rich golden
yellow in autumn. There are some attractive
cultivars: *A. c.* 'Rubrum', has young leaves
which are tinged red around the margin, and
A. c. 'Aureum' has leaves which are yellow in
spring, lime-green in summer, and yellow
again in autumn. Propagation is by softwood
cuttings in early summer or by layering.

Acer griseum

Paper-bark maple
HEIGHT: 20ft (6m) • Hardy
FLOWERING SEASON: Spring

This slow-growing tree has trifoliate leaves
which are dark green on the upper surface
and blue-green beneath, before turning red
and scarlet in the autumn. On young trees
some leaves remain in place all winter. The
buff-colored bark on the trunk and branches
rolls off in large pieces to reveal light,
orange-brown, new bark beneath. The fruits
are gray-green and covered in soft, downy
felt. Propagation is difficult, but seed sown in
autumn is the most successful method.

Acer palmatum var. dissectum

Japanese maple
HEIGHT: 15ft (4.5m) • Hardy
FLOWERING SEASON: Spring

A slow-growing large shrub or small tree
grown for the delicate palm-like leaves
deeply divided into five or seven lobes, which
can range in color from pale green to deep
reddish-purple. Most forms produce vivid
autumn leaves, and some are also prized for
their brightly colored bark. The thin,
delicate leaves are prone to wind damage.
Propagate from seed sown in early spring or,
for named varieties, from softwood cuttings
in June.

Ampelopsis glandulosa var. brevipedunculata 'Elegans'

HEIGHT: 20ft (6m) • Hardy
FLOWERING SEASON: Mid/late spring

Vigorous climbers grown mainly for their
attractive autumn foliage, they are ideal for
growing against walls and fences or up a
pergola. The broadly oval, coarse-textured
leaves are three- to five-lobed, bright green
with prominent purple veins in the summer,
before turning a golden orange-yellow in
autumn. The plant supports itself with
curling tendrils, and has small inconspicuous
flowers which are followed by small fruits.
Propagation is by semi-ripe cuttings taken
in summer.

Azolla filiculoides

Floating water fern
HEIGHT: 1in (2.5cm) • Moderately hardy
FLOWERING SEASON: Summer

This deciduous perennial, floating water
fern, is grown for its decorative foliage. The
finely divided leaves or fronds vary from
pink to bronze-red in full sun, and from pale
green to blue-green in shade, particularly in
autumn when they can make the surface of
the water look as if it is on fire. It is ideal for
controlling algae by reducing light beneath
water, but if it is not kept in check it may be
invasive. Remove portions with a net if
necessary. Propagate by redistributing clusters of the new plantlets when they appear.

Bassia scoparia f. trichophylla

Burning bush
HEIGHT: 3ft (1m) • Half-hardy
FLOWERING SEASON: Late summer

A popular annual usually grown for its masses of pale green, pointed, narrow and
strap-shaped leaves. In autumn the leaves
turn a vivid crimson red which lasts until the
plant is killed by the autumn frosts. It is this
autumn color which gives the plant its common name of burning bush. The small green
flowers are quite inconspicuous. The cultivar, *B. s.* 'Childsii', has a neater habit. Also
called *Kochia inconspicua*. Propagation is by
seed sown under glass in spring and planted
out in position.

Berberis dictyophylla

Barberry
HEIGHT: 6ft (1.8m) • Hardy
FLOWERING SEASON: Late spring

A deciduous, upright shrub with thin erect stems. When young the new shoots are covered with a waxy, gray bloom giving an attractive 'whitewash' effect. In spring yellow flowers are produced in small clusters on the previous year's shoots, to be followed in autumn by small red berries. The elliptical leaves, which are pale green on the upper surface and bluish-green beneath, turn scarlet in autumn. Propagation is by semi-ripe cuttings taken with a heel in late summer.

Betula ermanii

Birch
HEIGHT: 25ft (8m) • Hardy
FLOWERING SEASON: Late spring

This graceful tree has beautiful, peeling bark which is orange-brown changing to a pinkish creamy-white. A vigorous tree, it comes into growth early in the year, producing oval, mid green leaves which are heart-shaped and deeply veined. They are subject to damage from late spring frosts if the site is exposed. *B. e.* 'Blush' syn. *B. costata* and *B. e.* 'Grayswood Hill' are fine cultivars. The leaves produce good autumn color. Propagate by grafting under protection in early spring.

Celastrus orbiculatus

Oriental bittersweet/Staff vine
HEIGHT: 30 ft (9m) • Hardy
FLOWERING SEASON: Summer

A vigorous climber useful for growing over buildings such as garages and sheds, or through large trees and shrubs. The oval leaves have a pointed tip and are carried on short stalks, they are mid green, with good yellow autumn color. The twining stems are light gray-green changing to light creamy-brown with age. Small green flowers are carried in clusters of up to four in early summer. Propagation is from semi-ripe cuttings taken in summer.

Ceratostigma willmottianum

HEIGHT: 3ft (1m) • Moderately hardy
FLOWERING SEASON: Midsummer

This deciduous shrub forms a dome of dense twiggy growth. In spring the first sign of new growth are the tiny coral-red buds that open into dark green, diamond-shaped, narrow leaves along the stems, pink at first, later turning green. In early July the small, clear blue flowers show in rather tight heads at the end of the shoots, and flowering continues over a long period. In autumn the leaves turn a rich fiery red. It likes full sun and grows best in well-drained soil. Cut out dead wood in the spring. Propagate from heel cuttings taken in late summer.

Cercis canadensis 'Forest Pansy'

Eastern redbud/Judas tree
HEIGHT: 10ft (3m) • Moderately hardy
FLOWERING SEASON: Late spring

An outstanding slow-growing large shrub or small tree. The deeply veined, broad, heart-shaped leaves which are glossy green when young develop a slight blue sheen later and turn red and yellow in the autumn. The pretty, small, bright-pink, pea-shaped flowers are produced in vast quantities, followed by small pod-like fruits in autumn. The tree often leans over because the root system is very brittle. Propagation is by seed sown in spring. Coral spot may cause death of leaves.

Chiastophyllum oppositifolium

HEIGHT: 8in (20cm) • Hardy
FLOWERING SEASON: Late spring/early summer

A hardy evergreen perennial which consists of clusters of creeping rosettes with a lax, trailing habit. The mid green, large, broadly oblong and succulent leaves have serrated edges and bronzed margins in autumn. In late spring and early summer there are sprays of small, yellow flowers which hang like strings of beads from erect, slender red stems rising 6in (15cm) above the leaves. This plant needs shade and a moist, well-drained soil that does not dry out completely. Propagate by soft tip cuttings in early summer or seed sown in autumn.

Coronilla valentina ssp. glauca

Crown vetch
HEIGHT: 3ft (1m) • Not reliably hardy
FLOWERING SEASON: Spring/summer

This evergreen shrub has a dense, bushy
habit, with a mass of gently arching, greenish-
brown, woody stems. The bluish-gray leaves
are divided into five or seven round leaflets.
The small, fragrant flowers are yellow, pea-
like and are carried in small clusters above
the leaves on thin green stalks. The cultivar
C. v. ssp. g. 'Variegata' has creamy-white
splashes on the leaves. Propagation is by softwood cuttings in summer. In some years this
plant may be severely attacked by blackfly.

Cotinus coggygria

Smoke plant/Venetian sumach
HEIGHT: 8ft (2.5m) • Hardy
FLOWERING SEASON: Summer

A rounded shrub with a tangle of thin,
whippy, gray-green branches which bear
round leaves carried in thin leaf stalks
(petioles). The light green leaves color
brilliantly in shades of yellow, orange and red
in autumn. The small, fawn-colored flowers
are carried in loose, feathery panicles.
C. c. 'Royal Purple', has dark, plum-purple
foliage and produces light red autumn tints.
Propagate by layering long shoots in late
summer, or semi-ripe heeled cuttings.

Crataegus crus-galli

Cockspur thorn
HEIGHT: 15ft (4.5m) • Hardy
FLOWERING SEASON: Summer

A wide-spreading, small tree, with wicked-
looking thorns often up to 3in (8cm) long.
The broadly oval leaves are glossy green and
produce an attractive display of autumn
color, with shades of yellow, orange, and
brilliant scarlet. The large clusters of white
flowers are followed by scarlet fruits which
last on the tree well into winter. There is also
a thornless variety, C. c-g. var. pyracanthifolia.
Propagation is by seed sown in autumn, but
germination may take up to two years.

Decaisnea fargesii

HEIGHT: 20ft (6m) • Moderately hardy
FLOWERING SEASON: Spring/summer

This large deciduous shrub with an erect,
open habit, has branches which are semi-
arching. The large leaves, which are a light
gray-green and made up of up to twelve
small, spear-shaped leaflets, turn an attractive
yellow in the autumn. Large clusters of lime-
green flowers are followed in autumn by
strange pod-like fruits. These are metallic
blue in color and contain black seeds
suspended in a thick clear mucilage. It likes a
sheltered sunny position and good soil that
does not dry out. Propagation is by sowing
the fresh seed in autumn.

Disanthus cercidifolius

HEIGHT: 10ft (3m) • Hardy
FLOWERING SEASON: Autumn

This is a medium-sized deciduous shrub
with a rounded habit and dense, twiggy
branches. The bluish-green leaves are
broadly oval and almost heart-shaped. In
autumn they turn yellow, orange, soft crimson and claret-red before falling. The
flowers, which have small, strap-like, dark-
red petals, are produced in pairs just as the
leaves start to fall. It needs partial shade and
moist, rich, neutral to acid soil for the colors
to be at their best. Propagation is by layering
in spring or by fresh seed sown in winter and
placed in a cold frame.

Dregea sinensis

HEIGHT: 10ft (3m) • Not reliably frost hardy
FLOWERING SEASON: Summer

Formerly known as Wattakaka sinensis, this is
a woody-stemmed climber with a loose,
twining habit. The mid green, heart-shaped
leaves, which are gray-green on the under
side, turn yellow along the margins in
autumn. The small, trumpet-like, fragrant
flowers appear in clusters and have star-
shaped openings that are creamy-white with
red dots and splashes followed by slender
seed pods. This plant must have a sheltered
site to survive. Propagation is by softwood
cuttings in summer, or seed sown under
protection in spring.

Euonymus fortunei 'Emerald 'n' Gold'

HEIGHT: 6-10ft (1.8-3m) • Hardy
FLOWERING SEASON: Early summer

These popular plants often have narrow, oval, mid green leaves which produce very attractive autumn colors. The flowers are inconspicuous but the winged fruits can be brightly colored and very striking. *E. europaeus* 'Red Cascade' has leaves which turn a rich scarlet in autumn and produces large quantities of rosy-red fruits which hang on the plant all winter. Propagation is by semi-ripe cuttings with a heel, taken in August. No regular pruning is required.

Festuca glauca

Blue fescue
HEIGHT: 10in (25cm) • Hardy
FLOWERING SEASON: Summer

This is a low-growing, tussock-forming little grass with tufts of bristle-like, blue-gray leaves. It maintains its pattern and color throughout the winter and adapts well to exposed, windy sites. The purple flower spikes are carried above the leaves in summer and remain to provide decoration long after flowering has finished. It is easy to grow in any sunny position and likes well-drained soil. It is lime tolerant. Propagate by division and replanting in spring.

Ficus carica

Common fig
HEIGHT: 5ft (1.5m) • Moderately hardy
FLOWERING SEASON: Summer

This is a small tree or large shrub, with light green stems when young, turning gray-green as they age. The large, deciduous, palm-like leaves are mid to gray-green turning butter-yellow in the autumn. A versatile plant, it can be grown on a fence, or as a free-standing bush, but a wall which gives some frost protection is best. The cultivar *F. c.* 'Brown Turkey' regularly produces brown-green fruits in late summer. Propagation is by semi-ripe cuttings taken in summer.

Fraxinus angustifolia 'Raywood'

Narrow-leaved ash
HEIGHT: 45ft (15m) • Hardy
FLOWERING SEASON: Spring

This is a fast-growing deciduous tree of dense, fairly upright habit, and a bark which is dark gray, with closely networked ridges, which become deep and knobbly with age. The leaves are usually blue-green, pinnate and opposite, with up to thirteen spear-shaped leaflets joined by a strong central midrib. In autumn the leaves become plum-purple before falling. Likes sun and fertile well-drained soil that does not dry out. Propagate by seed or grafting, but named cultivars must be grafted in March.

Hakonechloa macra 'Alboaurea'

HEIGHT: 2½ft (75cm) • Hardy
FLOWERING SEASON: Autumn

This lovely clump-forming grass has long narrow, ribbon-shaped leaves growing alternately along a red-tinted stem and giving a light, arching 'mop head' effect. The leaves are very striking, being a combination of warm golden-yellow, finely striped with narrow green lines, and sometimes tinged bronze along the edges. In autumn they become tinged with bronze-red along the margins and makes a spectacular sight. It bears inconspicuous flower spikes in autumn. It prefers a cool site. Propagate by division in early spring.

Hamamelis mollis

Chinese witch hazel
HEIGHT: 7ft (2m) • Hardy • pH
FLOWERING SEASON: Winter/spring

This distinctive deciduous shrub produces its wonderfully fragrant flowers in winter. The frost-hardy flowers are spidery in appearance, with small, strap-like petals chiefly in shades of yellow, although some cultivars have darker flowers. The large mid green leaves are broadly oval and make a magnificent display in autumn, turning yellow and copper before falling. Likes sun or semi-shade and fertile, well-drained, peaty, acid soil. Propagation is by softwood cuttings taken in late summer or by grafting in midwinter.

Helleborus argutifolius

Christmas rose/Lenten rose
HEIGHT: 2½ft (75cm) • Hardy
FLOWERING SEASON: Winter/spring

This hardy evergreen perennial forms a compact mound of tough, leathery leaves which are mid to pale green with a spiny margin. In autumn the older leaves turn bronze-yellow along the margins. The large flower heads are made up of many cup-shaped, yellow-green blooms. The weight of these heads often causes the stems to collapse. Cut back such stems after flowering. Propagation is by seed sown in summer and placed in a cold frame.

Imperata cylindrica

HEIGHT: 2½ft (75cm) • Hardy
FLOWERING SEASON: Autumn

A hardy perennial grass with erect, slender stems. In autumn it produces light, wispy, silvery-white flower spikes up to 8in (20cm) long, which often persist throughout the winter. The mid to dark green leaves are flat and narrow, tapering gradually to a pointed tip. The cultivar *I. c.* 'Rubra' which is the plant most widely available in nurseries, has leaves which are flushed with bright ruby red changing to dark burgundy in autumn and winter. Will flourish in any well-drained soil and prefers some sun. Propagation, like all grasses, is by division and replanting in early spring.

Lagerstroemia indica

Crape myrtle
HEIGHT: 5ft (1.5m) • Not reliably hardy
FLOWERING SEASON: Summer/early autumn

This very attractive shrub has rigid, erect branches, which are gray-green when young, turning duller with age. The foliage consists of broad, spear-like leaves arranged in groups of three on short stalks, they are mid green with very prominent veins, and turn a vivid yellow in autumn. In summer and autumn trusses of white, pink or purple flowers are produced. This plant must have some protection during winter. Propagation is by semi-ripe cuttings taken in summer.

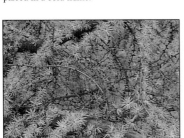

Larix decidua

European larch
HEIGHT: 55ft (18m) • Hardy
FLOWERING SEASON: Spring

This vigorous, deciduous conifer has rosettes of light green, needle-like leaves which become darker through the summer and change to a golden yellow before falling. The bark is a greenish gray-brown and fairly smooth when the tree is young, often becoming deeply ridged and an attractive pinkish-brown with age. Grows in almost all soils and conditions. Though easily propagated by seed sown outdoors in the spring, this tree is really too large for all but the very biggest gardens.

Lindera obtusiloba

Spice bush
HEIGHT: 20ft (6m) • Hardy
FLOWERING SEASON: Early spring

A large deciduous shrub that comes from Japan and is grown for its broadly oval, glossy, dark green, three-lobed aromatic leaves which turn butter yellow with rich pink tints in autumn. The small, deep yellow, star-shaped flowers are produced in spring before the leaves emerge and are followed by small round black berries. Likes semi-shade and moist acid soil. Propagation is by seed sown in spring or by layering in early summer, although rooting may take up to eighteen months.

Liriodendron tulipifera

Tulip tree
HEIGHT: 100ft (30m) • Hardy
FLOWERING SEASON: Summer

A large, vigorous tree with a spreading habit, and gray-green bark. The large, deep green leaves are very distinctive, with deep lobes and a very square tip. In the autumn they turn a bright golden-yellow. The large, magnolia-like flowers are tulip-shaped, greenish-white and splashed with orange markings. The cultivar *L. t.* 'Aureomarginatum' has deep green leaves with a golden-yellow margin. It likes fertile well-drained slightly acid soil. Propagation is by seed sown in spring or by summer budding.

Malus tschonoskii

Crab apple
HEIGHT: 40ft (12m) • Hardy
FLOWERING SEASON: Late spring

This attractive tree has a strong, vigorous, and characteristically erect, conical habit. The mid green leaves are broadly oval and covered with a dense felt of gray hairs on the underside and along the young shoots as they develop. In autumn the tree produces a magnificent display of yellow, orange, scarlet and purple colors. The small, single flowers are white flushed pink. Propagation is by budding in summer or grafting in spring. Apple canker can infect the tree.

Miscanthus sinensis 'Strictus'

Zebra grass
HEIGHT: 4ft (1.2m) • Hardy
FLOWERING SEASON: Summer

This vigorous, clump-forming ornamental grass has bold, glossy leaves with golden bands running across them. They turn yellow and later bronze in autumn. The flower-heads will only form in a hot summer and are useful for drying and using in floral arrangements. The usual method of propagation is by division in March, when the clump is split into smaller portions of 4-5 shoots. Though generally pest- and disease-free, over-feeding can cause soft weak growth to develop.

Nyssa sylvatica

Tupelo
HEIGHT: 25ft (8m) • Hardy
FLOWERING SEASON: Summer

A handsome, slow-growing, deciduous tree from north America that is broadly conical in shape with horizontal branches upturned at the tip. The oval leaves taper to a point; they are a dark, glossy green in summer, turning to shades of rich scarlet, orange and yellow in autumn. This tree rarely comes into leaf before May, when the risk of a frost is all but gone. Unsuitable for limy or dry soils. Propagation is by seed sown in autumn and overwintered in a cold frame.

Ophiopogon planiscapus 'Nigrescens'

Snake's beard
HEIGHT: 10in (25cm) • Hardy
FLOWERING SEASON: Late summer

This evergreen perennial has arching, strap-like, spidery clusters of leaves which are almost black and remain throughout winter. The flowers appear in short sprays of tiny mauve bells tucked between the leaves, to be followed by shiny black berries in autumn. Creeping underground stolons gradually establish this plant as a dense thicket. Grows in sun or partial shade and fertile well-drained soil. Propagate by fresh seed sown in autumn or by division in spring.

Paliurus spina-christi

Christ's thorn
HEIGHT: 12ft (4m) • Moderately hardy
FLOWERING SEASON: Summer

This large, deciduous shrub makes a dense thicket of slender, green, thorny shoots. The leaves are broadly oval, glossy and bright green. Tiny, greenish-yellow flowers are produced in short, dangling clusters, to be followed by woody, winged, yellow-green fruits in autumn. Propagation is by softwood cuttings in summer or seed sown under protection in autumn. This plant is slow to establish, and may require some winter protection. It also needs full sun, and a light, free-draining soil.

Persicaria affinis

Knotweed
HEIGHT: 10in (25cm) • Hardy
FLOWERING SEASON: Summer/autumn

The short, mat-forming knotweeds, such as this one, give a low, bold flash of color at the front of the border. The plant makes a wide clump of creeping stems with narrow, dark green leaves, and in late summer and autumn produces spikes of rose-pink or red flowers. There are a number of cultivars: *P. a.* 'Dimity' has white flowers flushed pink and scarlet foliage in the autumn; *P. a.* 'Donald Lowndes' has deep pink flowers all summer long. Propagation is by division in early spring.

Prunus incisa

Fuji cherry
HEIGHT: 15ft (4.5m) • Hardy
FLOWERING SEASON: Spring

This is a shrubby deciduous species with slender erect branches. The mid green leaves are small, prominently toothed around the margins and turn beautiful shades of yellow and orange in autumn. The flowers, which appear before the leaves, are deep pink in the bud, opening to form small pink-tinged white blooms. This tree makes an excellent hedge. Propagation is by softwood cuttings taken in early summer. The bacterial fireblight may cause young shoots to shrivel.

Ptelea trifoliata

Hop tree
HEIGHT: 22ft (7m) • Hardy
FLOWERING SEASON: Early/midsummer

A deciduous, large shrub or small tree, with a bushy, low-spreading habit and a tangle of thin, gray-green branches. The dark green aromatic leaves are made up of three narrow oval leaflets, which turn butter yellow in autumn. In summer, clusters of very fragrant, small, star-shaped, yellowish-green flowers appear, followed by bunches of pale green winged fruits. Propagation is by seed sown in autumn, or by softwood cuttings taken in summer for cultivars.

Rhus typhina

Stag's horn sumach
HEIGHT: 15ft (4.5m) • Hardy
FLOWERING SEASON: Summer

This wide-spreading, suckering shrub, develops a scrawny, flat-topped appearance as it ages. The young shoots are a furry velvety-brown. The large, dark green leaves are made up of many small leaflets, evenly arranged along a slender leaf stalk. In autumn the leaves turn a rich orange and reddish-purple. The flower spikes are reddish-brown in color and are carried like candles on the shoot tips. They last throughout the winter. Propagation is by root cuttings taken in late winter.

Rubus phoenicolasius

Japanese wineberry
HEIGHT: 6ft (1.8m) • Hardy
FLOWERING SEASON: Early summer

An attractive shrub with an open habit and gently arching, orange-red stems, which look very pretty in winter. The mid green leaves, which are sub-divided into three leaflets, have a slightly felty texture with a silvery-green undersurface. They turn a soft yellow in autumn. Clusters of single, pink, rose-like flowers are followed by bright red, edible fruits in autumn. Prune out flowering shoots in winter to encourage new shoots to develop from the plant base. Propagation is by semi-ripe cuttings taken in early summer.

Rubus tricolor

Bramble
HEIGHT: 2ft (60cm) • Hardy
FLOWERING SEASON: Summer

This evergreen bramble makes an excellent ground-cover plant that is fairly low-growing. It has glossy, dark green leaves, and produces cup-shaped, papery white flowers in summer. The raspberry-like fruits are scarlet and edible. Will grow under most conditions but does best in fertile well-drained soil in sun or in partial shade. Propagate by tip layering or by taking semi-hardwood cuttings in late summer. Generally pest-free, but it is sometimes prone to gray mold and rust.

Sorbus 'Joseph Rock'

Mountain ash/Rowan tree
HEIGHT: 25ft (8m) • Hardy
FLOWERING SEASON: Early summer

A deciduous upright tree with ascending branches and long pointed buds which are bright red and sticky in spring. The leaves consist of up to seventeen small, light green oval leaflets, which turn yellow and orange in autumn. The small, creamy-white flowers are produced in dense clusters in summer, followed by densely packed bunches of bright yellow fruits. These would last into late winter but are generally eaten by the birds. Propagation is by seed sown in spring or budding in summer.

Tiarella wherryi

Foam flower
HEIGHT: 12in (30cm) • Hardy
FLOWERING SEASON: Spring/summer

Stephanandra tanakae

HEIGHT: 7ft (2m) • Hardy
FLOWERING SEASON: Midsummer

A medium-sized shrub that produces a wealth of long, arching branches which are a rich nut-brown. The broadly oval, mid green leaves are sharply toothed and turn deep yellow and orange in early autumn. In winter the bare, brown stems are very showy. The tiny yellow and white flowers appear at the tip of each shoot in June and July. Likes sun or semi-shade and moist well-drained soil. Propagation is by hardwood cuttings taken in winter, or by digging up rooted suckers when the plant is dormant.

This is an excellent evergreen ground-cover perennial with masses of pretty maple-shaped leaves that form a dense mat over the soil. In summer the leaves are pale to mid green, but take on coppery tints through autumn and winter. It is rather slow growing. In spring clusters of creamy-white or pink flowers are carried above the leaves on spikes. This plant does well in a semi-shaded position and is perfect for the woodland garden. It gows in any soil but likes soil that is moist and does not dry out. Propagation is by division in early autumn or spring.

Toona sinensis 'Flamingo'

HEIGHT: 65ft (20m) • Hardy
FLOWERING SEASON: Spring/summer

This is a fairly fast-growing deciduous tree, with attractive pinnate leaves which are a bronzy-pink in spring, deep green through the summer and butter yellow in autumn. The white, fragrant flowers are produced in spikes up to 12in (30cm) in length. The cultivar *T. s.* 'Flamingo' has vivid pink young leaves which turn cream and eventually bright green. Propagation is by root cuttings taken in late winter and placed in a cold frame or by seed sown in autumn. 'Flamingo' must be grafted.

More Plants for Autumn and Winter Interest

Many deciduous shrubs and trees are grown especially for their autumn color. For many people the colors of autumn are the loveliest in the whole year and the plants listed in this chapter and below are just a few of those that will give pleasure to everyone as the year comes to its close. A number of trees produce their best color when grown in slightly acid soil and some plants, particularly those which have variegated leaves, are best grown in sun. These details are given in the plant descriptions. Plants that flower in winter are another of nature's bonuses and every garden should contain at least two, they are often beautifully fragrant.

TREES

Acer negundo 'Flamingo'
  A. platanoides
(Most acers produce brilliant autumn hues)
Aesculus pavia
Amelanchier canadensis
Arbutus × *andrachnoides*
Cercidiphyllum japonicum
Crataegus (in variety)

Cryptomeria japonica
Ginkgo biloba
Hamamelis × *intermedia*
Koelreuteria paniculata
Liquidambar styraciflua 'Worplesdon'
Malus hupehensis
Ostrya carpinifolia
Oxydendrum arboreum
Parrotia persica
Populus alba
  P. × *canadensis* 'Serotina'
Prunus (in variety)
  P. sargentii
Pseudolarix amabalis
Pterocarya fraxinifolia
Pyrus calleryana
Robinia pseudoacacia
Sorbus (in variety)
Stewartia sinensis
Taxodium distichum

SHRUBS

Berberis (in variety)
Calluna vulgaris
Cornus kousa var. *chinensis*
  C. nuttallii
Daboecia cantabrica
Enkianthus campanulatus
Erica carnea 'Springwood White'
  E. × *darleyensis* 'Darley Dale'
Euonymus fortunei cvs
Fothergilla major
Pyracantha 'Mohave'

Pyracantha 'Watereri'
Rhododendron (azaleas – deciduous varieties)
Spireae japonica 'Goldflame'
Symphoricarpos × *doorenbosii*
Vaccinium corymbosum
Viburnum opulus
  V. plicatum 'Lanarth'
  V. tinus

PERENNIALS & CLIMBERS

Epimedium grandiflorum
Holboella coriacea
Humulus lupulus 'Aureus'
Miscanthus sinensis
Parthenocissus henryana
  P. tricuspidata
Vitis coignetiae
  V. vinifera 'Purpurea'

SCENTED PLANTS

No garden is complete without a number of scented plants. Ideally, there should be a selection that provides the garden with scent at all seasons of the year. Both aromatic plants, with pungent foliage, and scented flowering perennials and shrubs are included in this chapter.

ABOVE: *Verbena 'Novalis', one of a large group of colorful, scented plants generally grown as annuals.*

OPPOSITE: *A pink azalea contrasts with the blue of the forget-me-nots to make a scented corner in a spring border. Many of the best garden effects like this corner happen by chance and are not planned.*

ABOVE: *Old-fashioned and species roses are among the best of the scented roses, but most of them only flower once a year. Growing roses among other plants will help to extend the appeal of the scented garden. Here the shrub rose R. 'Zigeunerknabe' is grown with salvias.*

Luckily for gardeners many plants have a delicious scent but some plants are especially prized for their fragrance and no garden should be without some of these, ideally with one or two flowering at the different seasons of the year. Appreciation of fragrance is subjective and that there is a wide range of types of scent: from sweet and cloying, like that of hyacinths, to spicy and musky like that of sage.

It is not always the flower that is the scented part of the plant. With some plants, as with the incense rose (*Rosa primula*), Russian sage (*Perovskia atriplicifolia*), or mint for example, it is the foliage that is the principal provider of scent. Usually foliage is at its most aromatic when crushed, and it is a good idea therefore to position plants with aromatic foliage close to a path or, if they are small enough, in cracks in paving stones so that they are crushed underfoot or brushed as you walk past. A bush of scented viburnum or mock orange (philadelphus) just outside a window will fill the whole house with scent, as will any of the scented climbers such as the fragrant honeysuckles (only some are scented), jasmine, wisteria or the evergreen *Trachelospermum jasminoides*.

Most herbs are aromatic, lavender, santolina, sage, nepeta and artemisia, in particular, and they can all be planted in a silver-leaved border.

The flowers of many scented plants are well known to all. Everyone immediately thinks of roses when they think of scented plants, but some varieties are not so well scented. There are many varieties available which are so avoid the non-scented ones if this is important to you. The old-fashioned roses, including the Albas, are among the most fragrant roses and have recently become extremely fashionable, although they only flower once a year. New breeds of rose, like the 'English' roses, developed by David Austin, have the attributes of old roses in form and scent with some of the repeat-flowering habits of modern roses. There are literally hundreds of roses available and the rose section (pages 54–7) includes a selection of most of the varieties available.

If the garden is large enough, it is well worth growing some of the scented flowers and foliage for drying, either for flower arrangements or to incorporate as potpourri. In this way you extend the enjoyment you get from the scent over a very long season. Flowers that pick and dry well for pot pourri are roses, most of the herbs and a number of the perennials in particular helichrysum, the everlasting flower.

If you are planning a big summer border, in which color is the main objective do not forget to include some of the scented perennials as well. It will increase your enjoyment of the border immeasurably. Alternatively, a few of the scented shrubs can be grown at the back of the border, if the scented perennials do not fit in with your plan. All gardens should contain a philadelphus for its wonderful summer scent if there is room.

Some plants are winter flowering and although your opportunity for appreciating their scent outdoors may be less, you can pick them for indoor use. Chinese witch hazel (hamamelis) is one such subject, as are some of the daphnes. *Elaeagnus × ebbingei* is another winter-flowering scented plant, and although the flowers are too small to notice, the scent is suprisingly strong, so it may take some time to determine where it is coming from.

BELOW: *A corner of a charming cottage garden full of scented plants. Salvias and rock roses mingle with the purple broom while lavender makes a fragrant edging in the background.*

Allium caeruleum

Ornamental onion/Ornamental garlic
HEIGHT: 2ft (60cm) • Hardy
FLOWERING SEASON: Summer

A clump-forming, summer-flowering bulb
which has small, bright blue, flowers held
together in a tight ball on the tops of long
stems. It has narrow dark green leaves.
Alliums grow in any soil although they do
best in soil that is well-drained and does not
become waterlogged. They like a sunny
position. The colors range from white
through pink to blue. Plant the bulbs in the
autumn and propagate by sowing seed in
autumn or division in spring.

Bulbs & Tubers

Bulbs and tubers are among the easiest and
most rewarding of all garden plants. Once
planted they can, and indeed often are,
forgotten, until they emerge the next year.
This section covers tubers as well as the
favorite bulbs of spring and there are a
number of plants which should be found
in all gardens. They will increase and
provide pleasure for many years repaying
the initial outlay many times over.
Most bulbs are reasonably tolerant as to
soil and position but if you can only give
them heavy, rather waterlogged,
conditions, it is a good idea to lift bulbs
like tulips and replant them again the
following spring. Treat them in the same
way as tuberous plants like dahlias. Buy
good quality bulbs from a good supplier
and don't plant mixed lots as they will all
flower at slightly different times and look
pretty odd. All bulbs will benefit from a
foliar feed when they have finished flowering to help them build up their strength
and they should all be planted deeply, at
least three times the depth of the bulb.
And if they are grown in grass let all the
foliage die down before you cut the grass.

Allium giganteum

Ornamental onion/Ornamental garlic
HEIGHT: 4ft (1.2m) • Hardy
FLOWERING SEASON: Summer

A spectacular sight when grown in a herbaceous border, *A. giganteum* can reach a height
of 6ft (1.8m) when grown in favourable
conditions. It carries its distinctive mauvy-
purple flowers in a dense spherical ball and is
robust and clump-forming. Other good
species are, *A. rosenbachianum*, pink, and *A.
nigrum*, which has unusual whitish florets
held on a flat head. *A. flavum*, which is yellow, and *A. oreophilum*, deep pink, are small
alliums suitable for the rockery.

Alstroemeria aurea

Peruvian lily
HEIGHT: 2½ft (75cm) • Hardy
FLOWERING SEASON: Summer

A genus of summer-flowering tuberous
perennials known as Peruvian lilies which
have showy, multi-colored flowers in
summer. *A. aurea* has orange flowers with
short dark red markings and narrow lance-
shaped, dark green leaves. The most popular
sort are *A.* Ligtu Hybrids which have widely
flared flowers in varying shades of pink,
orange, peach, pale-red and creamy-white
often marked with contrasting colors. Likes
sun and well-drained soil. Plant the tubers
10in (25cm) deep and mulch in the autumn.

Amaryllis belladonna

Belladonna lily
HEIGHT: 2½ft (75cm) • Moderately hardy
FLOWERING SEASON: Autumn

An autumn-flowering bulb which has a stout
deep red stem and carries funnel-shaped,
fragrant, pink flowers. The leaves appear
after the flowers and are mid green, long,
strap-like and semi-erect. Most people asso-
ciate the name amaryllis with the large bulbs
grown in pots but they are correctly known
as hippeastrums. *A. belladonna* needs a
sheltered position in sun and likes light,
fertile, well-drained soil. The bulbs must be
planted at least 8in (20cm) deep. It must not
be disturbed and likes a mulch in autumn.

Anemone ranunculoides

Wood anemone
HEIGHT: 8in (20cm) • Hardy
FLOWERING SEASON: Summer

This little wood anemone will naturalize
and spread in the right conditions. The leaves
are deep green, and lobed. The flowers are
about 1in (2.5cm) across, and bright yellow.
A. nemorosa, the true wild wood anemone of
Great Britain, is white and *A. n.* 'Robinson-
iana' is blue. They grow best in humus-rich
soil in light shade. Plant the rhizomes in
autumn about 1in (2.5cm) deep. Propagate
by division in late summer. Prone to attacks
from flea beetles, caterpillars and aphids, and
to various viral disorders.

Arum italicum

Cuckoo pint/Lords and Ladies
HEIGHT: 18in (45cm) • Half-hardy
FLOWERING SEASON: Inconspicuous

This handsome foliage plant, a native of
Europe and North Africa, is ideal for the
winter garden. The spear-shaped, dark green
leaves are attractively marbled with cream
and it has a yellowish-green flower spathe in
early spring. The leaves are much used by
flower arrangers. By summer the foliage has
vanished, leaving a spear of bright scarlet
berries. They grow best in sun or semi-shade
and moist well-drained soil. Propagate by
dividing the tubers in autumn.

Arum italicum 'Marmoratum'

Cuckoo pint/Lords and Ladies
HEIGHT: 12in (30cm) • Hardy
FLOWERING SEASON: Spring

This plant appears in autumn when glossy
green, cream and gray veined spear-shaped
leaves are thrust up on mid green stalks. The
leaves die down in late summer. The flower
spathes, which appear in April or May, are
pale yellow-green and hooded, terminating
in a pointed tip. In early autumn a short
yellow-green stem is all that remains and on
the top third is a dense cluster of glowing
(poisonous) red berries. Propagate in
autumn by division and separating offsets.

Camassia leichtlinii

Quamash
HEIGHT: 3ft (1m) • Hardy
FLOWERING SEASON: Summer

This is one of five species in a genus of bulbs
that are native to North America. Known as
the quamash, it was used by the Indians for
food. It has strappy green leaves and flower
stems bearing spires of bright lavender-blue
or white flowers in summer. *C. l.* Caerulea
Group have purple-blue flowers. Plant in
heavy moist soil in autumn, about 4in
(10cm) deep. The plants like sun or partial
shade. Propagate from offsets in autumn or
by seed sown in autumn.

Camassia quamash

Common camassia/Quamash
HEIGHT: 2½ft (75cm) • Hardy
FLOWERING SEASON: Late spring

This is an attractive, clump-forming, late
spring bulb with mid green leaves which are
tall, erect and strap-shaped, and end in a
sharp point. The small, star-shaped flowers
are carried in large showy spikes on tall, leafless, stalks. The flowers vary from white
through blue to purple. This bulb is perfect
for growing in damp areas close to streams
and water courses. Divide the plants when
dormant to prevent overcrowding. Propagate
by removing the offsets from the sides of the
parent bulb in September.

Canna indica 'Indian Shot'

Indian shot
HEIGHT: 3ft (1m) • Tender
FLOWERING SEASON: Midsummer

Robust, showy, rhizomatous perennials,
which are grown out of doors in the summer
as bedding plants in the milder parts of the
country. They have bold, oval, pointed,
green or reddish-bronze leaves with showy
flowers generally red, orange or yellow in
color. Put the plants in a cold frame in May
and plant out in June. They like well-
cultivated rich soil and require frequent
watering during the growing period. Lift
and store tubers when the leaves die down.
To propagate divide the tubers in winter.

Cardiocrinum giganteum

Giant lily
HEIGHT: 6ft (1.8m) • Hardy
FLOWERING SEASON: Summer

Known as the giant lily, *C. giganteum* makes
an eye-catching addition to any bog garden.
Plant the bulbs just below the soil's surface
in humus-rich moist soil in partial shade.
The slightly drooping, creamy white, funnel-
shaped fragrant flowers can be up to 6in
(15cm) long. Each flower stem, which may
have several flowers, is borne aloft on stout
leafy stems in summer. The flowers are
followed by decorative seed-heads. After
flowering the bulb dies, but offsets of the
main bulb will flower eventually.

Chionodoxa luciliae Gigantea Group

Glory of the Snow
HEIGHT: 6in (15cm) • Hardy
FLOWERING SEASON: Spring

Spring flowering bulbs which are suitable for naturalising in rock gardens or in woodland areas. They are effective colonisers. The bulbs have two leaves and the six-petalled starry flowers which grow on a leafless stem are blue with a white center. There are white and pink forms. *C. sardensis* has deep blue flowers. Plant the bulbs in August in ordinary garden soil 3in (7.5cm) deep and about the same distance apart.

Clivia miniata

HEIGHT: 16in (40cm) • Frost tender
FLOWERING SEASON: Spring/summer

This handsome evergreen grows from thick roots. Both leaves and flowers are striking: the leaves are long, strap-shaped and a glossy dark green. They grow in opposite ranks clasping the flower stem which bears waxy orange or yellow flowers in a dense cluster in late spring or early summer. Generally grown as a house plant. It needs protection in winter – grow it in containers and wrap the container base in bubble plastic or something similar to overwinter it outdoors; avoid freezing. Propagate by seed or division.

Colchycum speciosum 'Album'

Meadow saffron
HEIGHT: 8in (20cm) • Hardy
FLOWERING SEASON: Spring/autumn

Colchycums are charming plants, mainly autumn flowering, sometimes wrongly called the autumn crocus. *C.s.* 'Album', a rare, beautiful species, is pure white. Large semi-erect basal leaves develop in late winter or spring. *C. luteum* is a spring flowering species with yellow flowers. *C. autumnale*, the meadow saffron, has purple, pink or white flowers in September. They like an open sunny position and well-drained garden soil. Propagate by seed or division in the autumn.

Crinum × powellii

Cape lily
HEIGHT: 3ft (1m) • Moderately hardy
FLOWERING SEASON: Late summer

A large late-summer flowering bulb with a long neck which produces a group of strap-shaped leaves and fragrant, funnel-shaped, pink flowers held on leafless stems.
C. bulbispermum has white or pinkish-red flowers and *C. moorei* is deeper pink. They should be planted 6in (15cm) deep in April in well-drained soil in a sheltered sunny position, preferably a south-facing wall. In the winter cover with 3–4in (7.5–10cm) of ash. Propagate by offsets taken in the spring but these will take 3–4 years to flower.

Crocosmia 'Lucifer'

Montbretia
HEIGHT: 2½ft (75cm) • Hardy
FLOWERING SEASON: Late summer

These colorful plants have a dense, clump-forming habit, and spread by producing corms on the end of long underground stems. They have erect, deeply-veined, sword-like, mid green leaves and, in late summer, the upright green stems carry two rows of small tubular flowers. Cultivars include *C. × crocosmiiflora* 'Emily MacKenzie', with deep orange and crimson flowers, and the early flowering, *C.* 'Lucifer', with flame red flowers. Likes well-drained soil and a sunny open site. Propagate by division in spring.

Crocus chrysanthus 'E A Bowles'

Crocus
HEIGHT: 4in (10cm) • Hardy
FLOWERING SEASON: Early spring

Crocuses are one of the most spectacular harbingers of early spring, flowering from February onwards. 'E A Bowles' is one of the most beautiful, with old gold petals and a dark bronzy throat. There a large number of cultivars, *C. vernus* ssp. *albiflorus* 'Remembrance' is the deepest purple and *C. c.* 'Snow Bunting' has creamy white outer petals with a mustard yellow throat. Plant in a sunny open site 2in (5cm) deep. Propagate by sowing seed or division in autumn.

Crocus laevigatus

Crocus
HEIGHT: 3in (7.5cm) • Hardy
FLOWERING SEASON: Autumn/winter

There are many different species of crocus from different parts of Europe and Asia Minor, but this particular species is a native of Greece. It has pale mauve to whitish flowers with purple veins and an orange throat; unusually, it is highly scented. There is a cultivar, *C. l.* 'Fontenayi', which has deep mauve and buff flowers, slightly later in the year. Crocuses benefit from shelter from the wind and do well in the rock garden. Prone to damage by birds and mice.

Crocus vernus ssp. *albiflorus* 'Pickwick'

Crocus
HEIGHT: 3in (7.5cm) • Hardy
FLOWERING SEASON: Early spring

A common sight in early spring, this is one of the most popular crocuses with long pale purple flowers. Crocuses will grow and flower freely in ordinary garden soil and prefer leaf mold to be added to the soil rather than manure. Plant new bulbs in August or September in a sunny position in informal groups with small clusters at the end of larger plantings. Do not disturb the plants once they are established.

Cyclamen coum

Hardy cyclamen/Sowbread
HEIGHT: 3in (7.5cm) • Hardy
FLOWERING SEASON: Winter/early spring

Tuberous perennials which have small delicate flowers in varying shades of white, pink, mauve and red. They flower in late winter and early spring. *C. c.* ssp. *coum album* is white. The leaves are plain or marbled and rounded in shape. There are a number of hybrids available. Although they do best in moist organic soil, cyclamen thrive in thin soil under deciduous trees as long as they are given some mulch or top dressing. They self-seed and may need dividing every five years.

Cyclamen hederifolium

Hardy cyclamen/Ivy-leaved cyclamen
HEIGHT: 6in (15cm) • Hardy
FLOWERING SEASON: Autumn

The autumn flowering species of the hardy cyclamen, these little perennials have attractively marked rounded leaves and small, shuttlecock-shaped, pink flowers borne aloft on short stems. There is also a white form, *C. h. f. album*. They do well in the shade of trees or large shrubs in light, humus-rich soil, and, in the right conditions, may form extensive colonies through the spread of seeds. They are prone to quite a few pests and diseases, and the corms are particularly attractive to mice.

Dahlia 'Bluesette'

Water lily dahlia
HEIGHT: 4ft (1.2m) • Half hardy
FLOWERING SEASON: Summer

Dahlias are a large and popular genus of plants which provide vivid color in the border. 'Bluesette' has glossy dark green leaves and dark pink colored flowers with a gold center. Other popular forms of dahlia are cactus, decorative, ball and pompom, all of which refer to the shape of the flower heads. There are ten in all. They grow best in a sunny position and fertile well-drained soil. All forms except dwarf dahlias require staking. Lift the tubers when the flowers die and store in a frost-free place over winter.

Dierama pendulum

Angel's fishing rod/Wandflower
HEIGHT: 4ft (1.2m) • Moderately hardy
FLOWERING SEASON: Summer

An evergreen summer-flowering corm, *D. pendulum* has long pendulous stems from which hang deep pink bell-shaped flowers in long racemes. The leaves are long and grass-like and die down partially in winter. The plants look best beside water but prefer a sunny position. They like moist well-drained soil. *D. pulcherrimum* has pink flowers with white stripes. Propagate by dividing the corms in spring or sowing seed in autumn. The corms resent being disturbed and may take two years to flower after transplanting.

Eranthis hyemalis

Winter aconite
HEIGHT: 4in (10cm) • Hardy
FLOWERING SEASON: Early spring

The winter aconite, much valued for its early flowering, is a tuberous-rooted, hardy perennial, with pale green, deeply cut leaves. In the early spring it produces small, buttercup-like, yellow flowers which are surrounded by a collar of green, frilled leaves. This is an excellent plant naturalizing in a shaded or semi-shaded situation. It does best in moist woodland conditions. Divide in spring as soon as the flowers have died down and replant immediately.

Erythronium dens-canis

Dog's tooth voilet
HEIGHT: 6in (15cm) • Hardy
FLOWERING SEASON: Spring

Dwarf bulbous plants which are normally found in woodland gardens and have recently been revived as a garden species. The flowers of the species are purple-pink. Of the best-known cultivars, *E. d-c.* 'Purple King' is pink with blue anthers and *E. d-c.* 'Rose Queen' is rose-pink while *E. californicum* 'White Beauty' is white and *E.* 'Pagoda' a clear yellow. They need moist soil with plenty of organic matter, and some shade. If left undisturbed, they will colonize.

Freesia

HEIGHT: 2ft (60cm) • Half hardy
FLOWERING SEASON: Summer

The sweetly scented freesia, long popular as a cut flower, can be grown outdoors in the garden from specially prepared corms. These should be planted in mid-spring, and will then flower in the summer of the same year. After the leaves have died down the corms must be lifted and overwintered for replanting the following year. Plant in light sandy soil in a sunny and sheltered site. Propagate from offsets or grow from seed. Aphids and caterpillars will sometimes attack plants grown outdoors.

Fritillaria meleagris

Snake's head fritillary/Meadow fritillary
HEIGHT: 12in (30cm) • Hardy
FLOWERING SEASON: Spring

A spring flowering bulb which has narrow gray-green leaves and solitary bell-shaped flowers prominently marked with checks in colors varying from pink to purple and white. It grows best in moisture-retentive soil and is good for naturalizing in grass meadowland where it will self-seed freely. They like some shade. There is a lovely white cultivar *F. m.* 'Aphrodite'. Plant bulbs 4in (10cm) deep in the autumn and propagate by sowing seed in autumn or taking offsets in the summer.

Galanthus elwesii

The giant snowdrop
HEIGHT: 8in (20cm) • Hardy
FLOWERING SEASON: Late spring

This snowdrop differs from the common snowdrop in being slightly taller with broader leaves and larger flowers that are deep green on the inner petals and it appears later in late spring. *G. elwesii* does well under deciduous trees as it benefits from light in the winter, but is happier in shade the rest of the year. It likes rich moist soil. Always plant or move snowdrops just after flowering. They are occasionally affected by narcissus fly maggots, and by eelworms, and they can also succumb to gray mold.

Galanthus nivalis

Common snowdrop/Fair maids of February
HEIGHT: 8in (20cm) • Hardy
FLOWERING SEASON: Spring

Late winter- or early spring- flowering bulbs which have narrow strap-like leaves and small white flowers with a green tip at the end of each inner petal. Snowdrops colonize freely and establish themselves under trees and in grassland. Plant the bulbs 2in (5cm) deep in September and, if they are grown in grassland, do not mow until the leaves have died down completely. Like all bulbs they will benefit by the application of liquid manure or fertilizer to the leaves after the flowers have died.

Galtonia viridiflora

Cape hyacinth
HEIGHT: 4ft (1.2m) • Moderately hardy
FLOWERING SEASON: Spring

A clump-forming, summer-flowering, bulb which has large, gray-green, semi-erect, tulip-like leaves, and tall spikes which carry up to thirty, hanging, funnel-shaped, pale green, whitish-tinged flowers. They need a sunny, sheltered site and fertile moist well-drained soil that does not dry out in summer. The plants die down in the winter and are propagated by lifting and division in spring. Plant the bulbs in spring at least 5in (12.5cm) deep and 15in (35cm) apart.

Hippeastrum 'Apple Blossom'

Amaryllis
HEIGHT: 18in (45cm) • Tender
FLOWERING SEASON: Winter/spring

While it is technically incorrect to call hip-peastrums amaryllis, so many people do that this is the name they are known by and sold under. They are spectacular greenhouse bulbs which come from tropical America and Brazil. There are many kinds in colours varying from white through pale pink to orange and red. Feed the bulbs when flowering has finished and then place the pots on their sides in winter to dry off when the leaves have died down.

Hyacinthoides non-scriptus

Common bluebell
HEIGHT: 10in (25cm) • Hardy
FLOWERING SEASON: Spring

The common bluebell does best in partial shade, at the outer edge of a tree canopy, for example, in humus-rich soil. In the right conditions it will naturalize well and is ideal for planting in a small woodland area of the garden. Bluebells can be grown from seed scattered on a bed of leaf-mold, where they will not be disturbed, but they will take several years to develop into flowering bulbs. Generally pest- and disease-free, although they can be attacked by rust.

Hyacinthus orientalis

Hyacinth
HEIGHT: 8in (20cm) or more • Hardy
FLOWERING SEASON: Spring

Hyacinths are among the most strongly scented of all garden flowers, giving off a rich fragrance from their spires of densely packed tubular flowers in various shades of white, cream, blue, mauve and pink. Apple-green, strappy foliage surrounds the flower spires. There are many good named cultivars including 'Delft Blue', a strong cerulean blue, and 'L'Innocence' which is a clump-forming pure white hyacinth whose leaves appear after flowering. Propagate by offsets in autumn.

Leucojum vernum

Snowflake
HEIGHT: 6in (15cm) • Hardy
FLOWERING SEASON: Spring

Snowflakes are closely related to snowdrops which they much resemble. The favorite kind is *L. vernum* which has rather large drooping flowers, white with green tips at the end of each petal. It flowers in March. The summer snowflake, *L. aestivum,* reaches a height of 20in (50cm) and flowers in May and *L. autumnale,* which has pink tips on the end of the flowers, flowers in September. They prefer sandy loamy soil. Plant in September at least 3in (7.5cm) deep but they may take some time to get established.

Lilium 'Casa Blanca'

Lily – Asiatic hybrid
HEIGHT: 3ft (1m) • Hardy
FLOWERING SEASON: Summer/autumn

These colorful bulbous plants have shapely, trumpet-like blooms with six petals which curl open to produce flowers ranging in size from 1in (2.5cm) to 10in (25cm) across depending upon the variety. In addition to the brilliant display of color, many lilies are very fragrant and make excellent cut flowers. The leaves are pale to dark green, some are narrow, almost grass-like and grouped at the base of the plant, while others produce leaves in clusters (whorls) at intervals along the stem. Propagate from scales in autumn.

Lilium regale

Regal lily
HEIGHT: 5ft (1.5m) • Hardy
FLOWERING SEASON: Summer

This handsome lily has large, highly-scented, funnel-shaped flowers in midsummer, borne in clusters on top of tall stems. It has large, bright yellow stamens and pinkish-tinged backs to the petals. It does best in full sun, in ordinary soil, but makes an excellent container plant. Ideally, the stems should be discreetly staked. Plant the bulbs in autumn at three times the depth of the bulb. Propagate from offset bulblets in autumn. Prone to attack by aphids and lily beetle.

Muscari armeniacum

Grape hyacinth
HEIGHT: 6in (15cm) • Hardy
FLOWERING SEASON: Spring

Very attractive little spring-flowering bulbs which have semi-erect basal leaves and tight heads of deep blue flowers carried on spikes. The flowers have a musky fragrance. They like ordinary well-drained garden soil and a sunny position. As plants they do best in the less formal parts of the garden as the leaves become an untidy mass. Plant the bulbs as early as possible covered by at least 2in (5cm) of soil. Once planted they can be left undisturbed for several years.

Narcissus 'Golden Ducat'

Daffodil
HEIGHT: 15in (35cm) • Hardy
FLOWERING SEASON: Spring

Daffodils are botanically known as narcissus. They appeal to everyone with their bright promise of spring and the golden sunshine of summer to come. The varieties are bewildering and the genus is classified into twelve divisions. 'Golden Ducat' is a bright yellow, double-flowered form from group 4 which flowers in mid-spring. All daffodils need to be planted as early in the year as possible, with at least 6in (15cm) of soil on top of the bulbs.

Narcissus 'Ice Follies'

Daffodil
HEIGHT: 15in (35cm) • Hardy
FLOWERING SEASON: Spring

One of the group 2 large-cupped narcissi, 'Ice Follies' has slightly pointed perianth (the outer part of the flower) petals and a large flat crown or cup which opens pale lemon and ages to an ivory white. It produces a large number of lovely flowers. All daffodils should be dead-headed after flowering and they benefit from an application of liquid fertilizer to the leaves after the flowers have died. They will flourish in all soils and like sun or light shade but they do best in fertile well-drained soil.

Narcissus 'Kilworth'

Daffodil
HEIGHT: 15in (35cm) • Hardy
FLOWERING SEASON: Spring

'Kilworth' is another group 2 daffodil with large pale white perianth and a vivid orange red cup with a spot of intense green in the eye. All daffodils are fragrant but the sweetest smelling come from the jonquil, tazetta and poeticus groups with smaller, less showy, flowers often borne in clusters on the stem. It is important not to cut daffodils down before the foliage has died away as this will weaken the bulbs. If they are not planted deeply enough or cut down too soon they may well be 'blind' the following year.

Nerine bowdenii

Guernsey lily
HEIGHT: 15in (35cm) • Moderately hardy
FLOWERING SEASON: Autumn

A autumn-flowering bulb which carries its head of five or six bright pink flowers on an upright stem. The leaves are strap-like and mid green. They used to be considered plants for the greenhouse only as they come from South Africa but they are perfectly hardy in the milder parts of the country given the shelter of a south- or west-facing wall. They like light sandy soil and full sun. Propagate by seed sown in autumn or by offsets detached in August. Plant these in small pots and treat as newly potted plants.

Nerine sarniensis var. *curvifolia* f. *fothergillii*

Guernsey lily
HEIGHT: 2ft (60cm) • Moderately hardy
FLOWERING SEASON: Autumn

Varieties of *N. sarniensis* have up to ten heads of flowers in colors ranging from orange through pink to white. They are not so hardy as *N. bowdenii* and need more protection in hard winters. Once planted nerines should not be disturbed as they grow best when they are pot-bound. They take some time to establish themselves but they make a wonderful sight in autumn when the garden is looking rather bare.

Scilla siberica

Siberian squill
HEIGHT: 4in (10cm) • Hardy
FLOWERING SEASON: Spring

An early spring-flowering bulb which has four strap-like glossy mid green leaves and bell-shaped, lilac-blue flowers carried on a short spike. Scillas will grow in any garden soil but prefer sandy well-drained loam and sun or partial shade. Plant them in rockeries or at the edge of the lawn in the shrubbery where they will colonize and make a display of bright blue color early in the year. Propagate by division in late summer or by sowing seed in the autumn.

Triteleia hyacintha

Spring star flower/Missouri hyacinth
HEIGHT: 15in (35cm) • Hardy
FLOWERING SEASON: Late spring/early summer

A late spring- or early summer-flowering bulb which carries large heads of white flowers like alliums, tinged with blue or purple early in summer. It has long narrow semi-erect spreading basal leaves which are mid green. They must have light well-drained soil and will not flourish in heavy clay unless the soil is very carefully prepared. They die down at the end of summer. Propagate by sowing seeds or by taking offsets in the autumn.

Tulipa 'Golden Age'

Late-flowering tulip (Group 5)
HEIGHT: 18in (45cm) • Hardy
FLOWERING SEASON: Spring

Botanically speaking, tulips have been classified into fourteen divisions, which can be divided into early flowering, mid-season flowering, and late flowering kinds (these make up the first eleven divisions) and the species *Kaufmanniana*, *Fosteriana* and *Greigii* and their hybrids. The mid-season tulips which flower in April and May are the most suitable for exposed positions as they are weather resistant. 'Douglas Bader' is a lovely pale-pink variety and 'Prominence', deep red, but the color range is extensive.

Tulipa 'Pink Impression'

Darwin Hybrid tulip (Group 4)
HEIGHT: 2ft (60cm) • Hardy
FLOWERING SEASON: Spring

Tulips are the most tolerant bulbs and will grow in all types of soil as long as there is reasonable drainage. They are best when they are planted in groups and like daffodils it is a mistake to plant mixtures as they will all flower at slightly different times. 'Pink Impression' is a Darwin Hybrid which flowers at the end of April. They are the largest tulips yet produced. Tulips will colonize freely and are increased by lifting and dividing the bulbs in the autumn. In very wet areas lift and store the bulbs in winter.

Zantedeschia aethiopica

Arum lily/Calla lily
HEIGHT: 2½ft (75cm) • Moderately hardy
FLOWERING SEASON: Summer

The epitome of the garden lily which carries large white flower spathes in midsummer each enclosing a club-shaped spadix above large, evergreen, arrow-shaped, semi-erect, deep green leaves. *Z. aethiopica* likes sun or partial shade and moist, free-draining soil. It will grow beside a pool as a marginal water plant in up to 6in (15cm) of water. It needs to be sheltered from strong winds and in cold areas is best grown in pots and lifted in winter. Plant the tubers 6in (15cm) deep and propagate by taking offsets in winter.

Artemisia absinthium

Wormwood
HEIGHT: 3ft (1m) • Hardy
FLOWERING SEASON: Summer

This shrubby species of wormwood has the typical silvery-gray, aromatic leaves of the genus, which are finely dissected and feathery. The cultivar 'Lambrook Silver', as its name implies, is particularly silvery. The small, button-like, yellow flowers are borne in late summer. It does well in any sunny position in good garden soil. Propagate from semi-hardwood cuttings in late summer. Can be prone to root aphids and blackfly, leaf miner, and rust.

Buddleja 'Pink Delight'

Butterfly bush
HEIGHT: 10ft (3m) • Hardy
FLOWERING SEASON: Summer

The butterfly bush, so-called because its flower spikes are attractive to butterflies, is a deciduous shrub with light green leaves and a spreading habit. The species plant, *B. davidii* has pale-purple flowers borne at the end of arching branches. Cultivars have a range of flower colors from the purple 'Black Knight' to the pure white 'White Cloud'. It benefits from hard pruning in early spring. Propagate from half-ripe cuttings in late summer or from hardwood cuttings in autumn.

Chamaecyparis lawsoniana

Lawson's cypress
HEIGHT: 50-80ft (15-25m) • Hardy
FLOWERING SEASON: Inconspicuous

Known as false cypress, the genus *Chamaecyparis* are widely used trees with aromatic foliage. Some species make excellent hedging and there are also dwarf forms that are ideal for window boxes and rock gardens. *C. l.* 'Gnome' is a small 20in (50cm) cultivar which is bun-shaped with bluish foliage, but in the main false cypresses are tall and erect. *C. l.* 'Lane' is about 47ft (15m) high, with golden-yellow aromatic foliage. Does well in acid soil in sun or shade.

Chimonanthus praecox

Wintersweet
HEIGHT: 8ft (2.5m) • Hardy
FLOWERING SEASON: Winter

Known as wintersweet, from the season in which its richly fragrant flowers appear, this shrub has glossy, oval, dark green leaves. The yellow, cup-shaped, purple-centerd flowers, which are highly scented, bloom on bare branches. 'Grandiflorus' has larger, deep yellow flowers; 'Luteus' has bright yellow ones. Ideally it should be grown on a south- or west-facing wall or fence, and it needs full sun and rich well-drained soil. Propagate by cuttings, taken from softwood in summer or by layering a shoot in autumn.

Clematis armandii

Early-flowering clematis
HEIGHT: 10-15ft (3-4.5m) • Frost hardy
FLOWERING SEASON: Early spring

This twining climber is both evergreen and scented. The leaves are long, oval and glossy, and the flowers are white, six-petalled, small and star-like with yellow stamens. It should be pruned after flowering, to ripen wood for the next season's flowers. It will need support on trellis or on wires, a sheltered south- or west-facing site, and does best in rich, well-drained soil with the roots shaded. It is very vigorous when established. Propagate from seed sown in autumn. May be troubled by aphids, mildew and clematis wilt.

Convallaria majalis 'Albostriata'

Lily-of-the-valley
HEIGHT: 8in (20cm) • Hardy
FLOWERING SEASON: Late spring

Lily-of-the-valley is very fragrant, the perfume filling the air in spring wherever large drifts have naturalized. A herbaceous perennial, it will spread quickly in cool shade and while it will grow in any soil it prefers moist soil that has plenty of leaf mold. The leaves are broad, dark green and grow in pairs, and the spires of white, scented bell-shaped flowers rise between them. 'Albostriata' has a white-striped leaf. Divide well-grown clumps from autumn to spring.

Convallaria majalis var. *rosea*

Lily-of-the-valley
HEIGHT: 8in (20cm) • Hardy
FLOWERING SEASON: Spring

The lily-of-the-valley is an excellent plant for creating drifts of scent in shady corners of the garden. It should naturalize well given the right conditions: partial shade, soil containing plenty of leaf-mold and ample moisture. The little bells of white flowers are deliciously scented. There are a number of cultivars including *C. m.* 'Fortin's Giant' which has slightly larger flowers and the variety, *C. m.* var. *rosea* which is pink. Divide well-grown clumps from autumn to spring.

Daphne odora

HEIGHT: 5ft (1.5m) • Frost hardy
FLOWERING SEASON: Midwinter/early spring

A good shrub to scent the winter garden, this particular daphne has very fragrant, deep pinky-purple and white flowers borne in clusters between the glossy evergreen oval leaves. 'Aureomarginata', a more hardy cultivar, has cream margins to the leaves. This shrub propagates easily from cuttings taken with a heel in autumn, and can also be grown from seed sown in autumn. Prefers fertile well-drained moist soil and does not like being moved. Prone to mottling and distortion of the leaves from virus disorders, which may affect flowering as well. Aphids may sometimes attack the young shoots.

Dianthus 'Pink Mrs Sinkins'

Pink
HEIGHT: 12in (30cm) • Hardy
FLOWERING SEASON: Summer

Old-fashioned pinks, of which 'Pink Mrs Sinkins' and 'Mrs Sinkins' are two, are among the most strongly scented of all pinks. 'Mrs Sinkins' is fully double with white, fringed petals. Pinks have a low, spreading habit and produce large numbers of flowers. The stems and foliage are silvery green. They do best in sun and in an alkaline soil. Pinch out the flowers in their first year to build a strong plant. Propagate from seed, by taking cuttings in summer or by layering.

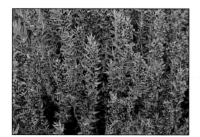

Hyssopus officinalis

Hyssop
HEIGHT: 18in (45cm) • Hardy
FLOWERING SEASON: Summer

Hyssop is a herb from the eastern Mediter-ranean region. The thin pointed leaves, which are aromatic, are arranged in pairs up the stems; the small, purplish-blue flowers are also borne along the length of the stems. There is a white form *H. o. f. albus* and a pink form, *roseus*. It likes full sun and fertile well-drained soil. Can be grown as a low hedge, in which case pinch out the growing tips to encourage bushy growth and trim lightly in spring. Propagate from seed or from basal cuttings, taken in spring.

Iris graminea

Spuria iris
HEIGHT: 8in (20cm) • Hardy
FLOWERING SEASON: Summer

I. graminea belongs to the group known as Spuria irises, which are beardless irises with a rhizomatous rootstock. It has grassy leaves that are about a foot tall, and the flowers, which are plum-scented, have red-purple standards (the raised part of the flower) and bluish-purple veined white falls (the lower part of the flower). Plant in autumn in a sunny position or semi-shade in good garden soil. Do not disturb after planting. Propagate by dividing and cutting the rhizomes. Prone to various viral disorders.

Iris unguicularis

Algerian iris
HEIGHT: 9in (23cm) • Hardy
FLOWERING SEASON: Autumn/winter

This beardless iris, known as the Algerian iris, has delicately scented lavender flowers with a yellow flash on the fall (lower part), and long dark green strappy leaves. It usually starts flowering early in autumn and continues until the following spring. It does best in a sunny, sheltered situation in well-drained, sandy soil but it is tolerant both of acid and alkaline conditions. Propagate by dividing and cutting the rhizomes in early autumn. Prone to attack by slugs and snails, and to a range of viral disorders.

Lathyrus odoratus

Sweet pea
HEIGHT: 4ft (1.2m) • Hardy
FLOWERING SEASON: Summer

The sweet pea species will grow up to 10ft (3m) high but the dwarf sweet pea Knee-hi will grow to about 4ft (1.2m) and the Bijou series grows to about 18in (45cm). Sweet peas will twine their leaf tendrils around a support, producing the delicate, sweetly scented flowers in a range of colors. The very small strain Little Sweetheart is ideal for edgings. Give them a sunny site and lots of organic matter in the soil. Prone to attacks by slugs and aphids, and to viral disorders.

Laurus nobilis

Sweet bay tree
HEIGHT: 18ft (6m) • Hardy
FLOWERING SEASON: Inconspicuous

The sweet bay, a native of the Mediterranean, has glossy, dark green, lance-shaped leaves that are highly aromatic, and used in cooking particularly for flavoring soups and stews. Bays make excellent formal standards for containers and tubs, and can be clipped into geometric shapes. The variety 'Aurea' has golden-yellow leaves. Small greenish-yellow flowers are borne in spring, but usually go unnoticed. Propagate from heel cuttings taken in late summer. Prune container-grown bay trees in summer. Bays can be infested by scale insects.

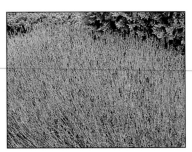

Lavandula angustifolia 'Hidcote'

Lavender
HEIGHT: 2ft (60cm) • Hardy
FLOWERING SEASON: Summer

An evergreen bushy shrub with dark purple flowers which are very fragrant and narrow, aromatic, silver-gray leaves. It makes an excellent low hedge. Lavenders come from the Mediterranean and do best in light soil that contains plenty of leaf mold or manure and full sun. They may well be damaged by frost if grown on heavy soil and they do not like being waterlogged. To propagate take cuttings from the side shoots in late summer.

Lavandula × intermedia

Old English Lavender
HEIGHT: 2-3ft (60-90cm) • Hardy
FLOWERING SEASON: Summer

Lavender is one of the best scented plants with its highly fragrant flowers and foliage. Old English lavender is a variant of *L. × intermedia*. It is a vigorous plant with grayish-green leaves. Dutch lavender (also *L. × intermedia*) has wider, whiter leaves. The stems, with silvery-green narrow leaves, form a dense clump which can be clipped into shapes. It does best in full sun in light soil. *L. stoechas*, the French lavender has deep purple flowers surmounted by violet bracts. Propagate from cuttings in early autumn after flowering.

Lonicera japonica

Japanese honeysuckle/Burmese honeysuckle
HEIGHT: 30ft (9m) • Hardy
FLOWERING SEASON: Summer/autumn

Known as the giant Burmese honeysuckle, this is one of the most vigorous species, of which two cultivars are most often grown: 'Aureoreticulata' has yellow-veined green leaves and long-tubed fragrant white flowers, which yellow as they age. The other popular cultivar, 'Halliana', also has very fragrant flowers. As twining climbers, honeysuckles need a suitable support, and they do well in either sun or partial shade, in any good garden soil. Prune after flowering. Propagate from semi-ripe cuttings in summer.

Magnolia grandiflora

Laurel magnolia/Bull bay
HEIGHT: 13ft (4m) or more • Moderately hardy
FLOWERING SEASON: Summer

This big evergreen shrub is one of the best magnolias – there are more than 120 species in the genus. It has large, handsome, glossy green leaves that have russet felting on the underside. It bears huge, highly scented, dish-like flowers in a creamy white, from mid- to late-summer. It is almost always grown as a wall shrub, where it has protection from cold winds. Prefers neutral to acid soil. Propagate from heeled semi-ripe cuttings in summer. Generally pest-free, but prone to some viral disorders.

Mahonia × media 'Charity'

Oregon grape
HEIGHT: 10ft (3m) • Hardy
FLOWERING SEASON: Late autumn/early spring

This evergreen shrub is particularly good
value for winter, with its strongly scented
racemes of bright yellow flowers. There are
several species and cultivars that are worth
growing for scent, of which 'Charity' is just
one: others are *M. lomariifolia* and *M. japonica*
Bealei Group. Mahonias do well in shade or
partial shade, and prefer fertile, moist soil.
Propagate by sowing seeds when ripe,
layering the branches in spring or from
semi-ripe cuttings in summer.

Malus hupehensis

Hupeh crab
HEIGHT: 33ft (10m) • Hardy
FLOWERING SEASON: Early summer

This crab apple, which has a vigorous habit,
is unusual in that it has scented flowers,
which are quite large – about 1in (2.5cm)
across and single followed by reddish-tinged,
yellow fruits in early autumn. *M.* 'John
Downie' is another excellent crab apple with
orange-red fruits in autumn. Plant new trees
in the autumn or spring, and keep the area
around the trunk grass-free until the tree is
established. Will adapt to partial shade, but
feed well in spring. Prone to attacks by caterpillars, and to the same diseases as ordinary
apple trees, in particular apple scab.

Mentha suavolens 'Variegata'

Mint
HEIGHT: 2ft (60cm) • Hardy
FLOWERING SEASON: Summer

Common mint, or *M. spicata*, is the one
most often used in cookery, but apple mint,
M. suavolens has the most highly scented
leaves. The attractively variegated cultivar,
M. suavolens 'Variegata', has creamy-white
margins to the leaves, and small, bluish-
mauve flowers in summer. All forms of mint
are best grown in moist, slightly shaded conditions, and in a place where their root run
can be constricted. Propagate by division
in the dormant season.

Myrtus communis

Common myrtle
Height: 10ft (3m) • Tender
Flowering SEASON: Summer

The common myrtle is a Mediterranean
shrub that is normally grown in containers in
cooler climates. It is grown for its neat, evergreen leaves, which are also aromatic. White
flowers, about 1in (2.5cm) across, are borne
in summer, and occasionally blue-black fruits
follow in autumn. There are other sorts:
'Variegata' has creamy-tinted leaves, and
M. c. ssp. *tarentina* is more dwarf. In warmer
areas it can be grown against a sheltered wall.
Propagate from heeled cuttings of non-flowering shoots in summer.

Nicotiana × sanderae

Tobacco plant
HEIGHT: 3ft (1m) • Half-hardy
FLOWERING SEASON: Summer

The tobacco plant has wonderfully scented
flowers, which fill the evening air with their
fragrance. *N.* × *sanderae* has several cultivars,
among them 'Sensation Mixed' in colors
including white, cream, carmine and yellow;
the flowers stay open all day instead of opening only in the evening, as the species does.
The cultivar 'Lime Green', has almost fluo-
rescent looking yellowish-green flowers.
Sow seed in spring under glass. Prefers sun
and well-drained soil. Generally disease-free,
but may be liable to attack by aphids.

Nicotiana sylvestris

Flowering tobacco
HEIGHT: 5ft (1.5m) • Half-hardy
FLOWERING SEASON: Late summer

This large perennial is often grown as an
annual, principally for its small white
tubular flowers at the end of long stems
which give off a heady perfume in the
evening in the late summer. The flowers
form in sprays at the ends of the stems,
above the mid green, rough oval leaves. It is
easily grown from seed in early spring. Like
all tobacco plants it does best in sun and
fertile, well-drained soil. Generally pest-
and disease-free, although slugs may attack
the young shoots.

Origanum vulgare

Wild marjoram
HEIGHT: 12in (30cm) • Hardy
FLOWERING SEASON: Summer

The common marjoram grows in the wild on hillsides around the Mediterranean. Its aromatic leaves are used to flavor soups and stews. The pinkish-purple flowers are borne in dense clusters at the end of the flowering stems in summer. There is a golden-leaved cultivar, 'Aureum'. Likes a sunny position and well-drained soil. Sow from seed or take cuttings of basal shoots in late spring. Marjoram for drying for culinary use should be picked before the flowers open.

Osmanthus × burkwoodii

HEIGHT: 6ft (1.8m) • Hardy
FLOWERING SEASON: Late spring

A hybrid between *Osmanthus delavayi* and *O. decorus*, this makes a good hedging plant. It has evergreen mid green leaves and clusters of tubular, white, very fragrant flowers in late spring. It is more compact in habit than *O. delavayi*. For hedging, plant about 18in (45cm) apart in sun or partial shade. It prefers fertile well-drained soil that contains some peat and has some leaf mold or compost added when planting. If planted as a hedge trim in midsummer, prune shrubs when the flowers fade. To propagate, take half-ripe cuttings in summer or layer branches in autumn.

Pelargonium crispum

Geranium
HEIGHT: 2ft (60cm) • Tender
FLOWERING SEASON: Summer/autumn

This pelargonium is grown primarily for its foliage, which is small, dense and almost frilly in appearance. The leaves have a subtle lemon scent. The delicate pale pink flowers are relatively small, and are borne in clusters all summer. The cultivar, 'Variegatum', with silvery edges to the leaves, is particularly attractive. Plant out after the last frosts in a sunny position. Feed during flowering. Propagate from tip cuttings in late summer. Prone to mold and rust.

Pelargonium tomentosum

Peppermint geranium
HEIGHT: 1-2ft (30-60cm) • Frost tender
FLOWERING SEASON: Summer

This pelargonium is grown for its large, gray-green, fragrant peppermint-scented leaves, hence its common name, peppermint geranium. The flowers are borne in clusters, and are small and white. The leaves can be used to flavor drinks and fruit tarts. It should be grown in partial shade, not full sun like other pelargoniums, and the growing tips should be pinched out to keep a neat, bushy shape. Prefers well-drained neutral to alkaline soil. Propagate from cuttings from spring to autumn. Dislikes over-watering.

Philadelphus 'Beauclerk'

Mock orange
HEIGHT: 6ft (1.8m) • Hardy
FLOWERING SEASON: Late spring

This hybrid mock orange is a hardy, deciduous, spreading shrub. The flowers are single, fragrant and creamy-white with a dark red blotch. The leaves are light green and pointed. Plant in sun or part shade between autumn and spring. Generally soil tolerant but prefers fertile well-drained loam. Prune after flowering, taking care not to remove young shoots, which will bear flowers next year. Propagate by taking half-ripe cuttings in late summer or hardwood cuttings in autumn. Sometimes prone to leaf spot.

Philadelphus coronarius

Mock orange
HEIGHT: 10ft (3m) • Hardy
FLOWERING SEASON: Late spring

Often called, mock orange, this free-flowering shrub is covered in large, white cup-shaped flowers in summer, which have a wonderfully heady scent. It is a spreading shrub, almost as wide as it is tall, and does well in dry situations. A golden-leaved culti-var, 'Aureus', is very popular but needs to be grown in partial shade. Prune out old wood after flowering. Propagate from half-ripe cuttings in late summer or from hardwood cuttings in winter. Generally pest-resistant, but can be prone to leaf spot.

Primula auricula 'Adrian'

Alpine auricula
HEIGHT: 6in (15cm) • Hardy
FLOWERING SEASON: Spring

Native to the European Alps, the flowers of this species of primula have distinctly marked golden centers, which are carried in branching heads on an upright stem. The leaves are grayish-green and form a cluster around the stems. There are a number of different cultivars in a variety of colors. These primulas do best in well-drained soil with plenty of humus, in sun or partial shade. Take cuttings in summer. Prone to attack from caterpillars and cutworms.

Rhododendron luteum

Azalea
HEIGHT: 10ft (3m) • Hardy • pH
FLOWERING SEASON: Late spring

This species was formerly classified as an azalea, but it is now classed as a rhododendron. One of a huge genus of over 800 species, ranging from the massive to the miniscule, *R. luteum* is one of the very fragrant species. It has bright, yellow, tubular flowers about 5cm (2in) wide, which are borne in large trusses. It is the parent of numerous hybrids. Rhododendrons need peaty, acid soil and some shade. Propagate by layering. Prone to attacks by leafhoppers, and azalea gall.

Rosmarinus officinalis 'Jackman's Prostrate'

Rosemary
HEIGHT: 6ft (1.8m) • Frost hardy
FLOWERING SEASON: Summer

The foliage of rosemary, a culinary herb, is richly aromatic. The leaves are small and spiny, and the small, bright, pale-blue flowers are borne along the length of the stems. 'Miss Jessopp's Upright' is a compact, upright shrub, while the Prostratus Group hybrids are very low growing. Rosemary benefits from regular trimming and if grown as a hedge, trim after flowering. Propagates easily from heeled cuttings in summer.

Santolina chamaecyparissus

Lavender cotton
HEIGHT: 2ft (60cm) • Hardy
FLOWERING SEASON: Summer

Lavender cotton, as santolina is also known, makes attractive mounds of silvery-gray aromatic foliage. It can be treated as a low hedging plant or grown as a border edging. Small yellow flower buttons are borne profusely in midsummer. A smaller variety, *S. c.* var. *nana*, is sometimes grown in the rock garden. Santolina needs full sun and well-drained soil that is not too rich. For hedging, pinch out the growing tips to encourage bushiness. Propagate from cuttings in midsummer.

Sarcococca hookeriana

Christmas box/Sweet box
HEIGHT: 5ft (1.5m) • Hardy
FLOWERING SEASON: Winter

This sweetly scented evergreen shrub is another useful addition to the winter garden, flowering as it does in winter. The small white flowers are not very significant; they appear in the leaf axils, almost obscured by them. The leaves themselves are narrow, pointed and glossy green. Black fruits are borne after flowering. It can be grown in shade or sun, but it needs a fertile soil that does not dry out. Propagate by taking semi-ripe cuttings in summer or by sowing seed in autumn.

Syringa × chinensis

Rouen lilac
HEIGHT: 8ft (2.5m) • Hardy
FLOWERING SEASON: Late spring

This bushy lilac, known as Rouen lilac, makes a useful informal deciduous hedge in a town garden. A hybrid between *S. persica* and *S. vulgaris*, it makes a dense shrub with the typical fragrant lilac-purple flowers borne in upright panicles and the typical oval, tapering, mid green leaves. Plant in sun or part shade in fertile, preferably alkaline, soil. Remove the flowers in the first season to create a stronger shrub. Propagate from half-ripe cuttings in late summer. Prone to scale insects and to forms of blight.

Syringa vulgaris 'Congo'

Common lilac
HEIGHT: 15ft (4.5m) • Hardy
FLOWERING SEASON: Late spring

Lilac, as this deciduous shrub is also known, bears large panicles of scented flowers in a range of colors from white to deep purple. This cultivar has deep purplish-pink flowers which open from paler buds. The leaves are heart-shaped and dark green. Lilacs need alkaline soil and sun to flourish, and prefer the soil fertile and well-drained. If required prune after flowering. Propagate from soft-wood cuttings in summer. Susceptible to leaf miners, leaf spot and lilac blight.

Tagetes patula

French marigold
HEIGHT: 12in (30cm) • Half-hardy
FLOWERING SEASON: Summer

This marigold, known as the French marigold, has rust-colored or bright yellow single or double flowers, and there is a wide range of varieties, some dwarf. The feathery, deep green foliage gives off a pungent scent when crushed. A half-hardy annual, it is normally grown from seed sown in warmth in early spring. Plant out the seedlings after the last frosts. Does best in rich soil, but will succeed in poor soil. Deadhead to encourage a longer flowering period.

Verbena × hybrida

HEIGHT: 12in (30cm) • Tender
FLOWERING SEASON: Summer/autumn

These hybrids are treated as summer-flowering annuals, much in favor for window-boxes and hanging baskets, as they produce a wealth of flowerheads in many bright colors ranging from white, pink, purple and red to blue. There are tall and dwarf types, and cultivars that comprise several colors, such as Sparkle Mixed which is bushier and more dwarf in habit. Likes sun and well-drained soil. Pinch out the leading shoots of young plants for bushier growth. Susceptible to aphids.

Viburnum × burkwoodii

HEIGHT: 8ft (2.5m) • Hardy
FLOWERING SEASON: Spring

This evergreen viburnum has bronze-tinged foliage and very highly scented flowers, which are pink when in bud, opening to wide flat heads of white flowers throughout spring. There is a variety, 'Park Farm Hybrid', which has larger flowers and 'Anne Russell' has very fragrant flowers. The older leaves turn bright red in the autumn. Grows in most soils but prefers slightly acid soil which does not dry out and full sun. Thin out old wood in late spring. Propagate from lateral shoots in summer. Can be prone to aphid and whitefly attacks and scale insects.

Viburnum carlesii

HEIGHT: 4ft (1.2m) • Hardy
FLOWERING SEASON: Late spring

This deciduous viburnum has ovate mid green leaves that are slightly rough and produces highly fragrant rounded heads of waxy pink flowers which turn to white in late spring. There are cultivars with different characteristics: 'Aurora' has pale pink flowers, opening from reddish buds, as does 'Diana', which also has a more compact habit. Grow in full sun, in moist garden soil. It is a good idea to grow a number of viburnums together. Propagate from heel cuttings in late summer or layer shoots in autumn. Prone to aphid attacks.

Viburnum farreri

HEIGHT: 8ft (2.5m) • Hardy
FLOWERING SEASON: Winter

Formerly known as *V. fragrans*, this is one of the relatively few scented winter-flowering shrubs, it has bright green oval toothed leaves that are bronze-tinged when young. The heavily scented white flowers with a pink tinge are borne in hanging clusters from autumn through mild periods in the winter to the spring. The cultivar 'Candissimum' has light green foliage and pure white flowers. Grow in full sun, in moist garden soil. Propagate from heel cuttings in late summer or layer shoots in autumn. Prone to aphid attacks.

Viola odorata

Sweet violet
HEIGHT: 6in (15cm) • Hardy
FLOWERING SEASON: Spring

Known as the sweet violet, and native to
many temperate parts of the world, this small
plant spreads quickly by means of runners, to
form colonies. It has small, heart-shaped,
mid green leaves and lightly scented, violet-
blue, pansy-like flowers in early spring.
There are a number of cultivars, including
V. o. 'Alba' which is a winter-flowering
white violet and *V.* 'Czar' which is a dark
purple. Plant in autumn or spring in partial
shade. Sow from seed in spring.

Wisteria sinensis

Chinese wisteria
HEIGHT: 100ft (30m) • Hardy
FLOWERING SEASON: Late spring

This wisteria, known as Chinese wisteria,
is one of the most vigorous climbers. It has
long drooping racemes of pale violet flowers
that are lightly scented and cover the whole
plant profusely. The leaves are attractive,
light green, with about twelve leaflets. There
is a white cultivar, 'Alba' and *W. venusta* var.
violacea has violet flowers. Plant in moist,
rich soil on a south- or west-facing wall if
possible. Can also be trained into a standard.
Propagate from heel cuttings in late summer.

Wisteria sinensis 'Alba'

Chinese wisteria
HEIGHT: 100ft (30m) • Hardy
FLOWERING SEASON: Late spring

The white cultivar of the Chinese wisteria,
W. s. 'Alba' shares the characteristics of the
species plant. New plants require careful
training and pruning. After the first year
select three to five shoots to form the main
frame of the plant, cut them back by half and
tie them to support wires. At the end of the
summer cut all the thin whippy shoots back
to five buds and in winter, shorten all
growths to two buds. Wisterias seldom
flower within the first five years.

More Scented Plants

Large numbers of garden plants are scented
and in many ways it might be easier to make
a list of those which are not. The only
plants to avoid are perhaps, ligustrum
(privet) whose flowers have an overpower-
ing, rather nasty, smell in the summer and
those plants aptly called *foetidissima* (fetid –
stinking). Many roses, but not all, have a
lovely scent as do the majority of bulbs and
tuberous plants which appear in their own
section at the beginning of this chapter. We
have therefore not included any roses or
bulbs in the lists below nor have we added
any plants as there simply isn't room to list
more than a tiny fraction of those available.
We have included plants with fragrant
foliage like salvias as well as those with
fragrant flowers.

TREES AND SHRUBS

Abelia × *grandiflora*
Carpentaria californica
Caryopteris × *clandonensis*
Cercidiphyllum japonicum
Choisya ternata
Clethra arborea
Coronilla valentina ssp. *glauca*

Corylopsis pauciflora
Crataegus (in variety)
Cytisus battandieri
Deutzia scabra 'Plena'
Eucalyptus gunnii
Fothergilla major
Genista aetnensis
Hamamelis × *intermedia*
Laburnum × *watereri* 'Vossii'
Lavandula angustifolia
Lonicera nitida
Osmanthus delavayi
Philadelphus coronarius 'Variegatus'
Phillyrea latifolia
Phlomis fruticosa
Populus balsamifera
    P. × *candicans* 'Aurora'
Prunus (in variety)
Rhododendron – *azaleas* (in variety)
Robinia pseudoacacia
Ruta graveolens 'Jackman's Blue'
Salvia officinalis Purpurascens Group
Skimmia japonica
Spartium junceum
Styrax officinalis
Syringa × *henryi*

PERENNIALS AND CLIMBERS

Centaurea moschata
Crambe cordifolia
Dianthus 'Doris'
Erysimum cheiri
Galium odoratum

Jasminum officinale
Lathyrus grandiflorus
    L. latifolius
Lonicera × *brownii* 'Dropmore Scarlet'
    L. periclymenum 'Belgica'
    L. × *tellmanniana*
Petasites japonicus
Romneya coulteri
Saxifraga cuneifolia
Trachelospermum jasminoides
Wisteria floribunda

ACKNOWLEDGEMENTS

The publishers would like to thank the following picture libraries and photographers for supplying the pictures used in this book.
The pictures are numbered according to their position on the page and are identified by the page number first and position second. The position is numbered 1-6 reading from top left to bottom right on each page.

SUE ATKINSON & SUE ATKINSON LIBRARY
14/4-5, 15/1-5, 16/3-4-5, 17/-4, 18/3, 19/2-4-6, 20/4, 21/1-2-6, 22/1-5, 24/2-3-4-5-6, 25/1-2-3, 30/1-2-3-4, 31/4-5-6, 32/1-4-5-6, 33/3-4, 34/1-2, 35/1-4-5-6, 36/3, 37/1-3-6, 38/1-2-3-4-6, 39/2-4-5-6, 40/1-4-6, 46/4-6, 47/3-4-5, 48/3-6, 49/1-4-5-6, 50/1-5, 51/1-3-4, 52/2-4, 53/2, 62/1-2, 63/2-6, 64/1-4, 65/1-2, 65/5-6, 66/1-3-5, 67/3-4, 68/1-2-5, 69/3, 74/1-3-4, 75/1-2-4-5-6, 76/1-2-4-5, 77/2-3-4-5-6, 78/1-2-3-4-5, 79/2-5-6, 80/1-2, 80/4-6, 81/1-3, 86/3-6, 87/-2-5-6, 88/1-2-4-5-6, 89/3-4-5, 90/2-3-5, 91/4-6, 92/1-6, 93/1-6, 94/2-5, 95/1, 100/4, 101/1-2-5, 102/3-5, 103/2-4-5-6, 104/1-2-3-4-5-6, 105/2-3, 106/1-3-5-6, 107/2, 108/1-2-4-5-6, 109/1-2-3, 114/6, 115/1-6, 116/1-2-4-5-6, 117/1-2-3-4, 118/2-4, 119/5-6, 120/1-2-3, 121/2, 129/1-2-4-5, 131/4, 133/2, 139/1-2, 140/2-5, 142/5, 143/6, 144/1, 146/1-3-5, 147/3-6, 148/1-2-5-6, 149/3-4-5-6, 150/1-4-6, 151/1-2-3,-4-6, 152/1-2-4, 153/1-3

DAVID AUSTIN ROSES
54/1-5, 55/2-5, 56/5, 57/3-5

GILLIAN BECKETT
16/2, 17/2, 18/4, 20/3, 21/5, 33/1, 36/4, 37/2, 39/3, 40/5, 41/2-3, 46/1, 54/3, 55/6, 74/2, 80/5, 94/3, 100/3, 102/4, 105/6, 115/4, 118/3, 132/1, 142/2, 143/1-2-5, 144/3-4-5, 145/1, 146/2, 148/4

THE GARDEN PICTURE LIBRARY
30/1, 34/2, 47/4, 92/5, 115/3, 118/1

BOB GIBBONS/NATURAL IMAGE
19/3, 20/6, 37/4, 47/1, 48/5, 69/2, 91/1, 95/2, 105/4, 119/4, 126/4, 127/2, 128/1, 132/2, 139/5, 140/1, 141/4-5

JOHN GLOVER
14/2, 15/3, 18/5, 19/1, 31/2, 33/6, 40/3, 48/4, 49/3, 92/3-4, 93/4, 100/6, 105/4, 126/2, 128/2, 130/6, 132/3, 138/3-5, 140/3, 141/2, 142/6, 143/3, 144/6, 150/3

BRIAN MATTHEWS
23/4, 34/4-5, 36/2, 40/2, 50/4, 51/5, 94/6, 100/1-2, 130/1, 131/6, 139/4, 143/4, 147/1-2, 153/2

PETER MCHOY
14/6, 15/2-6, 16/1, 17/5-6, 18/1-2-6, 22/3-6, 23/1-6, 24/1, 30/6, 35/3, 36/5, 39/1, 47/2-6, 48/1-2, 49/2, 50/6, 51/6, 53/1-3, 62/3-6, 63/3-4, 66/6, 67/5, 68/4-6, 69/1, 74/5-6, 75/3, 77/1, 79/3, 80/3, 86/2,-5, 87/3-4, 89/6, 90/1-4-6, 94/4, 101/3-4, 102/1-6, 105/1, 107/4-6, 114/2, 115/2, 116/3, 117/5, 119/3, 120/4-5, 121/3, 126/5-6, 127/1, 128/5, 129/6, 130/4, 131/3, 132/6, 139/3, 1 142/1, 146/4-6

HARRY SMITH COLLECTION
14/1-3, 15/4, 16/6, 17/3, 19/5, 20/1-2-5, 21/3-4, 22/2-4, 23/2, 23/3, 30/5, 31/1-3, 32/2,-3, 33/2-5, 34/3-6, 35/2, 36/1-6, 37/5, 38/5, 41/1, 46/2-3-5, 50/2-3, 51/2, 52/1-3-5-6, 54/6, 55/3, 56/4, 57/2-4, 62/4-5, 63/1-5, 64/2-3-5-6, 65/3-4, 66/2-4, 67/1-2-6, 68/3, 76/3-6, 78/6, 79/1-4, 81/2, 86/1-4, 88/3, 89/1-2, 91/2-3-5, 92/2-5, 93/2-3-5, 94/1, 95/3, 100/5, 101/6, 102/2, 103/1-3, 105/5, 106/2,-4, 107/1-3-5, 108/3, 114/1-3-4-5, 115/3-5, 117/6, 118/1-5-6, 119/1-2, 120/6, 121/1, 126/1-3, 127/3-4-5-6, 128/3-4-6, 129/3, 130/2-3-5, 131/1-2-5, 132/4-5, 133/1-3, 138/1-3-6, 139/6, 140/4-6, 141/1-3-6, 142/3-4-2, 145/2-3-4-5-6, 147/4-5, 148/3, 149/2, 150/2-5, 151/5, 152/3-5-6

The publishers have tried to credit all agencies and photographers whose pictures appear in this book and apologize for any omissions.

Index of Plants

Fremontodendron 'California Glory'

Geranium 'Johnson's Blue'

List of Common Names

Most plants have common names and these are shown throughout the book in the plant details. Charming though they are these are not an accurate guide to ordering or buying plants. Many plants are known by more than one name and names vary in different parts of the country or world. Where no common name is listed the plant does not have one that is acknowledged.

Viburnum plicatum 'Mariesii'

Waldsteinia ternata

NOTES

NOTES

NOTES

NOTES

NOTES

NOTES

NOTES

NOTES